DATE DUE

THE WELLNESS GUIDE
TO LIFELONG FITNESS

UNIVERSITY OF CALIFORNIA AT BERKELEY

The Wellness Guide to Lifelong Fitness

by Timothy P. White, Ph.D.

Professor and Chairman of the Department of Human Biodynamics
University of California at Berkeley

and the Editors of the
University of California at Berkeley
Wellness Letter

REBUS NEW YORK

Distributed by Random House

THE UNIVERSITY OF CALIFORNIA AT BERKELEY WELLNESS LETTER

The Wellness Guide to Lifelong Fitness is an illustrated comprehensive guide to
a practical low-key, low-impact approach to fitness for men and women of all ages, at any fitness
level. It comes from the publishers of America's top-rated health newsletter, the
University of California at Berkeley Wellness Letter.

The *Wellness Letter* is an eight-page monthly newsletter that delivers brisk, useful coverage on health,
nutrition, and exercise topics—in language that is clear, engaging, and nontechnical. It's a unique resource
that covers fundamental ways to prevent illness. For information on how to order this award-winning
newsletter from the world-famous School of Public Health at the University of California at Berkeley,
write to Health Letter Associates, Department 1107, 632 Broadway, New York, New York 10012.

REBUS

© Health Letter Associates, 1993

Library of Congress Cataloging-in-Publication Data

White, Timothy P.
The wellness guide to lifelong fitness / by : Timothy P. White and
the editors of the University of California at Berkeley wellness
letter.
p.   cm.
At head of title: University of California at Berkeley
Includes index.
ISBN 0-929661-08-7
1. Exercise. 2. Physical fitness.   I. University of California,
Berkeley.   II. University of California, Berkeley, wellness letter.
III. Title
RA781.W47   1993   93-19083
613.7' 1--dc20   CIP

Printed in the United States of America
10 9 8 7 6 5 4 3 2 1
Distributed by Random House, Inc.

This book is not intended as a substitute for medical advice. Readers who suspect they may have
specific medical problems should consult a physician about any suggestions made in this book.

THE WELLNESS GUIDE TO
LIFELONG FITNESS

Thomas Dickey
Editor

Susan Bronson
Executive Editor

Nona Cleland, Mary Crowley,
William Dunnett, Carl Lowe
Senior Editors

Linda Epstein
Text Editor

Robert Hernandez
Copy Editor

Jacqueline Damian, Jane Jeffs
Contributing Editors

Carney W. Mimms III
Chief of Research

Dale Ogar
Managing Editor

Susan Paige
Editorial Assistant

Judith Henry, Robin Schiff
Art Directors

Timothy Jeffs, Francine Kass
Associate Art Directors

Karin Martin, Sara Bowman,
Deborah Ragasto
Designers

Steven Mays, David Madison,
Andrew Eccles
Photography

Nola Lopez
Photo Stylist

Rodney M. Friedman
Editor and Publisher

Barbara Maxwell O'Neill
Associate Publisher

Charles L. Mee, Jr.
Editor in Chief

THE UNIVERSITY OF CALIFORNIA AT
BERKELEY WELLNESS LETTER

Rodney M. Friedman
Editor and Publisher

Shirley Tomkievicz, Michael Goldman
Medical Writers

Dale A. Ogar
Managing Editor

Bette Ponack Albert, M.D.
Medical Editor

Jeanine Barone, M.S.
Sports Medicine and Nutrition Editor

Jane Margaretten-Ohring, R.N.
Associate Medical Editor

Tom R. Damrauer
Librarian/Researcher

Barbara Maxwell O'Neill
Associate Publisher

*The following consultants helped design
the exercises in this book:*

Ralph Anastasio, M. A. *(Strength
Training with Machines)* has a master's
degree in exercise physiology and physical education and is certified both as an
exercise program director and an exercise test technologist by the American
College of Sports Medicine.

Paul Asmuth *(Swimming)*, a world
champion swimmer, has won every major swimming marathon at least once
and also set a men's world record for
swimming the English Channel.

Marshall Clark *(Running)* has trained
United States Olympic marathoners,
and has coached track and field at San
Jose State University, the University of
Montana and Stanford University.

Risa Friedman, M.A., *(Stretching and
Strength Training in Parts II and III)* is
certified in health fitness instruction by
the American College of Sports Medicine, the American Council on Exercise
and the Laban-Bartenieff Institute of
Movement Studies.

Wayne Glusker *(Walking)* is a former
national race walking champion and a
member of the Athletics Congress Race
Walk development committee.

John Howard *(Cycling)* has been on
three United States Olympic cycling
teams and is an eleven-time United
States Cycling Federation and National
Off-Road Bicycle Association National
Champion. He also holds two world
speed records in cycling.

Nancy Klitsner, M.A., *(Exercise Routines in Part IV)* holds a master's degree
in applied physiology. She is the Man-
hattan Health and Fitness Coordinator
for the New York City Department of
Parks and Recreation.

Jean Ann Scharpf, M. A. *(Aerobic
Movement)* is an exercise physiologist
and Professor of Physical Education at
Suffolk Community College in Selden,
New York.

Jessica Wolf *(Exercise Routines in Part
IV)* is a certified teacher of the Alexan-
der Technique. She also holds a master's
degree in movement analysis from the
Laban-Bartenieff Institute of Movement
Studies.

CONTENTS

Now that the fitness boom has been underway for more than a decade, what have we learned? Throughout the United States, millions of Americans have been taking advantage of health clubs, tennis courts, jogging tracks, swimming pools, home exercise equipment and all manner of road races and triathlons. Every day, an estimated 50 million people are making choices about an activity, a program or a piece of equipment in an effort to obtain benefits ranging from more vigor and alertness to a lowered risk of heart disease and premature mortality. Yet for all the tremendous surge in enthusiasm over exercise, probably just as many people have fallen by the wayside. Part of the reason is that plenty of them pushed too hard and too fast. In the 1980s, high-impact aerobics classes and high-mileage training dominated the fitness landscape, and at times it seemed as if you had to be in almost perfect shape even to begin an exercise program.

But as exercise programs have proliferated, research on them has gained in sophistication, and studies conducted over the past 10 years are redefining the standards of what makes physical activity beneficial. Drawing on that knowledge, this book will help you rethink what fitness means from a wellness standpoint—for the purpose of protecting and promoting good health. The plan of the book also reflects the following trends that have emerged from research findings and the consensus of leading experts.

The elements of fitness

Running, cycling and other aerobic activities have been given the most emphasis during the past decade because they enhance cardiorespiratory endurance—the aspect of fitness that provides the most impressive health benefits. Aerobic exercise, which is covered in Part I of this book, will continue to be the cornerstone of fitness programs. Yet many people in long-term aerobic programs may lose muscle mass and flexibility, particularly in their upper bodies.

Physical fitness, as experts in the field have emphasized, actually has four components.

•*Cardiorespiratory endurance* is reflected in the sustained ability of the heart and blood vessels to carry oxygen to your body's cells.

•*Muscular fitness* consists of both strength—the force a muscle produces in one effort—and endurance—the ability to perform repeated muscular contractions in quick succession.

•*Flexibility* refers to the ability of your joints to move freely and without discomfort through their full range of motion.

•*Body composition* refers to how much of your weight is lean mass (muscle and bone) and how much is fat.

Each of these components can be measurably improved with appropriate types of exercise. Recently, there has been an increasing emphasis on exercising to enhance muscular fitness and flexibility. Consider this: While a decade ago a very small proportion of women worked out with weights, a recent Gallup survey found that 15 percent of women who exercise regularly include some kind of weight training. The new interest in strengthening muscles is also evident in the growing number of low-impact aerobics classes that utilize light weights. And the American College of Sports Medicine has altered its exercise guidelines to include strength training along with aerobic exercise for healthy adults.

But the emphasis isn't on pumping heavy weights to build hulking muscles. Rather, the College recommends resistance training of moderate intensity at least twice a week, in workouts that can take as little as 15 minutes per session. The "resistance" can be provided by barbells or weight machines. You can also use your own body weight as resistance, as in calisthenics such as push-ups, sit-ups, and pull-ups. All of these methods are demonstrated in Part III.

Being fit means being active in a variety of pursuits. Jogging and aerobics classes, the premier exercise activities of the 1980s, continue to attract participants. But as the nation and its fitness habits mature, people have been shifting to all manner of activities, from fitness walking to ballroom dancing. Two classic low-impact activities, swimming and cycling, continue to gain in popularity. At the same time, others are choosing new types of strenuous sports, from mountain biking to biathlons and triathlons that combine different activities. Exercisers are also cross training—combining different (usually complementary) types of exercise to create a more rounded, less boring program. Step-aerobics is one innovative form of exercise turning up at health clubs: It's like low-impact aerobic dance, except that participants step up and down on low platforms, often holding light weights.

Easy does it. The notion that exercise training should be painful or exhausting has lost its validity, and a growing number of physicians, physiologists and fitness experts affirm that more moderate forms of exercise are sufficient to improve fitness and health. Using just 1,000 calories a week in moderate exercise and daily activities can provide fitness and health benefits. And as long as it expends these calories, almost any activity will do—even activities like bowling, golf or active housework offer some health benefits for people who have been sedentary.

One additional reason for this move toward gentler exercise is the rising incidence of injuries associated with some popular activities, particularly aerobic dance and running. Moderate workouts not only reduce the risk of injuries, but, equally important, they are also accessible to people who are intimidated by—or who have given up on—highly strenuous regimens.

Moderate exercise doesn't mean that it's best to do as little as possible. The most significant health benefits that exercise can provide—lower blood pressure, greater cardiorespiratory im-

provements, a sense of well-being, more energy, among others—come only from sustained, regular workouts. But a long-term study conducted by the University of Minnesota showed that a moderate level of activity does have clear-cut advantages over a sedentary lifestyle. The subjects in the study were men at high risk for heart disease, and researchers found that those who engaged daily in such activities as gardening, dancing, home exercise and other so-called moderate exercise activities reduced the risk of a fatal heart attack by as much as one third over a seven-year period.

How fit are you?

Each of the four elements of fitness described above can be tested to assess your own level of fitness and to monitor your progress every month or two. The tests can help you determine the areas to concentrate on to get where you want to be. A high score in one element of fitness doesn't balance out a poor score in another—your long-term goal should be to score well in all elements.

Cardiorespiratory endurance
Rockport one-mile walking test (page 27)

Flexibility
Sit-and-reach test (page 200)

Muscle strength and endurance
Three-part strength test (page 281)

Body composition
Body mass index (see box, page 10)

It's never too late. More and more studies are showing that exercise may inhibit, arrest, or even reverse many of the declines associated with aging. According to a long-term study of thousands of Harvard graduates aged 45 to 84, men middle aged and older who take up moderately vigorous activities such as tennis, swimming, jogging or brisk walking have up to a 41 percent reduction in coronary artery disease. In effect, the exercisers in the study could expect to live 9 or 10 months longer, on average, than those who remained sedentary. Men who were at highest risk and began to exercise probably gained more time, while others may have gained less.

Another study, published in the *Journal of the American Medical Association,* found that an eight-week weight-training program allowed frail 86- to 96-year-olds to build muscle mass and become more mobile and self-sufficient. And comparisons of the mental agility of younger people and healthy older people who exercise at about the same level show that the elders react about as fast as their juniors and significantly faster than their sedentary peers.

As this message sinks in, we're likely to see more people in their 60s, 70s, and 80s starting or continuing to exercise. Older people who start exercising have to take more time and work at a lower intensity to build cardiorespiratory function and muscle strength and endurance. But it doesn't matter if you never really exercised before—the benefits will still accrue.

How to use this book

The pages that follow will steer you through the often confusing variety of options in exercise activities, and provide you with guidelines for choosing clothing and equipment. In each chapter, you'll see how to perform fitness-related activities and exercises safely and effectively. The routines have been designed by experts and are shown in step-by-step photographs, so that you are less likely to get injured or to be overcome with either fatigue or boredom—the chief reasons why people who are initially enthusiastic about exercise end up dropping out.

You will find guidelines for self-assessment tests for gauging your current level of fitness and monitoring your progress, guidelines for starting a fitness program, advanced routines if you are already fit, advice on how to stay motivated, warm-ups and cool-downs and tips on how to minimize exercise-related aches and pains. The book's final section (Part IV) presents useful ways of incorporating fitness into a variety of day-to-day situations.

Your Body Mass Index

How to determine a person's "desirable" weight is still a matter of controversy, but most experts agree that the preferred way to arrive at your healthy weight is to measure the proportion of fat in your body. You can estimate this by calculating your body mass index—the figure you get by dividing your weight in kilograms by the square of your height in meters. This is the most useful figure because it minimizes the effect of height and provides reasonable guidelines for defining overweight.

Calculate your body mass index by following the steps below. Weigh yourself in shorts or underwear. A calculator, while not necessary, will help. Round off numbers after the decimal point to the nearest hundredth.

1. To convert your weight to kilograms, divide the pounds by 2.2 (the number of pounds per kilogram): _____. (For example, 150 pounds = 68.18 kilograms)

2. To convert your height to meters, divide height in inches (without shoes) by 39.4 (the number of inches in one meter): _____. (For example, 5' 9" = 69" = 1.75 meters). Take this figure and square it: _____. ($1.75^2 = 3.06$)

3. Divide the result of (1) by (2): _____. (For example, 68.18/3.06 = 22.28) *This is your body mass figure.*

For men, desirable body mass ranges from 20 to 25. Above about 29 is obese; above 40 is extremely obese.
For women, desirable body mass is 19 to 24; obesity begins at about 27, and extreme obesity is above 39.
For both men and women, values below 19 are underweight.

How to enjoy exercise—safely

People who have been inactive often take up exercise training enthusiastically, and they tend to forget—or ignore—certain measures that can reduce the risk of injury. And even veteran exercisers may skip basic precautions that can help minimize aches and pains. The guidelines and tips here and on pages 12-14 can help protect you from exercise-related injuries and will also make being active more enjoyable.

1. **"NO PAIN, NO GAIN" IS A MYTH.** Exercise should require some effort, but not undue discomfort. Beware of any exercise instructor who says that exercise must hurt (or "burn") to do any good. If you have continuing pain during an exercise, stop and don't do it again unless you can do so painlessly. (If the pain occurs in the chest or neck area, seek medical attention right away.) General muscle soreness is another matter; sore muscles need not make you stop exercising, but they might make you slow down temporarily.

2. **DON'T OVERDO IT.** Studies show that the most common cause of injury is exercising too aggressively—the "too much, too soon" syndrome. Even if you consider yourself in relatively good shape, start any new exercise at a relatively low intensity and gradually increase your level of exertion over a number of weeks.

3. **USE ADEQUATE FOOTWEAR.** Wearing improper or worn-out shoes places added stress on your hips, knees, ankles and feet—the sites of up to 90 percent of all sports injuries. Choose shoes suitable for your activity (see page 15) and replace them before you wear them out and they lose their shock-absorbing ability.

4. **WATCH YOUR FORM AND TECHNIQUE— ABOVE ALL, MINIMIZE "HIGH IMPACT" MOVEMENTS.** In most activities, strained muscles and joints can result from poor form, whether it's the repetitive, jarring movements of some aerobics routines, landing on the balls of your feet (rather than your heels) when running or constantly cycling in high gears. In the chapters that follow, pay attention to the step-by-step pictures and directions—they are designed to protect your shins and calves, lower back, ankles and knees, all areas that are vulnerable to strain.

5. **DON'T BOUNCE WHILE STRETCHING.** "Ballistic" stretching, in which you perform quick, pulsing movements, actually increases the risk of muscle tears and soreness. To improve flexibility, do "static" stretches, which call for gradually stretching through a muscle's full range of motion until you feel resistance (as explained more fully in Chapters 7 and 8).

6. **WARM UP AND COOL DOWN.** Most authorities agree that it's essential to warm up first and to cool down following an exercise session. Doing so can help improve your performance and also minimize the chance of injury (see below).

Before you begin

The American College of Sports Medicine recommends that healthy women over 50 years old, and men over 40, who wish to start a vigorous exercise program should first consult a physician. Younger people should also see a physician if two or more risk factors or symptoms for heart disease are present (such as recurrent chest pain, high blood pressure or cholesterol levels, smoking or obesity). And at any age you should consult a physician first if you have any cardiovascular, lung or joint-muscle condition.

The right way to warm up

Many people still think that the way to start an exercise session is by stretching. Not so. Stretching cold muscles can injure them. Whether you're running, playing a sport, doing calisthenics or lifting weights, warm up first, then stretch. A proper warm-up raises blood flow to muscles, increases tissue temperature, and promotes joint lubrication so muscles and joints are more pliable—all of which help avoid putting undue strain on muscles, tendons and ligaments.

You should first perform a *general warm-up* by exercising the large muscle groups of the body at a light pace for 5 to 10 minutes—with activities like brisk walking, jogging, running in place or riding a stationary bike. This helps promote cardiovascular function, and so helps prevent placing your heart at undue risk for abnormal function. Always perform a general warm up before you stretch or work with weights.

Specific warm-ups involve the same muscles and joint movements that you are planning to train in your exercise session—for example, if you are exercising your lower legs, you would first stretch key muscles around the hip, knee and ankle joints. Or, for tennis, you might perform stretches for the shoulder, back and leg muscles involved, and then lightly hit balls in a less vigorous rehearsal of the activity you're about to perform. Many of the chapters that follow contain suggestions for specific warm-ups.

After exercise, cool down by slowing down gradually, exercising at a relaxed pace for at least five minutes. It also helps to gently stretch the muscles you've been using. Never stand still immediately after vigorous exercise. In cold weather, try to warm up and cool down indoors. Many exercisers find that when it's cold outside, they can also stretch more fully indoors.

The need for fluid replacement

During any prolonged period of exercise, the continuous action of your muscles generates a tremendous amount of heat—as much as 10 times the amount your body produces at rest. This heat production can raise your internal temperature rapidly, but your body has a remarkable ability to dissipate heat buildup. Cooling occurs primarily through the evaporation of sweat, which cools the skin and the blood that circulates just below the skin. The cooled blood then flows to other regions in your body, cooling them. The system works much like the radiator and coolant in a car engine.

The fluid you lose through sweating needs to be replaced—and this is particularly important in hot and humid weather, when you can easily lose more than a quart of water in an hour. Neglecting to replace lost fluids in hot weather can result in dehydration and more severe forms of heat stress such as heat exhaustion and heat stroke (see the next page).

Unfortunately, many exercisers don't drink anything until they're thirsty. But if you are sweating heavily, thirst is satisfied long before you have replenished lost fluids.

• For optimal hydration during strenuous exercise in hot, humid weather, drink at least 16 to 20 ounces of fluid two hours before exercising and another 8 ounces 15 to 30 minutes before.

• While you exercise, sip 4 to 6 ounces every 15 to 20 minutes.

• After exercising, drink enough to replace the fluid you've lost. One way to ensure adequate fluid replacement is to weigh yourself before and after you exercise, and then drink one pint of fluid for each pound you've lost.

• While heat buildup may be slower when you exercise in cold weather or in water, you still lose fluid from sweating. Therefore, it's important to replace fluids just as regularly when you swim or work out in the cold as you do in the heat.

For years, many exercise physiologists recommended water as the ideal replacement beverage, asserting that it is better absorbed than beverages that contain sugar, whether fruit juices, soft drinks or specially formulated "sports drinks." But during the past decade, researchers have found that drinks containing a low percentage of sugar are usually as well absorbed as water. Moreover, during strenuous endurance exercise lasting more than two hours, sugared beverages may help your body maintain its carbohydrate stores, maintain normal blood volume sugar levels, and thus delay fatigue.

Keep in mind, though, that sports drinks are nutritionally similar to diluted juice or soft drinks, only more expensive. Sports drinks promise to replace the electrolytes (sodium and potassium) lost in sweating. But except under the most extreme circumstances, there is no need to replace them by consuming special drinks or mineral supplements.

In the end, it's a matter of personal preferences. Fruit juices and soft drinks contain more than 10 percent sugar, so they need to be diluted to supply the optimal concentration of carbohydrates—5 percent to 10 percent—for endurance exercise. Higher concentrations impair gastric emptying. Carbonated beverages are also fine unless they make you feel bloated.

Beer and other alcoholic beverages, however, are poor choices; they promote dehydration, hamper coordination and impair performance. If caffeinated beverages help you with mental performance, they may also help you with physical performance. But if you're not accustomed to caffeine, be careful, since caffeine combined with prolonged exertion can sometimes boost heart rate and blood pressure excessively. Also, caffeine is a diuretic and thus may increase urination, so increase your intake of other fluids.

Most of us prefer cold fluids, but there's no other advantage to them; cold beverages will rarely cause cramping or a "stitch."

The most important thing is to drink—even if you don't feel thirsty.

Being active in heat and humidity

Drinking plenty of fluids is the most important step to minimize the effects of hot and humid weather. At the very least, neglecting to compensate for fluid loss can cause lethargy and nausea, interfering with your performance. In endurance activities like brisk walking, running, strenuous hiking, cycling and cross-country skiing, water loss can be severe, potentially producing heat exhaustion or heat stroke. The former condition is a result of dehydration and is signaled by such symptoms as headache, nausea, loss of coordination and sometimes chills. Heat stroke is far more serious, since it involves a failure of the body's cooling mechanism and can result in neurological damage or death.

However, replacing the fluid lost through sweating is only one of several measures you should take to exercise safely in the heat. Indeed, under humid conditions, sweat doesn't evaporate as readily and so contributes much less to cooling the body.

Dress for the heat. Your exercise clothing should be light-colored, loose-fitting and made of lightweight, absorbent material such as cotton. As this material becomes sweat-soaked, it actually provides a cooling effect. Changing to dry clothing during a workout or when playing a game like tennis makes little sense for proper temperature regulation in hot weather.

Exercise and air pollution

Since you breathe faster and more deeply when you exercise, you also take in more atmospheric pollutants—notably ozone, smog's major component. At this time, there is no way to predict who can tolerate ozone and who can't, and at what levels ozone poses a health risk. People with asthma and allergies should be especially careful of exercising in polluted air, but everyone can benefit from the following precautions:

• Check air quality reports on the radio or TV. When pollution levels are high, exercise prior to 10 a.m., before ozone has a chance to build up.

• Avoid exercising near heavy or even moderate traffic. If possible, exercise in open, windy areas where pollutants are easily dispersed.

• When pollution levels are high, reduce the intensity and duration of your exercise sessions.

Use common sense. Try to exercise in the early morning or late afternoon or early evening to avoid the worst of the heat. And during very hot spells, consider alternatives like swimming or exercising indoors in an air-conditioned space.

Take time to adjust. Most cases of heat illness occur among exercisers during their first exposure to hot weather, before their bodies have become acclimatized to heat—a gradual physiological adjustment that allows the body to lose unwanted body heat more efficiently during exercise. The best way to acclimatize is to increase your exercise time gradually in hot weather over a period of several days. It takes the average individual 7 to 14 days to acclimatize fully, though well-trained athletes often need only a few days.

As the body acclimatizes, the amount of sweat production increases (especially on the limbs), and its composition changes such that more sodium is retained in the body. Blood plasma volume increases, thereby improving skin blood flow. As a result of these and other adjustments, the body can maintain a lower temperature and heart rate at a given exercise intensity.

Exercising in the cold

For most people, cold weather doesn't have to mean the end of outdoor exercise. Running, cycling or walking in winter can be as much fun as skiing. All you have to do is be aware of potential hazards and how to sidestep them.

The two main dangers of exercising in the cold are frostbite and hypothermia. Be on guard for the numbness and discoloration of frostbite—particularly on your hands, ears, toes and face. Hypothermia, which involves a dangerous drop in body temperature, is mostly a risk when you're out in very cold weather for many hours, especially if you're wet, injured and/or not moving around enough to stay warm. Early warning signs include shivering, muscle weakness, a sense of elation and feeling intoxicated. Dressing properly and taking other precautions described here are your best safeguards.

Breathing cold air can be risky for those who suffer from angina, asthma or high blood pressure—they should check with a physician before exercising in the cold. For such people, wearing a ski mask or scarf pulled loosely in front of the face will help warm up inhaled air.

The most common problem isn't that exercisers wear too little clothing in the cold, but too much. Exercise raises body temperature significantly—even a moderate workout can make you feel that it's 30° warmer than it really is. This can cause your clothes to become damp with sweat, and result in a risk of hypothermia once you stop. So when you're about to run on a 25° day, dress for about 55°.

Wear several layers of loose-fitting, thin clothing. This helps insulate you by trapping the heat you generate. And you'll be able to take off layers if you become too warm. Remove layers as soon as you start to sweat and tie them around your waist or stow them in a day pack.

Start with thermal underwear made of a fabric that draws sweat away from your skin (such as polypropylene, Capilene or Thermax). Next wear a wool sweater, synthetic turtleneck and/or pile jacket. Keep legs warm with sweat pants, lycra tights or leg warmers. For the outer layer, wear a jacket made from synthetic material—like Gortex—that's waterproof, wind-resistant and yet breathable (so that moisture isn't trapped inside). An ordinary windbreaker is okay for a short workout in dry weather.

Since you lose so much heat through your head, wear a wool or synthetic cap or a hood. For hands, mittens are warmer than gloves since they keep fingers together and have less surface area from which heat can escape. You can also wear inner liners made of synthetic material that draw sweat from your skin. In severe cold, protect small patches of exposed skin—nose, cheek bones, ear lobes—with petroleum jelly.

Shoes should offer good traction and shock absorption, especially when you run on frozen ground. They should also have a little extra space inside to trap warm air and, when it's really cold, to let you wear an extra pair of socks.

The wind can penetrate clothes and remove the insulating layer of warm air around the body. Compensate for a strong wind with proper clothing and by running or riding against the wind on your way out, then with it behind you on the way back—you'll do the most work before you're tired and sweaty.

Keep moving. If you stop exercising for any reason and remain outdoors, you must keep moving to stay warm or compensate by adding layers of dry clothing.

Specialized athletic shoes have proliferated during the last decade. With all the varieties available, it's helpful to realize that there are two basic kinds of athletic shoes—running shoes and tennis-type shoes. Active people generally need both kinds, and athletes may require other specialized shoes for their sport as well.

Running shoes. These are good for activities that primarily involve forward movement. Light weight and often thickly cushioned, shoes for runners have a durable, deeply patterned outer-sole; a thick heel wedge; a firm, shock-absorbent mid-sole; and a breathable upper. (See illustration, page 68.)

A study at Tulane University found that all running shoes lose about 30 percent of their shock absorbability after 500 miles of use, regardless of the brand, price, or construction. If shoes can't be repaired, replace them. (See Shopping Tips at right).

Tennis-type shoes. These are designed for any activity that primarily involves side-to-side movement, such as tennis, basketball and other racquet sports. Heavier and stiffer than running shoes, they usually have a herringbone outer-sole and reinforcement under the toes for stop-and-go action.

Aerobics shoes. Because aerobic dance calls for multidirectional, high-stress movement, these shoes combine the features of running and tennis-type shoes. You can use tennis-type shoes in aerobics classes, but not running shoes.

Walking shoes. Shoes for everyday walking should have a rigid shank for support. Rubber heels are a must—they absorb shock and are replaceable. If you plan to purchase shoes for hiking or orienteering, be sure they provide adequate ankle support. Shoes specially designed for long treks may also have curved soles to facilitate the rocking motion of walking and extended heel counters at the backs.

Cross-training shoes. If you engage in a variety of fitness activities and do not wish to purchase shoes for each type, cross-training shoes combine characteristics of many types of shoes, including cushioning and heel support for walking and jogging, and ankle support and added stability for lifting weights or playing a stop-and-start game like basketball.

SHOPPING TIPS

• If you have an old pair of shoes, take them with you when you shop for a new pair; a knowledgeable salesperson can evaluate the wear pattern to help you choose a suitable shoe. Walk or lightly jog in the store. Remember to wear the appropriate socks.

• Examine new shoes carefully. Make sure they are the same length and width. Put the shoes side by side on a flat surface and look at them from behind: The uppers should be perpendicular to the sole; they should not lean to one side.

• Hold onto the front and back of the shoe and try to bend it. It should bend where the foot bends—at the ball; if the shoe bends at mid-foot, it will offer little support. Shoes for running and walking shouldn't bend too easily or be too stiff. Also, hold the heel and try to move the heel counter (the rounded rigid section at the back of the shoe); it shouldn't move from side to side.

• In general, if your foot rolls outward significantly when you run (a motion known as supination), you are probably better off with a shoe with a strong heel counter, a substantial yet somewhat soft mid-sole, a curved last (the basic shape of the shoe) and a flexible sole. If your foot rolls inward (pronation), you might benefit from a shoe with a good arch support, a straight last and a less flexible sole, especially along the inside edge.

SPORTS-SPECIFIC SOCKS

For people who take participation in physical activity seriously, there are socks designed for specific sports—from cycling and tennis to walking and skiing. The socks differ according to where protective padding is placed (ball, toes, instep, heel, arch or shin), how thick the padding is and which materials are used. Nearly all of these are made of Orlon, polypropylene or other synthetic materials that draw (or "wick") away perspiration.

Do you really need such socks? They do provide extra cushioning and can help decrease foot abrasion. But the sock is less important than the appropriate athletic shoe, since the shoe can make up for many shortcomings of a sock. All purpose socks that wick away moisture are sufficient for most people.

PART 1

THE FIT HEART

Building Endurance

Walking

Running

Swimming

Cycling

Aerobic Movement

CHAPTER 1

Building Endurance

*The basic element of fitness:
cardiorespiratory endurance*

O f all the elements of fitness, the most crucial is that of cardiorespiratory endurance—the sustained ability of the heart, lungs and blood vessels to take oxygen from the air and deliver it and other nutrients throughout the body to every cell. As this chapter makes clear, improving the cardiorespiratory system through exercise has a number of physical and psychological benefits, some of them immediate, others far-reaching.

How is endurance built?

Since there is no way to exercise the heart and lungs and blood vessels directly, you must engage in an activity or exercise that places a demand on the cardiorespiratory system. To achieve this, the exercise must utilize large muscle groups in the legs or the arms and shoulders; equally important, the exercise should also be continuously maintained for a sufficient period of time.

Short-term efforts such as sprinting or lifting a weight can't accomplish this because they scarcely require oxygen. Such activities are commonly known as *anaerobic,* a word derived from Greek words meaning "without oxygen." But when exercise extends beyond a minute or two, the active muscles get most of their energy from metabolic processes that require a continuous supply of oxygen. Such activities are *aerobic,* meaning "with oxygen."

The best aerobic exercises are brisk walking, distance running, swimming, cycling, aerobic movement, cross-country skiing, orienteering, rowing and jumping rope. Exercises like sit-ups, push-ups and other calisthenics, or such start-and-stop sports as volleyball and baseball, may build strength or coordination, but they offer little or no aerobic benefit, even when performed vigorously. Brisk workouts on strength-training machines can raise the heart rate, but because the individual exercises are brief and often work smaller muscles, such workouts ordinarily don't enhance the body's intake and delivery of oxygen; hence, they don't confer any improvement in cardiorespiratory endurance.

What does an aerobic exercise actually do?
In response to having to work harder during regular bouts of aerobic exercise, your heart becomes stronger and is able to pump more blood per beat. Consequently, your heart has to pump less often to deliver blood to your muscles at rest and during exercise. Your arteries become dilated so that more blood can be carried to the muscles involved in the exercise. The muscles themselves become more effective at removing oxygen from the blood, and in using fat as an energy source. We refer to these changes collectively as "the aerobic training effect."

Isn't exercising mainly helpful if you play sports? If you don't, why bother?
Many benefits are attributed to regular aerobic exercise in addition to improved performance in endurance sports. The most important benefit is reducing the risk of cardiovascular disease, the leading cause of mortality in the United States. Epidemiological evidence suggesting that exercise and physical activity reduce the risk of heart disease was first put forward in 1953. Since then, numerous studies have noted a relationship between physical activity and protection from cardiovascular disease.

Perhaps the most comprehensive series of studies on exercise and health is Dr. Ralph S. Paffenbarger's research on nearly 17,000 Harvard alumni, whose exercise habits and mortality rates were studied starting in the 1960s. Surviving subgroups are still being followed. Subjects who used up more than 500 calories a week in exercise—which included walking, stairclimbing and various sports—had a lower risk of coronary

heart disease (CHD) than those who were sedentary. And CHD risk declined steadily up to an expenditure of 3,500 calories a week (equivalent to walking six miles daily).

EXERCISE DIVIDENDS:
- *A stronger heart*
- *Improved levels of blood cholesterol*
- *Lower blood pressure*
- *Reduced body fat*
- *More energy*
- *Improved self-esteem*

Subsequent studies have shown that other groups in the population have benefited from being active—and that the greatest decrease in the number of deaths due to all causes is associated with adding a relatively modest amount of activity (equivalent to expending 200-250 calories daily) into a formerly sedentary lifestyle.

One of the best studies, conducted at the Institute for Aerobics Research in Dallas, surveyed more than 13,000 healthy men and women for an average of eight years and related their exercise and activity habits to overall mortality. The researchers found that those subjects who were the most sedentary were also the least fit (based on the results of treadmill tests) and had the highest mortality rates by far. The death rate dropped most significantly among the next-fittest group—those who performed the equivalent of walking briskly for 30 to 60 minutes per day. The fittest subjects—including people who jogged up to 40 miles per week—derived relatively minor additional health benefits.

In addition, women benefited as much as men. Indeed, being physically fit lowered the risk not only of heart disease among both men and women, but also cancer (for which there is less evidence) as well as all causes of death.

What is it about aerobic exercise that provides these benefits?
Weight loss is part of the explanation—obesity is associated with a higher risk of coronary artery

disease. The loss of weight, which can be one of the benefits of aerobic exercise, is associated with reduced risk of heart disease. But the beneficial effects of exercise on the blood lipids may also decrease the risk of heart disease. Although exercise usually does not lower total or LDL cholesterol levels, regular aerobic exercise—enough to expend more than 1,000 calories a week—reduces the levels of triglycerides (fatty acids) and raises the blood level of "good" HDL cholesterol, which carries cholesterol to the liver to be broken down.

It is now widely accepted that there is an inverse relationship between the level of physical activity and the incidence of cardiovascular disease—so much so that in 1992 the American Heart Association cited being sedentary as one of the important risk factors for cardiovascular disease. While exercise alone is not sufficient to prevent heart disease, it is a critical part of any prevention program.

Hypertension, or high blood pressure, is also less likely to develop among those who exercise than among those who do not. In their studies of Harvard alumni, Dr. Paffenbarger and his associates found that men who did not engage in regular, vigorous exercise were at a 35 percent greater risk of developing hypertension at some time in their lives than those who did. In addition, some studies have shown that regular exercise can bring systolic blood pressure down by 5 to 25 mmHg, and diastolic pressure down by 3 to 15 mmHg for those who already have high blood pressure. Again, weight loss partly explains the reduced blood pressure: Hypertension is three times more common among obese people than among those of normal weight.

Such exercise also helps in the management of diabetes because it aids in weight loss and can also lower blood sugar levels. And it also can increase bone density in women over 40, many of whom are at high risk of osteoporosis, the loss of bone that occurs among the elderly.

Do you really need to exercise to lose weight—isn't dieting much more important?

Although an estimated 65 million Americans are on a diet at any given time, research has shown that dieting alone will not help most of them lose weight on a long-term or permanent basis. Almost everyone who goes on a weight-reduction diet eventually quits—and regains the lost weight. What is worse, the regained weight often has a higher proportion of fat to muscle than the weight previously lost.

About a third of the weight lost from all types of diets conducted without exercise is lean tissue, not fat tissue. Furthermore, when you put the weight back on, you will gain back mostly fat tissue, not lean tissue, particularly if you have not been exercising. Going on and off diets constantly over a period of time can make you progressively weaker and, in terms of your fat-to-muscle ratio, "fatter."

Aerobic exercise contributes to weight loss in three ways. First, because you can maintain activity for an extended period, it uses more calories than activities like weight lifting. Secondly, if you perform an exercise long enough, your body draws increasingly on fat stores for energy. Finally, the exercise will help you build muscle tissue—and if you are trying to lose weight, what counts isn't just how many pounds you take off, but what kind of body tissue is lost. Research has shown that a proper low-calorie diet combined with exercise can help dieters maintain lean body mass—muscle, organ tissue and bone—while increasing the use of fat. As a result, your percentage of body fat decreases and you improve your fat-to-lean ratio.

Is it true that exercising can help you feel better?

Researchers have consistently found a strong link between regular exercise and "feeling better." Explanations for the phenomenon range from the psychochemical (exercise induces the release of morphine-like chemicals to the brain) to the psychological ("I exercise, therefore I'm in control of my life."). Whatever the reason, psychological tests have shown that those who start exercising become more self-confident and less anxious. In some cases, exercise can also relieve depression. In addition, reports of exercisers indicate that they often are able to cope with psychological stress better than nonexercisers. Though such research is difficult to undertake, objective measures of stress levels (such as pulse rate, blood pressure and muscle tension) tend to be lower in fit people.

People often say there is no point in exercising to lose weight because exercise just makes them hungry. Several studies have shown, however, that exercise actually decreases appetite. In one study, obese women participated in a moderate exercise program for eight weeks. Even though there were no limits on their caloric intake, the women ate less and lost an average of about 15 pounds each.

How much exercise do you need?

That depends on your goals. In order to achieve a training effect and thereby build cardiorespiratory fitness, the American College of Sports Medicine suggests performing aerobic exercise sessions *three to five times a week.* Depending on how fit you already are, and how intensely you exercise, *each session should last for anywhere from 20 to 60 minutes,* in addition to the warm-up and cool-down activities you perform. You also should exercise at your target heart rate—a level of intensity that raises your heart beat to within a certain range that is based on your age. (See page 28 for the easiest way to compute this.)

Exercising less than this will not help you achieve an adequate training effect for fitness. However, experts have recently begun making an important distinction between exercise as it affects health versus exercise for fitness. If you simply want to improve your health and increase your odds of living longer, you needn't be quite so rigorous about how intensely and how many minutes you exercise. What's important is being *physically active.*

In the Harvard study of 17,000 male graduates, for example, the subjects reported the various activities they engaged in and the time spent on each one, and researchers assigned energy costs for each activity—for example, 28 calories for climbing 70 stairs. Men who expended 2,000 calories a week in vigorous physical activity such as running and brisk walking had a 39 percent lower risk of heart attack than their sedentary peers did, and the active men lived, on average, two years longer.

Most people could expend 2,000 calories if they jogged for about 30 to 40 minutes five days a week, or walked five to eight hours per week. The findings of the Harvard study also showed that simply walking nine miles a week will reduce significantly your chances of developing heart disease.

Is one form of aerobic exercise better than another?

The answer to this question depends on what your goals and preferences are, and what kind of shape you're in to begin with. Virtually every aerobic activity can give you a training effect. The one possible exception is walking, which may not elevate the heart rate sufficiently for people who are already quite fit. On the other hand, recent studies have indicated that it isn't necessary to exercise at a high training intensity to reap certain health benefits. In several studies of walking, including one involving postal workers who had been walking an average of 25 miles a week for 15 to 28 years, researchers have found a link between walking and increased levels of HDL cholesterol.

Such a finding is significant because many exercise physiologists have reported that, to increase HDL levels significantly, you need to run or perform some other intense aerobic exercise. But these studies appear to indicate that walking or other low-intensity exercise, when done regularly, may provide the same benefit.

On what basis should you choose an exercise?

Probably the most important step is to determine which activities best fit into your everyday life. Studies show that people tend to stick with exercises that are accessible to them and are the most enjoyable to perform. Recent data also suggest that people who engage in informal exercise on their own are most likely to continue with their training for the long term. The less equipment or preparation you need, and the less you depend on going to a class or health club, the better are your chances of exercising regularly.

For example, while walking may not raise your heart rate to a training level as effectively as running, many people find that walking is easier to incorporate into their daily lives. Walking to work, or part way to work, is an option for many people who cannot change their clothes when they arrive, as they would probably need to if they ran to work, or who don't have access to a gym or health club. Walking is also less stressful than running for out-of-shape beginners, and walkers have a lower risk of injury.

Still, running is tremendously popular: In the United States, an estimated 25 million people run at least three times per week. Some runners find that competition motivates them to stick with an exercise program, and the existence of numerous races makes them prefer running to walking for their regular workouts.

You should also consider the other benefits specific activities offer. Swimming, for example, works many muscles in the upper body and has lower injury rates than running or cycling, though the latter are usually more accessible. The following chapters cover in detail the benefits and potential stresses of the most popular aerobic exercises.

How will you know that you are becoming fit?

The most precise determination of aerobic fitness is a laboratory test that measures the amount of oxygen you consume while walking briskly or running on a motor-driven treadmill or pedaling a stationary bicycle. This measurement is called "VO_2max," which refers to the maximum volume of oxygen the body is capable of taking in and using for one minute in the course of intense exercise. (Oxygen is designated "O_2".) A high VO_2max is a sign of fitness. The VO_2max values of elite long-distance runners, for example, can be two to three times greater than those of sedentary individuals.

Although a laboratory test of your VO_2max is the most accurate way to determine your present level of cardiorespiratory fitness, the walking test described on pages 26-27 is a reliable and safe substitute that you can perform to gauge your level of fitness.

One indication of improved cardiorespiratory fitness is that you will have a lower heart rate when you are at rest (your "resting heart rate") than you did before you began an aerobic exercise program. In other words, your heart is processing the same amount of blood with less effort than it did before you exercised regularly.

Although no one has proved that a low resting heart rate is good for you (and sometimes it is simply an individual variation from the norm, a symptom of a low-thyroid condition or certain cardiac disorders), it is most often associated with people who are cardiovascularly fit. Marathon runners frequently report resting heart rates ranging from the low 40s (beats per minute) to the mid-30s. The lowest recorded resting heart rate, measured in a world-class cross-country skier, is 27 beats per minute.

How long does it take for exercise training to produce some results?

Many researchers report psychological benefits—exercisers feeling better about themselves—within two to three weeks. And studies have shown that people who embark on a regular program of aerobic exercise experience the initial physiological benefits—including increased cardiovascular efficiency, improved muscle tone and renewed energy—in about six to eight weeks.

Of course, how quickly benefits appear depends on your level of fitness to begin with. If you have been sedentary for many months, your body may need several months to adjust physiologically to the demands of exercise.

Will exercise that makes you perspire heavily help you lose weight?

You do not "sweat off" fat. Vigorous exercise can make you sweat off up to three quarts of fluid hourly, the equivalent of six pounds of body weight. Once you replace that fluid, as you should during and after a workout, you will regain those six pounds.

Is it safe to exercise during pregnancy?

You ought to check with your physician, but, as a general rule, you can exercise regularly during most times of a normal pregnancy. Some studies indicate that women who exercise during pregnancy have fewer post-delivery complications than sedentary women. Walking, cycling, running and swimming are usually recommended for pregnant women.

If you stop exercising, will you lose all of the benefits you have worked for?

No matter how long you have been exercising, you must continue your exercise program in order to maintain the training benefits. But you can take a couple of weeks off without losing all you have gained.

In one study of athletes who had maintained their exercise programs for 10 years or more and then stopped training, researchers found that the athletes' aerobic capacities diminished gradually. After about 12 weeks, the athletes' maximal stroke volume—the amount of blood the heart can pump with one beat—was about the same as that of sedentary control subjects. Nevertheless, the athletes were able to return to their original aerobic capacities with only eight weeks of retraining.

Isn't it too late to get fit after age 55 or 60?

No—virtually anyone, regardless of age or physical condition, can benefit from exercise. In one study, men aged 63 and older were found to increase their VO$_2$max as much as 49 percent through training. However, if you are over age 50 and have been sedentary for some time, you need to start out particularly slowly.

Another potential benefit provided by less-than-strenuous exercise is for women over 40 who are concerned about osteoporosis, the loss of bone mineral mass that afflicts some 25 million Americans, most of them women. Almost any type of weight-bearing activity may help to maintain or increase bone mass. Walking, jogging, dancing or a modest weight-training program are often recommended.

Can exercise actually reverse "the aging process"?

Certainly not. However, physiologists have been struck by the similarities between the effects of sedentary living and aging, so much so that many scientists have concluded that many of the "normal symptoms of aging" may be, in part, symptoms of inactivity. Such effects include changes in the cardiovascular and respiratory system, cholesterol levels, bone mineral mass, joint flexibility, bowel function, immune system function, sleep patterns, sensory abilities and intellectual capacity.

By age 60, for example, blood flow to the arms and the legs is 30 to 60 percent slower and muscle power is 10 to 30 percent less than what it was at age 25. By age 70, the metabolic rate has declined by 10 percent from that of a 25-year-old, the speed at which nerve messages travel has dropped 10 to 15 percent, flexibility has declined 20 to 30 percent and bone mass has decreased by 15 to 30 percent. Each of these progressive dysfunctions can be postponed to some extent with regular aerobic exercise.

After 30 years of age, most people lose 8 to 10 percent of their VO$_2$max for every additional decade of life. By engaging in an aerobic conditioning program, however, people can not only reduce the decline in their aerobic power, but may actually raise their level of aerobic endurance to that of the average sedentary person 25 to 45 years their junior.

Can exercising too hard cause heart attacks?
The concern that running can place too much stress on the heart was sparked in 1984 by the death of marathon runner and best-selling author James Fixx, who died of a heart attack while running. A study published in 1987 reported 36 cases of heart attack or sudden death in marathon runners worldwide. These deaths dispelled a widely held notion that anyone fit enough to run a marathon, an extremely demanding 26.2-mile road race, simply could not have life-threatening coronary artery disease.

However, the same study found that 71 percent of the victims had experienced symptoms of cardiovascular disease but had ignored them, just as James Fixx was reported to have done. He had apparently refused to have a complete physical examination or to take a stress test, so that he was unaware of his condition. Indeed, Fixx had many risk factors that predisposed him to heart disease, and he may have lived an even shorter life had he not been a runner.

In the general population, exercise-related deaths are actually quite rare: One study of active males whose ages ranged from 30 to 64 revealed that the risk of their dropping dead while running was one in 7,620. And although physically active people have a slightly higher chance of dying from a heart attack while they are exercising than when they are not, their overall risk of sudden death is 60 percent less than that of sedentary men.

Among cardiologists and therapists, walking and running are now widely accepted as health-ful exercises for recovering cardiac patients. As long as patients are carefully monitored and do not have symptoms that indicate a potential problem, they can increase their training.

How can you keep exercise from becoming monotonous?
About 50 percent of people who are concerned enough with their health to begin exercise programs drop out within six months to a year—even cardiac patients, who stand to benefit the most from exercise, drop out at a rate as high as 70 percent. Studies show that those who withdrew from exercise programs reported that their workout routines were boring or the facilities were expensive and inconvenient. If you walk or run, expense and inconvenience will not be problems. And bicycling, or any exercise involving a machine, requires a one-time expense. In addition, exercises can be varied sufficiently to help keep your interest and motivation levels from flagging.

The most important step when starting an exercise regimen is to set realistic, attainable goals. If you are out of shape, don't try to run several miles or swim 50 laps in the first week or two. You are better off concentrating on the length of time you exercise, not on distance. Researchers have found that runners who aim for 30 minutes during an exercise session are more likely to keep running than those who go for mileage.

Studies indicate that testing yourself—as with the walking test on the next two pages—helps you stick to an activity as you see your fitness improve. Exercising with other people can also increase your enjoyment, and entering amateur races is yet another tool for motivation. The following chapters contain a number of tips for keeping exercise enjoyable and injury-free.

Rating Your Fitness Level

To determine how fit you are at present, and to monitor your progress during your exercise program, you can take the Rockport Fitness Walking Test. This test, which was developed for the Rockport Walking Institute by cardiologists and exercise scientists, is quite safe and can be taken by virtually anyone. However, if you are a woman over 50 years of age, or a man over 40, or if you have any signs of heart disease, you should consult a physician before performing it.

The walking test will give you a simple but accurate measurement of your cardiorespiratory fitness. The only equipment you need is a watch with a second hand or a stopwatch to clock both your pulse and your one-mile walking time.

You also need to find a location where you can measure off a mile and where there is a level surface—for instance, a track at a school or college; a YMCA or YWCA or a health club with an indoor track; or a level fairway on a golf course.

BEFORE YOU BEGIN

Practice taking your pulse. The best spot to measure your pulse is at the radial artery in your wrist. Use the sensitive tips of your index and middle fingers: First feel for the wrist bone at the base of the thumb, then move your fingertips toward your wrist. You will feel your pulse in a pocket of flesh.

Don't eat, smoke or drink coffee or tea for at least two hours before the test. And wear clothing that allows you to exercise comfortably, along with shoes that are suited to walking.

Be sure to warm up before you begin. Start out walking slowly, and gradually pick up the pace until you feel warm. Then do the stretches shown on pages 40-43.

Once you are warmed up, follow the steps on the opposite page.

ASSESSING THE RESULTS

After taking the test, see how your results relate to the graph for your age and sex, at far right. Draw a horizontal line to the right of your heartbeat, and a vertical line up from your walking time. Where the lines intersect is your fitness category.

If the results show that you are at a *low or below average* level of fitness, the aerobic exercise routines in this part of the book will help you improve your fitness level significantly. As your fitness builds, or if you have already reached an *average, above average* or *high* level of fitness, you can increase the exertion of an activity by adding weights or following the other guidelines for intensifying exercises that are given in the following chapters.

For reinforcement, take the test periodically—every month or two—to keep track of how your cardiorespiratory fitness is improving.

1-MILE WALK TEST

Step 1 Record your resting heart rate. Walk in place for 30 seconds, then use the tips of your second and third fingers to locate the radial artery in your wrist. First feel for the wristbone at the base of the thumb, then move your fingertips down your wrist until you find your pulse. Count your pulse for 15 seconds and multiply it by four to determine the rate per minute.

Step 2 Find a measured track or measure out a level mile. Then walk a mile as fast as you can. Record your time precisely at the end of the mile. (Walking speeds may vary in individuals, so you may want to repeat this test at a later date to make sure your first-mile time is typical for you.)

Step 3 Immediately record your heart rate at the end of the mile.

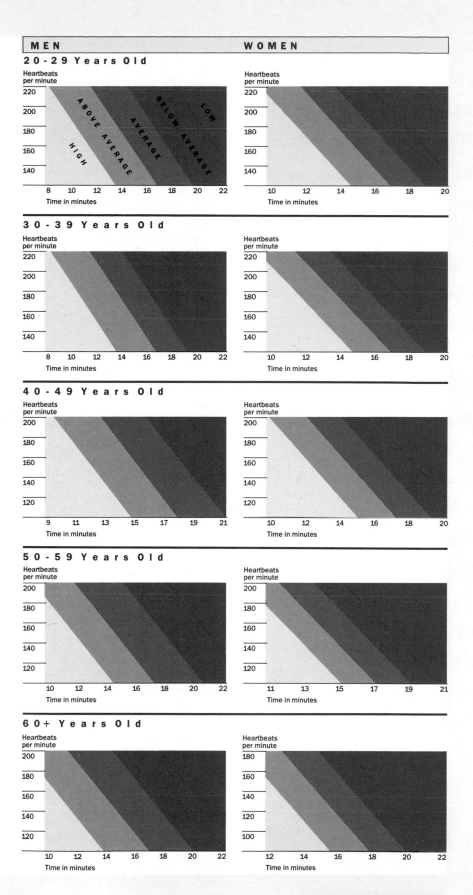

Choosing an Activity

A minimum requirement for an aerobic activity is that it provide continuous exertion of large muscle groups—the only way to work the cardiorespiratory system effectively. Any of the activities in the chart on the opposite page can do this. You can take up these activities at any age and continue them for a lifetime. And if exercising outdoors is not convenient, there are machines that allow you to perform most outdoor activities indoors (see pages 30-31).

Studies show that people tend to stick with exercises that are accessible to them and that they enjoy. It is senseless to embark on a program at a health club that is far from your home or office; chances are you will drop out. If you live near a YMCA, however, and you enjoy swimming, then you should seriously consider that as your primary activity. If you live in an urban area, then walking or jogging may be your best choice. In the country, it's easy to take up cycling.

HOW OFTEN AND HOW LONG

Once you have chosen an activity, it helps to follow these guidelines established by the American College of Sports Medicine:

If you are below average in cardiorespiratory fitness, you should aim at *three exercise sessions per week,* preferably on alternate days. Warm up for 5 to 10 minutes before each session. Increase the intensity of aerobic exercise until you are hitting your target heart rate (see at right) and maintain that pace for 20 minutes. Gradually decrease your activity to cool down. After two weeks, increase the duration of exercise at your target heart rate to 25 minutes, and after two more weeks to 30 minutes.

After six to eight weeks, if you wish to continue improving your cardiorespiratory fitness, you can increase the frequency and duration of your activity sessions. This is also necessary if you want to lose body fat. The optimal schedule is *four weekly sessions of 40 minutes each* (not including the warm-up and cool-down). Exercising more than this will not improve your fitness significantly, and it can increase your risk of injury if you are exercising at a high intensity. Indeed, unless you are an athlete, *exercising at a low to moderate pace for a longer time is better than exercising at a high pace for a short time.*

SETTING YOUR PACE

To achieve an aerobic training effect, the American College of Sports Medicine suggests that you exercise at a level of intensity called your *target heart rate.* The easiest way to calculate this rate is to subtract your age from 220—which is a person's theoretical maximum heart rate—then take 60 percent and 90 percent of that number (multiply the number by 0.6 and by 0.9)

The results are the upper and lower end of your target heart rate zone: While you perform aerobic exercise, your heart rate per minute should fall somewhere between these two numbers. For example, a 40-year old has a target heart rate of 108 to 162 beats per minute. (If you take medication for your heart or blood pressure, your target heart rate may be lower than determined by this calculation. Consult your physician.)

Don't let pulse taking and various computations make exercise frustrating. Once you've gained some experience, you may no longer need to take your pulse—you'll simply know how it "feels" to work out at your training heart rate. And if you find the above guidelines too strenuous at first—then do less. Although these are proven recommendations for improv-

ing fitness levels, researchers are still learning about how little a person "can get away with" and still become fitter. We do know that, compared to being sedentary, significant health benefits occur with less intense exercise—such as simply taking a brisk walk for 30 minutes.

CROSS TRAINING

Increasingly, people are choosing to get more enjoyment out of exercise by participating in more than one activity—a pursuit known as cross training. Not only does cross training allow you to exercise more muscle groups than sticking to a single activity does, but it also helps avoid the boredom of performing the same day-in, day-out routine. It can also provide highly used muscles some relief and thereby lower the risk of exercise-related injuries. For example, if instead of running four times a week, you alternated running sessions with swimming, you would give your leg muscles and joints a rest between runs.

Cross training doesn't necessarily condition your heart better than sticking to a single exercise. The main benefit of cross training is to condition different specific sets of peripheral muscles, thereby helping to improve overall muscle endurance.

If you decide to take up cross training, start slowly, as you would with any exercise activity. The best method is to pair activities that train different parts of your body: swimming with cycling, for example, or rowing with running. You can alternate activities on a daily basis, or switch over during a single workout: Instead of three or more 40-minute cycling sessions per week, cycle for 20 minutes and spend the other 20 running. And remember that you can use stationary exercise machines to mimic various activities.

An Exercise Guide

AEROBIC DANCE

This activity works all of your major muscles and can be performed either at home or in classes. If done at home, you can set your pace by your choice of music: Fast tempo music will make the session more vigorous. Be sure your workouts are low-impact—one foot should be on the floor at all times—to reduce your chance of injury.

Light:	120
Moderate:	200
Vigorous:	300

CYCLING

A superb conditioner for the lower body, cycling can be performed outdoors or on an indoor stationary bike that allows you to adjust how hard you pedal. Outdoors, the injury rate is low, though cyclists should always wear hard-shell helmets for safety.

5.5 mph:	130
10 mph:	220
13 mph:	320

RACQUET SPORTS

Unlike the rhythmic movements of other aerobic activities, racquet sports alternate high- and low-intensity movements. Squash, racquetball and singles tennis are most effective for burning calories and for overall conditioning.

Badminton:	175
Tennis:	210
Racquetball:	360
Squash:	420

ROWING

Whether you row in a shell on the water or use an indoor machine, rowing is a powerful aerobic conditioner. It burns calories at a high rate, has a low injury rate and strengthens the whole body, particularly the thighs and upper back.

Light:	200
Vigorous:	420

RUNNING

A highly efficient exercise, running is also convenient and inexpensive. Competitive long-distance runners have less body fat than any other group of athletes. Running puts stress on the knees, lower legs and feet, so be sure to wear good running shoes that fit correctly.

5.5 mph:	320
6 mph:	350
7.5 mph:	430
10 mph:	550

SKIING

Both downhill and cross-country skiing can be excellent conditioners. Cross-country burns calories more effectively since you need not stop at the bottom of each hill. Cross-country skiing also strengthens the shoulders and upper arms.

Downhill:	300
Cross-country:	200-560

SWIMMING

Many people, especially those who are overweight, find swimming an enjoyable exercise because it is free of weight-bearing stresses. The front crawl, or freestyle, is the most efficient stroke for an aerobic workout as well as being a good upper body conditioner.

25 yds/min:	180
40 yds/min:	260
50 yds/min:	375

WALKING

Certainly the most accessible exercise activity, walking is ideal if you are just starting an exercise program. You can increase the caloric expenditure of walking by increasing your pace and vigorously swinging your arms. Fast walking can burn more calories than running.

2.5 mph:	105
4.5 mph:	200
6 mph:	370

*Approximate caloric expenditure for a person weighing 150 lbs . Add 10 percent for every 15 lbs over this weight and subtract 10 percent for every 15 lbs under.

Home Equipment for Aerobic Exercise

Americans have spent billions of dollars on home exercise equipment, yet surveys show that the great majority of buyers of exercise equipment do not remain steady users. The best way to avoid wasting money on "fitness furniture" is to understand your goals, the different types of equipment and what they can and cannot do.

Obviously, you don't need to buy a machine to get an aerobic workout—just go out and jog, walk or cycle. But many people prefer to exercise indoors. Above all, exercising at home is convenient: you can squeeze it in before or after work, even while watching the evening news on TV. Thus a good machine at home can make it easier to stick to an exercise schedule and stay motivated. Home equipment is also an alternative to waiting in line for equipment at a health club, and it's handy when the weather is bad.

However, there's nothing magical about exercising with machines—any type of exercise you do that raises your heart rate to a training level, and that you perform long enough and often enough, will provide approximately the same aerobic benefits.

The chart on the opposite page describes the main types of aerobic exercise machines. Which one is right for you is largely a matter of personal preference. Some people dislike stationary bikes, for instance, while others become bored with any single piece of equipment. All of these machines can provide an excellent workout and help you expend an impressive number of calories, though some work primarily the lower body, while others provide a full-body workout. These machines will also help strengthen certain muscle groups.

They range from no-frill $100 models to state-of-the-art, computerized devices that can cost several thousand dollars. On an expensive machine, you may be paying a great deal for gadgets, such as monitors that calibrate your speed, distance and energy output. You don't need these to get a good workout, though they can certainly add some motivation and variety to an exercise routine.

SHOPPING TIPS

1. Before you buy equipment, always try it out to make sure it is comfortable, easy to use, and the right size for your body. Stores generally have floor models that you can test. Compare different models; try them out for at least a few minutes each. If you buy from a catalog, try out the model first at a store, a friend's house or a local health club. This is especially important for tall, short or very heavy people, who may not fit onto some machines.

2. Check construction. A machine shouldn't rock or wobble when you use it. If it is made of lightweight sheet metal or has many plastic parts, it may not withstand use. Flimsy rowing machines, for instance, have been known to collapse under the weight of 185-pound users. Look at display models to see how they have stood up to abuse. Bikes or other machines that fold may be convenient to store, but they may not be sturdy.

3. Shop at a reputable store or company with a knowledgeable sales staff. Salespeople may offer free instructions and should be able to answer any questions later after you get the equipment home. If you have to assemble a machine yourself, ask how difficult it is.

4. Think twice about buying bargain-basement equipment. A $99 exercise bike or rower may be uncomfortable, hard to use and perhaps dangerous. Of course, more expensive models aren't always better.

5. Make sure you need the fancy gadgets and trimmings (such as heart rate monitors and even video displays)—these can add greatly to the price. The simpler the equipment, the fewer the potential breakdowns.

6. The machine should have a warranty of at least 90 days. It's better if the warranty covers service as well as parts.

7. If marketing claims seem too good to be true—they probably are.

BEFORE YOU START

• The same health precautions for any exercise program apply to using a machine. If you are a healthy man over 40, or a woman over 50, or if you have high blood pressure or other risk factors for coronary artery disease, or back problems or other musculoskeletal problems, see your physician before starting any program using an exercise machine.

• Start slowly and with modest goals when using new equipment. Equally important, make sure you know how to use it. Each year thousands of people are injured while using exercise equipment.

• As with any exercise, the idea of "no pain, no gain" is both wrong and dangerous. Pain is a signal from your body that you should never ignore. Pay attention to your body and know when to stop.

• Always warm up (for instance, by running slowly in place or using your machine at a slow pace) and stretch before exercising to prevent muscle tears. Cool down afterward to avoid a sudden drop in blood pressure and, later, muscle soreness.

• Don't let unsupervised children play with equipment.

• Find a way to make using the machine enjoyable. One advantage of having a machine at home is that you can read, watch TV or listen to music while you're exercising.

Comparing Aerobic-Exercise Machines

MACHINE	WHAT IT DOES	WHAT TO LOOK FOR	COMMENTS
Exercise bicycle	Most models work only the lower body, but some have pumping handlebars for arms and shoulders. Some can be programmed for various workouts, such as climbing hills.	Smooth pedaling motion. Comfortable seat. Handlebars that adjust to your height. Pedal straps to keep your feet from slipping and to make your legs work on the upstroke too. Easy-to-adjust work load. Solid construction. Some models let you pedal backwards, which enhances working your hamstring muscles.	Puts less strain on joints than running. Adjust the seat so that your knee is only slightly bent when the leg is extended. To prevent knee problems, don't set the resistance too high: you should be able to pedal at least 60 rpm. Recumbent models let you sit back in a chairlike seat; this puts less strain on back, neck, and shoulders.
Bicycle trainer	This stand allows you to convert your regular bike for indoor use. Rear wheel typically rests on a roller.	One that is easy to mount your bike on; some don't require removal of front wheel. Wind-resistance designs simulate outdoor conditions.	Since this uses your regular outdoor bike, it is likely to be comfortable. The stand is less expensive than stationary bikes.
Treadmill	Some machines have adjustable inclines to simulate hills and make workouts more strenuous. Some can be programmed for various preset workouts.	Easily adjustable speed and incline. Running surface that is wide and long enough for your stride and that absorbs shock well. A strong motor, which can handle high speeds, and a heavy load.	Many models have side or front hand rails: some people like them for balance. To prevent a mishap, straddle the machine before starting it; slow it down gradually before you get off.
Stair Climber	Some larger models simulate real stair climbing. But most home models have pedals that work against your weight as you pump your legs; this puts less strain on your knees since you don't take real steps.	Smooth stepping action, large comfortable pedals and no wobble. Easily adjustable resistance. Comfortable handlebars or rails for balance. Some people prefer pedals that remain parallel to the floor, others like pivoting pedals. Models with independent pedals provide a more natural stepping motion.	Beginners shouldn't overexert themselves, since blood pressure and heart rate may rise quickly. Start with short steps and a slow pace. Put your entire foot on the pedal, not just the ball. Try to keep your knees aligned over your toes. Leaning on the rails or front monitor will reduce your energy expenditure.
Rowing machine	Provides a fuller workout than running or cycling; tones muscles in upper body. Most have hydraulic pistons to provide variable resistance; many larger models use a flywheel. One new model actually has a flywheel in a water tank to mimic real rowing.	Piston-type models have hydraulic arms and are cheaper and more compact than flywheel models, which have smoother action that's usually more like real rowing. Check that seat and oars move smoothly to reduce friction. Foot rests should pivot.	Proper rowing technique and cadence put little strain on body. If you have a back problem, consult your physician first. Make sure your legs, not your back, power your rowing motion. In early part of stroke, your arms should move forward before you bend your knees. When using a flywheel model, pull the bar into your abdomen, not to your chin.
Cross-country ski machine	Works most muscle groups. Simulates outdoor sport: feet slide in tracks, hands pull on cords or poles, either independently or in synchronized movements.	A base long enough to accommodate your stride. Adjustable leg and arm resistance. Smooth action. Machines with cords rather than poles may provide an especially strenuous upper-body workout.	Provides perhaps the best all-round workout. It may take some practice to coordinate your movements. Puts little strain on body; shouldn't aggravate knee problems.

CHAPTER 2

Walking

Techniques to make walking an effective aerobic conditioner

—

At first glance, walking may not seem like much of an exercise; after all, virtually everybody does it. Many exercise physiologists, however, contend that it is an ideal activity for anyone who wants to get into shape. A walking program is the safest and easiest way to start being active. And since it is versatile—you can vary the setting and the style of your workouts, the intensity, and you can even race—walking is also appropriate as a long-term exercise, even for those who are already in good physical condition.

Walking of any kind can be a social activity to share with friends or family. You can converse while you walk, and you can combine walking with other activities such as sightseeing, visiting or doing errands. And if you like participating in organized activities, there are numerous walking events and groups to join. In the United States, there are an estimated 10,000 walking events annually, from walk-a-thons to competitive race walks that attract thousands of participants. And there are more than 6,500 walking clubs across the nation.

Some shopping malls encourage exercise walking, and even mark out walking courses, give away T-shirts and promote walking clubs in many areas. Malls and other indoor locations are particularly suited to walkers recovering from heart attacks or elderly persons who need to exercise, yet require a climate-controlled environment for protection against inclement weather, pollutants and allergy-provoking pollen.

In addition to effectively conditioning you, walking—compared with running and most other aerobic exercises—is a low-impact activity that rarely leads to injury. Walking uses a heel-to-toe motion; your foot lands at the back of the

Walking vs. Other Activities

Calories expended by a 150-pound person per hour

Activity	Calories
Race walking	600
Uphill walking, 10% incline (3 mph)	500
Walking, 15-lb. backpack (4 mph)	410
Brisk walking (4 mph)	350
Slow running (5 mph)	550
Recreational tennis, singles	430
Swimming, slow crawl	400

heel, and pushes off at the end of the big toe. This spreads the force of impact over the widest possible foot area, relieving any one spot of excessive stress. It also allows the foot to roll forward and provide momentum for the body. Runners, on the other hand, often land more flat-footed with greater force and less roll, and then bounce into the air for a short period of time before striking the ground again. Walkers never lose contact with the ground: A walker's advancing foot lands before the rear foot leaves the ground.

Except for blisters, which are primarily the result of ill-fitting shoes, exercise walkers are troubled only by occasional mild shin splints—tenderness between the ankle and knee on the inner side of the shinbone—that can usually be treated with ice and a day or two of rest.

A major study, the Aerobics Center Longitudinal Study, followed more than 10,000 men for a little longer than eight years and correlated their exercise and activity habits with mortality from all causes. The researchers found that both walking and running have about equal benefit for reducing all-cause mortality.

The greatest advantage to walking as a means to fitness is also, ironically, its biggest drawback—walking is efficient, which means it does not require much energy. Because of this, you can walk for long periods without taxing yourself. At a casual pace, in fact, walking is more efficient than running: While a runner lifts himself off the ground, fighting gravity, a walker uses gravity to his advantage. The biomechanics of walking is similar to an egg rolling on end: You only have to add a tiny push with each roll to keep it moving. Researchers have noted that walking efficiency decreases and the energy you expend increases as you quicken your pace. While you use about the same number of calories to run a mile, regardless of speed, the faster you walk a mile, the more calories you burn.

This chapter will show you how to make walking an effective exercise, whether you simply want to improve your overall cardiorespiratory conditioning, to lose weight or to derive aerobic benefits from outdoor leisure-time activities like orienteering or backpacking. There are several different ways to walk for fitness, as the following pages demonstrate, and you can vary your walking sessions to suit either your mood or your training goals.

Can walking really exercise your heart? In one study of 343 people spanning the ages of 30 to 69, fast walking enabled nearly all of the women and about two-thirds of the men to reach their target heart rates.

There are also variations on walking you can turn to. Climbing stairs is another excellent way to keep in shape and add to your lifelong fitness routine. If you live or work in a high-rise building, for example, you should make it a habit to walk up and down some or all of the stairs instead of riding the elevator. Studies of several groups of office employees showed that those who made use of the stairs instead of depending on the elevators improved their fitness levels by 10 to 15 percent.

You can also condition your body by augmenting weekday exercise walking with more strenuous weekend hikes. Hiking and backpacking are pleasant pastimes that help you maintain your aerobic conditioning and produce other health benefits. One Appalachian Trail hiker was tested by exercise physiologists before and after his 87-day, 1,700-mile trek, during which he carried a backpack weighing 35 to 50 pounds. Because he was already in superb condition, his heart rate while hiking usually hovered somewhat below his target heart range, and his aerobic conditioning at the end of the hike was almost identical to his superb prehike level. But blood tests revealed that his HDL cholesterol, the "good" cholesterol that helps protect against arterial plaque, had risen from 54 to 74. This hiker's experience supports the research findings that frequent long-term activity—even if it is not within a formal workout setting or always intense enough to bring the heart to its target rate—can reduce the risk of cardiovascular disease.

You do not have to hike the Appalachian Trail to reap the benefits of backpacking: One study of 44 individuals aged 18 to 23 examined the effects of walking at a speed of 3.1 mph with a light backpack. It showed that walking for 30 minutes a day, five days a week for three weeks with a load of 6 to 13 pounds significantly improved aerobic fitness levels. Backpacking one or two days a week adds variety as well as vigor to a walking program. And while backpacking can be strenuous, it is also reasonably safe, provided that you don't push too hard going up hills and that your load is manageable: People of normal stature shouldn't carry more than 35 pounds.

Try water walking. You can do it anywhere— along a lakeshore or beach or in a pool—and you don't have to know how to swim. Because of the water's resistance, you don't have to walk as far as you would on land to obtain a comparable workout: Walking two mph in thigh-high water is the equivalent of walking three mph on land. Deep water provides more resistance, but you may do better in waist-high water since you won't tire so easily.

Orienteering is another walking activity that is becoming popular in America. Since an orienteerer's goal is to find a cross-country route between two points and then hike across terrain that may be quite rugged, this sport can be as challenging mentally as it is demanding physically. Those experienced in orienteering use a

WALKING TIPS

• If you are beginning a walking program, you should start by walking briskly or striding at a pace that raises your heart rate to within 60 percent of your maximum for about 15 minutes. Warm up for 5 to 10 minutes before starting the walk, and cool down for an equal time afterward. Be sure to swing your arms vigorously, which can help you expend 5 to 10 percent more calories.

• Walk on alternate days, gradually increasing your pace and distance until you can walk at a continuous, brisk pace for 20 to 60 minutes. Try striding: Lengthen your stride and aim for a faster pace (about 4.5 mph). As your pace increases, your feet will land closer to an imaginary center line stretching in front of you (see page 37).

• You can increase the effort of walking in other ways besides increasing your speed. Carrying hand weights (see pages 48-49) boosts the intensity yet allows you to maintain a comfortable pace. If you pump your arms while you carry hand weights, you will get a workout for your upper body as well as your lower body, and you will make your heart work harder. In addition to boosting the cardiorespiratory benefits of exercise walking, carrying weights while pumping your arms burns more calories than walking without weights.

• If you are just beginning a walking program, do not carry hand weights at first. You should be able to walk a mile in 15 minutes before you intensify your workout by carrying weights.

Walking Speed Conversion Table

STEPS PER MINUTE	MINUTES PER MILE	MILES PER HOUR
70	30	2.0
90	24	2.5
105	20	3.0
120	17	3.5
140	15	4.0
160	13	4.5
175	12	5.0
190	11	5.5
210+	<10	> 6.0

To estimate your walking speed, count how many steps you take per minute and compare the results with this table. This table is based on an average stride (2.5 feet long). If your stride is closer to 3 feet long, here's an easy way to estimate your speed: Count how many steps you take per minute and divide by 30. Thus if you are taking about 105 steps per minute, you are covering about 3.5 miles per hour.

map and compass to help guide them along country roads and paths, and through the woods, fields and mountains. The ability to find your way through the wilderness is an admirable skill, and pathfinding can be an excellent addition to your regular fitness routine. By practicing a few simple techniques, you can learn orienteering easily and chart your own course. You can also take part in organized orienteering events. (See pages 60-65 for a more complete description of orienteering and a sample cross-country course.)

If you enjoy the thrill of competing, or it helps you to feel motivated, you may want to try race walking, which is the fastest form of walking. A typical race walker can walk as fast as many people can run. The race walker's special gait, however, is as different from ordinary walking as walking is from running. While a runner's feet leave the ground to extend his stride, a race walker's stride is increased by rotational, or rolling, movements of the hips. (Early race walkers were called wobblies because of their style.) Race walkers can achieve speeds that would be impossible for other walkers to attain.

Since the crossover of efficiency between walking and running occurs between 5 and 5.5 mph, race walking at a faster speed burns more calories than running. Studies show that the body fat compositions and aerobic capacities of competitive race walkers are similar to those of marathon runners.

Race-walking technique is governed by a stringent set of rules designed to keep at least one of the race walker's feet in contact with the ground at all times. In other words, the heel of the lead foot must strike the ground before the toe of the back foot is lifted. This prevents "lifting," or rising up off the ground like a runner and thereby gaining unfair advantage over other race walkers.

You can race walk strictly for fitness, or you can train to enter races. Olympic athletes compete in long-distance walks of 20 kilometers (12.4 miles) and 50 kilometers (31 miles), but race walkers compete in walks of many shorter distances. Road-racing officials often allow separate entries for both race walkers and runners. By competing in running events, race walkers frequently derive impish pleasure from finishing

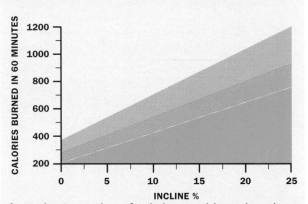

Calories Used Walking Uphill

Approximate number of calories used in an hour by a 150-pound person walking uphill at different speeds on various inclines. Most hilly streets have inclines of 10 to 25%.

2 MPH   3 MPH   4 MPH

ahead of many runners. Extremely popular in Mexico and Europe, race walking is now catching on in the United States. There are approximately 50,000 race walkers who regularly train and compete in this country, including many competitors over the age of 40.

While it is true that the impact force of the foot against the ground is quite low in casual walking, that impact probably increases substantially during more energetic fitness walking. In addition, while a runner's knee is usually bent on foot strike, allowing the muscles to absorb much of the force of impact, the walker's knee remains straight, and may therefore transmit more of the shock of foot strike to the upper body. Fitness experts suspect that, because of their gait and the speed at which they travel, race walkers probably risk the same injuries as runners. (For a description of the types of injuries that can be-

fall runners, and tips on how to minimize the risk of sustaining them, see pages 72-73.)

The only equipment essential for walking is a good pair of socks and shoes. You can purchase shoes designed for exercise walking. But almost any pair of flexible, well-fitted shoes with sufficient cushioning and stability will go a long way toward ensuring your comfort and minimizing your chance of injury.

The clothing you wear while you walk should be comfortable and nonrestrictive, such as loose-fitting street clothes or a warm-up suit. Race walkers usually wear the same outfits as runners. In winter, be sure to wear a wool cap and gloves to help you retain body heat, which is easily lost at the extremities. If you walk along paved roads, walk against the traffic and wear bright clothing during the day and reflective patches at night.

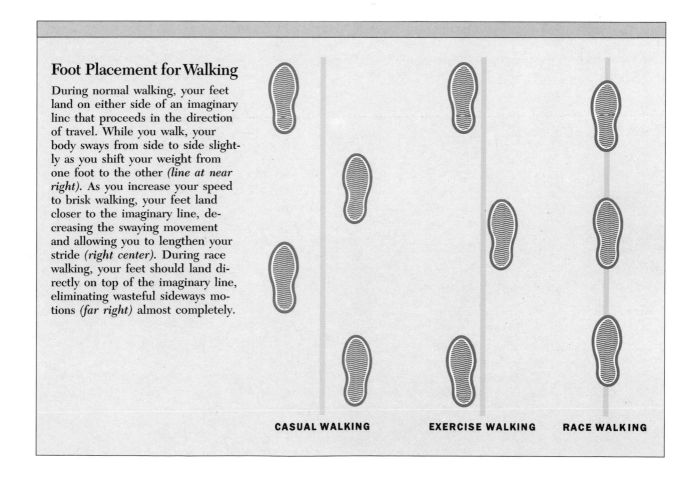

Foot Placement for Walking

During normal walking, your feet land on either side of an imaginary line that proceeds in the direction of travel. While you walk, your body sways from side to side slightly as you shift your weight from one foot to the other (*line at near right*). As you increase your speed to brisk walking, your feet land closer to the imaginary line, decreasing the swaying movement and allowing you to lengthen your stride (*right center*). During race walking, your feet should land directly on top of the imaginary line, eliminating wasteful sideways motions (*far right*) almost completely.

CASUAL WALKING   EXERCISE WALKING   RACE WALKING

Equipment

In addition to a good pair of shoes, walkers and runners can benefit from additional items such as those pictured at left. Many exercise walkers, for instance, enhance the benefits of walking by carrying hand weights such as those shown at bottom center. Many fitness enthusiasts and virtually all competitive walkers and runners wear digital wrist watches called chronographs. Besides displaying the time, a chronograph *(bottom center)* can function as a stopwatch for timing yourself.

Hikers who spend a whole day —or perhaps several days — on the trail must depend on a good backpack to carry supplies, and frame packs, such as the one shown opposite, take the weight off the shoulders and distribute it to the hips, buttocks and thighs. Day hikers, who may carry only a plastic water bottle and a sandwich or fruit, may prefer a fanny pack *(lower left)*, which is a belt with a pouch attached to the back so that it is light and snug.

If you hike in unfamiliar territory, you will also need a topographical map and a protractor compass similar to the examples shown here. Topographical maps clearly show geographical features, trails and elevations; the protractor compass, which has a housing that turns on a clear plastic rectangular base plate, allows you to align your map to magnetic north to find your way in the wilderness. *(See pages 60-65 for tips on how to use a map and compass.)*

Warm-ups and Stretches/1

Each walking session should be composed of three segments: warm-up, exercise and cool-down. The warm-up is the preliminary period or practice episode during which you begin to raise your heart rate and metabolic rate to the approximate level of the exercise session. In this way, your heart and muscles will be fully prepared to work for an extended period. In addition, a warm-up prepares you mentally and helps you fine-tune your motor skills for your workout.

Warming up is important, and it is really quite simple to perform. All you have to do is rehearse your activity at a slightly lower intensity than normal. Make it a practice to warm up for 5 to 10 minutes.

You should also stretch during your warm-up and again when you cool down at the end of your exercise session. Stretching will increase the range of motion in your joints and develop greater joint flexibility. The stretching routine shown on these two pages and the following two was designed specifically for walkers. Perform each stretch for a least 20 seconds. Be sure to repeat a stretch for one side of your body on the other side as well.

Perform heel raises to stretch and strengthen your calf muscles. Hold on to a stationary object for balance and stand on your toes. Then drop your heels to the ground. Perform at least 20 heel raises.

To stretch your side muscles, grasp your right elbow with your left hand over your head. With your feet apart and knees bent slightly, pull your elbow to the left until you feel a stretch.

Hold on to a stationary object with both hands. Extend your right leg behind you and bend your left knee. Lean forward until you feel a stretch in your calf and Achilles tendon.

Stabilize yourself against a stationary object with your left hand. Bend your right knee and grasp your right foot with your right hand. Pull your knee toward your buttocks until you feel a stretch in your thigh.

Sit on the ground and support yourself with your left arm *(above)*. Extend your right leg and place your left foot outside your right knee. Place your right elbow against your left knee and twist to the left.

Lie on your back with your legs extended. Bend your left knee and grasp it with both hands. Lift your head and draw your knee toward your chest until you feel a stretch in your thigh and buttock *(above)*.

Perform windmills to improve flexibility in your shoulders. Walk at a brisk pace and swing your arms in full circles, alternating sides as if you were performing the backstroke in the water.

To increase hip mobility, cup your hands together and swing them from side to side as you walk briskly. Use a crossover stride so that your left foot is placed on the outside line of your right foot, and vice versa.

Walking Stride/1

Normal walking is biomechanically efficient — that is, it does not require much energy. However, as your walking speed increases, your efficiency decreases. The faster you walk, therefore, the faster your heart beats and the more calories you burn. By the time you are walking at a pace of five miles per hour, you are burning about the same number of calories as if you were running. At higher speeds than this, it is easier and more efficient to run than to walk.

The key to walking efficiently at slow speeds is the biomechanics of the walking gait. As the photographs on these and the following pages show, the proper posture and stride will make your technique efficient.

While walking, you always keep at least one foot in contact with the ground. The foot on the ground supports the body while the raised foot swings forward. In addition, there is a brief period when both feet are in contact with the ground. At slow speeds, this gait conserves energy. At speeds above 3.5 miles per hour, however, it takes an increasing amount of energy to keep both feet on the ground. Therefore, to burn more calories and improve your fitness, you should walk as fast as you can comfortably.

Push off with your right foot and shift your weight to your left leg. During the left-leg support phase, your right leg is free to swing forward.

At the completion of the right-leg swing phase, strike the ground with your right heel and roll forward on your left foot. There is a moment of double support.

Shift your weight forward on your left foot and roll forward from the right heel. By the time you push off from your toes, your right leg supports your body.

Walking Stride/2

4

5

To get the most from walking, swing your arms forcefully with each stride. At your right heel strike *(1)*, raise your left hand to about chin level. As you begin to shift your weight onto your right foot during the double-support phase *(2)*, swing your left arm down for balance. Both arms are close to your sides *(3)* during midstance. As you shift your weight forward from your right foot *(4)*, swing your right arm up to balance your left leg. Then, just before your left heel strike *(5)*, raise your right hand toward chin level.

Increasing the Effort

Virtually anyone can improve his or her fitness by walking regularly. However, a person who is already well conditioned may have to walk uncomfortably fast in order to raise his heart rate to its training zone. (For an explanation of the training zone and how you can determine yours, see page 28.) For instance, one study showed that fit young men may have to walk at a pace of five miles per hour or more to achieve their training heart rates.

Fortunately, walking at high speed is not the only way to get a quality walking workout even if you are very fit. Studies show that you can increase your workload significantly by carrying hand weights of one to three pounds, so long as you swing your arms vigorously and maintain a brisk pace.

You can also increase the intensity by choosing hilly terrain as your walking course. It takes more than twice as much energy, for instance, to walk briskly up a moderate incline than it would simply to walk briskly along a flat stretch.

While carrying hand weights, be sure to swing them vigorously. When walking up hills, shorten your stride slightly. Do not slacken your pace but keep your head up while you lean into the hill.

Common Walking Mistakes

I t is important to maintain good form and posture while you walk. Keeping your head up, your pelvis back and your abdomen tight will improve your respiration and blood circulation.

Yet, because walking is such an automatic activity, many people exhibit poor posture while walking. Poor posture makes you unbalanced and forces the muscles in your head and body to strain to keep your balance. In addition to increasing fatigue, poor walking habits may result in lower back pain, shin splints and neck and shoulder aches.

These two pages show some common indicators of faulty posture. Monitor yourself from time to time to make sure you are not straining or tightening up, which may indicate fatigue or bad posture.

Slumping can cause neck and lower back pain *(right)*. Tighten your stomach, pull in your buttocks and swing your arms.

Neck and lower back pain can also result from watching your feet *(above)*. Keep your back erect and head up.

If your hands and teeth are clenched, then you are probably tense and stiff *(above)*. Concentrate on relaxing.

Using Weights

Do not walk with ankle weights *(below left)*, which may throw off your leg momentum. Avoid bending your elbows when using hand weights *(center)*; you might hit your head. Do not hold hand weights at your sides limply *(right)*, since that will not improve walking intensity.

Swinging your arms to the sides indicates you are throwing energy away from your direction of travel *(right)*.

Take smooth, even strides, but do not try to overreach your step, which can strain your muscles *(left)*.

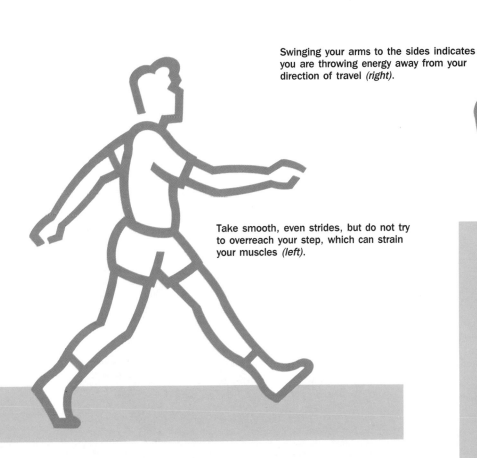

Race Walking/1

You can walk faster, and thus burn more calories in a shorter period of time, by race walking than by walking in any other style. The race walker minimizes the double-support phase to a fraction of a second and employs a rolling hip movement to extend the stride length and frequency.

Competitive race walking is governed by two basic rules to prevent "lifting," or rising off the ground with both feet. First, the advancing foot must make contact with the ground before the rear foot leaves the ground; and second, the supporting leg must be straight in the vertically upright position.

Start race walking slowly, so you can become accustomed to the gait.

Point your toes in the direction of your stride and swing your right leg forward, reaching with your hip and knee so that you strike the ground with your heel at about a 40-degree angle. Be sure that your leg is straight when your heel hits the ground. Push off with your left foot and keep your right leg straight as your body passes over it to begin the gait cycle again.

Arm movements are also important in race walking: They add thrust to each stride and assist in giving you balance and momentum. Although race walking may feel like an unnatural movement at first, with practice you should soon feel as if you were gliding lightly or even floating smoothly across the ground.

1

5

Keep your leg straight when your right heel strikes the ground *(1)*. Be sure your leg remains straight as your body assumes a vertically upright position *(2)*. Roll forward on your right foot and swing your left leg in front of you *(3)*. Push off with the toes of your right foot and extend your left leg *(4)*, making sure that it is straight at heel strike *(5)*. Swing your right leg forward *(6)* and roll toward your toes on your left foot *(7)*. Finally, push off on your toes and straighten your right leg for heel strike *(8)*.

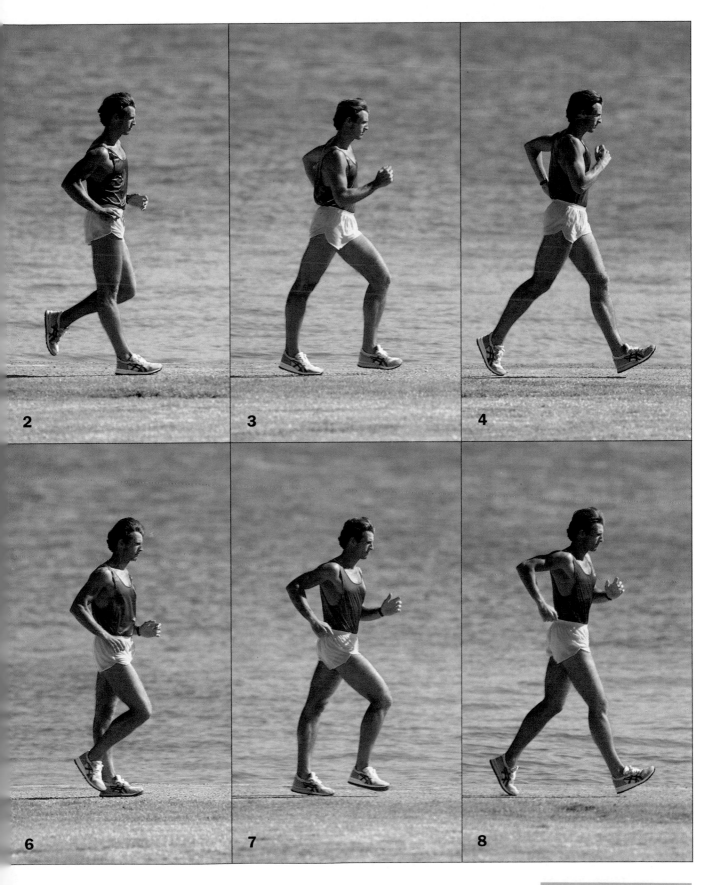

2

3

4

6

7

8

Race Walking/2

While race walking, one heel must strike the ground before the toes of your other foot lose contact. Plant your feet in a heel-to-toe alignment so that you will be walking along an imaginary line *(left)*.

1

2 **3** **4**

Bend your arms at a 90-degree angle, and keep your hands turned in and cupped slightly. Swing them from just behind your hips to mid-chest level *(1)*. During midstance, your hands should be in front of your hips *(2)*. As you swing your right leg forward, move your left hand forward for balance *(3)*. Return to midstance with the right leg supporting your body *(4)*.

Common Race-Walking Mistakes

In the beginning, you will have to pay particular attention to your walking form. And even after you have mastered race walking, and your technique has become second nature, you should review your form periodically to make sure you have not picked up any bad habits. Even top-ranked race walkers develop sloppy form, especially when they are fatigued.

Do not look down at your feet or watch your hands to see if you are race walking correctly. Instead, try to stay relaxed and loose. If you feel tension in your body, it may be caused by a mistake that is detracting from your performance. It is often a good idea to train with a partner, who can easily spot errors in your form that you do not notice.

Pictured on this page are the results of three common race-walking mistakes; on the facing page are three errors in technique that judges look for and can lead to your disqualification from a race-walking event or competition.

Walk erect with your buttocks in and your stomach muscles tight *(above)*. Excessive curvature of the spine can result in lower back pain.

Do not swing your arms across your chest, since it will cause excessive rotational movements of your shoulders and upper body *(left)*.

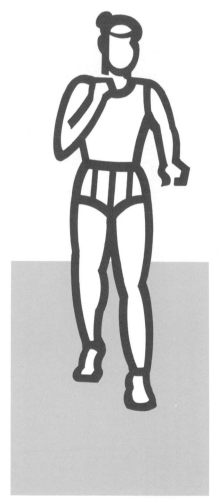

This results in a swaying, side-to-side motion and shortens the distance of each stride *(above)*. Plant your feet along an imaginary straight line.

Technical Errors

LIFTING Keep your rear foot on the ground until the heel of your leading foot makes contact *(left)*.

HANDS TOO HIGH Carrying your arms high and close to your chest raises your center of gravity and may mean you are lifting off the ground *(right)*.

BENT-KNEE FOOT STRIKE Make sure your knee is straight when your leading foot hits the ground *(left)*. A bent knee can lead to disqualification in a race-walking event.

Hiking

In the past 15 years or more, increasing numbers of Americans have participated in fitness routines such as walking and running and in wilderness pursuits such as camping and canoeing. Hiking combines the elements of both, providing a challenging workout for anyone who loves the outdoors. Although it is not possible for most people to take hikes daily, many exercise walkers find that weekend hikes and backpacking trips provide another dimension to their usual fitness workouts.

In addition to its value as a break in a walker's routine and as an adventure in itself, hiking can be a powerful aerobic conditioner. Although few studies have quantified the benefits of hiking, the experience of hikers themselves makes clear that hiking is a strenuous activity that demands a high degree of fitness. One group of hikers and researchers from the Georgia Institute of Technology, for instance, determined that hiking 150 miles in 13 days is the rough equivalent of running five miles in 40 minutes or less.

Orienteering/1

In addition to its practical value as a means to get around in the wilderness, orienteering—using a map and compass to find your path between two points of land—has special sports and fitness applications. Orienteering clubs across the nation regularly hold meets, in which entrants are given special topographic-style maps indicating a series of checkpoints, called controls, to find. Hikers must proceed from one control to the next to complete a course.

On most orienteering maps, the start of a course is drawn as a triangle, the finish as two concentric circles and controls as single circles. Control markers, usually white and red or orange flags, are placed on the course. Some control markers may be easy to find, while others may be placed behind a landmark. Lines connecting the control markers show the shortest routes between them, but not necessarily the most desirable ones. These two pages and the following four show a sample orienteering progression from an easily located control marker placed behind a tree.

Stand near the control marker and relate your map to the landscape *(right)*. On the map *(opposite, top)*, you are standing at the first control after the triangle in the middle of an open area. The top of the map is north, and you can see the line of trees and heavy vegetation (shown as green patches) to the north and east. Although the most direct route is through the vegetation, a more practical route may be to head north until you hit a trail (line of dashes), where you turn right. Then you can walk southeast to the top of a hill (thin brown contour lines). From there — the attack point — you can plot your route to the second control, which is a tree (small green circle in the center of the control circle). Having chosen your route, strike out in a northern direction *(opposite, bottom)* until you hit the trail.

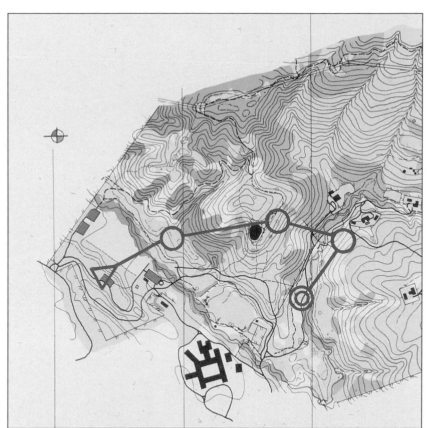

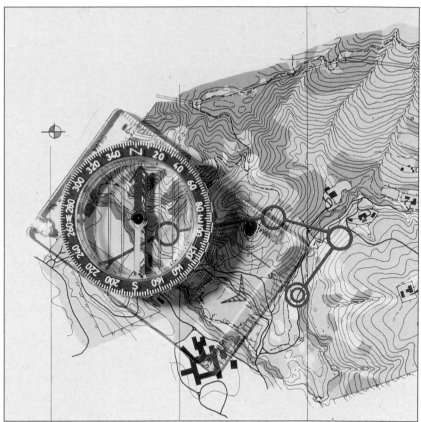

Orienteering/2

Once you have made it to the top of the hill, you have reached your attack point. If you cannot see the control, then kneel down and place the map on your thigh *(left)*. Place your compass on top of the map and orient the map so that the red compass needle points to the north end. Then position the base plate of the compass on the map so that one edge connects both where you are now, at the top of the hill, and your destination, the next control. Turn the housing of the compass so that the red needle points to both north on the map and north on the housing *(above)*. Since north on orienteering maps is actually magnetic north, to find the next control, merely follow the compass heading — in this case, 120 degrees— shown by the arrow on the compass base.

Orienteering/3

After you have set your bearing, stand up and hold the compass in front of you, with the arrow on the base plate pointing straight ahead *(above)*. Keeping the red compass arrow pointing north, walk in a straight line. If you continue walking in the direction you have plotted, you should soon see the tree indicated on the map. The control marker will be behind it *(right)*.

CHAPTER 3

Running

Still the aerobic activity of choice for millions

—

Running is *the* aerobic activity for conditioning the heart effectively and rapidly, along with most of the body's largest and most powerful muscles. Studies have shown repeatedly that running significantly improves cardiorespiratory fitness for almost everyone, including children and older people. According to one survey, the average VO_2max of elite distance runners is among the highest of all groups of endurance athletes, including competitive cyclists and rowers, elite swimmers and world-class cross-country skiers. Runners in the same survey also showed a lower percentage of overall body fat than any other group. In addition, several studies have shown that people who began running programs succeeded in lowering their blood pressure.

Running also seems to have a beneficial effect on a person's state of mind: Runners commonly report that if they are anxious, angry or depressed, they feel better after a run, and psychological tests confirm that running tends to reduce feelings of stress and anxiety.

Running is justly promoted by many physicians and sports-medicine practitioners as both a preventative and therapeutic activity. No wonder that the President's Council on Physical Fitness and Sports determined that running, when compared to 13 other popular forms of exercise, was the best activity for cardiorespiratory fitness, muscle growth, losing weight and relaxation.

In addition to its direct physiological and psychological benefits, running seems to encourage people to eliminate bad habits and adopt a healthier lifestyle. Researchers in Georgia surveyed 1,250 randomly selected male and female entrants in the Peachtree Road Race in Atlanta. The researchers found that 81 percent of the

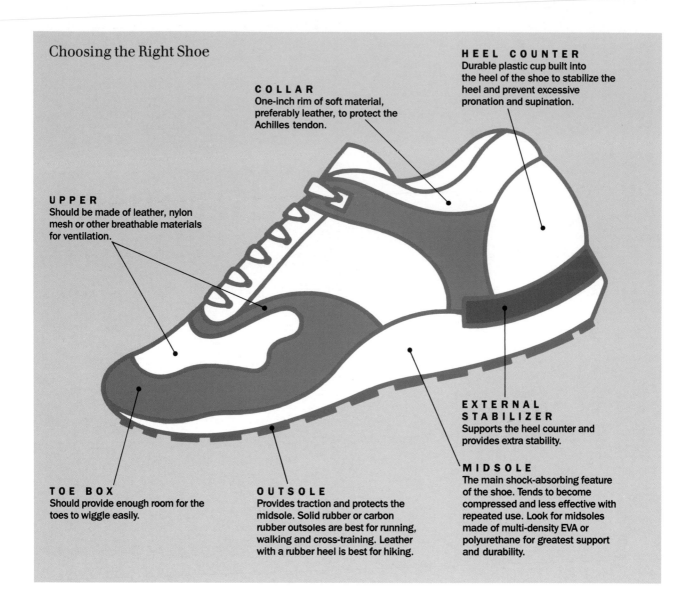

Choosing the Right Shoe

COLLAR
One-inch rim of soft material, preferably leather, to protect the Achilles tendon.

HEEL COUNTER
Durable plastic cup built into the heel of the shoe to stabilize the heel and prevent excessive pronation and supination.

UPPER
Should be made of leather, nylon mesh or other breathable materials for ventilation.

EXTERNAL STABILIZER
Supports the heel counter and provides extra stability.

TOE BOX
Should provide enough room for the toes to wiggle easily.

OUTSOLE
Provides traction and protects the midsole. Solid rubber or carbon rubber outsoles are best for running, walking and cross-training. Leather with a rubber heel is best for hiking.

MIDSOLE
The main shock-absorbing feature of the shoe. Tends to become compressed and less effective with repeated use. Look for midsoles made of multi-density EVA or polyurethane for greatest support and durability.

men and 75 percent of the women who smoked cigarettes when they began recreational running had given up the habit by the time they entered this 6.2-mile (10-kilometer) race. The researchers also determined that weight loss was associated with running: On the average, men who were overweight when they started running lost more than two pounds for every six miles they ran per week.

The key to many of these physiological benefits is the biomechanical action of the running stride. Although the gait for running is similar to that for walking, there are significant differences between the two. Speed is determined largely by how fast you move your legs—your stride rate, style and gait technique—and how far each step reaches—your stride length. When you walk, you always have at least one foot on the ground, and there is a brief period of double support, during which both feet are on the ground. Although this makes the walking stride highly efficient, it slows you down. In contrast, when you run, you literally take off into the air with each stride. The period when you are in the air, called the float phase, accounts for about 30 percent of your stride.

The great value of running as an aerobic conditioner derives in part from the effort required by three groups of the body's most powerful muscle groups for you to become airborne: the calves, hamstrings and the buttocks. Also, the quadriceps muscle along the front of your thigh is required to pull your knee forward and draw it up to prepare your leg for its next stride cycle.

Can running replace psychotherapy? A group of researchers at San Diego State University gave 12 men and women, aged 23 to 41, a series of initial psychological evaluations. After a one-year program of running three times a week for 45 minutes, the people were retested. In addition to showing cardiorespiratory improvement, the subjects were found to be more relaxed, assertive, happy-go-lucky and able to deal with abstract concepts more effectively.

Electromyographic measurements of the electrical activity in the leg muscles show that as you progress from walking to sprinting, your leg muscles become activated for longer periods of time. The hamstrings, for instance, are active during 10 percent of a walker's stance phase—when the foot is supporting the body—while the same tests show that the hamstrings are involved during 80 percent of a runner's stance phase. Similarly, the calf muscles work during 15 percent of a walker's stance phase compared to 80 percent of the runner's stance.

Some of the very factors that make running such a vigorous conditioner can also cause injuries. For instance, the ground reaction force, which is generated between your foot and the ground, either during push-off or upon impact, can amount up to 2.8 times your body weight during fast running and perhaps as high as 5.5 times body weight during sprinting. The force generated by foot-strike impact causes a vibration that travels very rapidly up your legs like a shock wave to the top of your head.

The human body, however, is able to make a number of biomechanical adjustments to accommodate the effects of this shock wave. When you run, your body increases the flexion of the hips, knees and ankles, thereby lowering its center of gravity. At heel strike, the runner's flexed knee and ankle allow the contracted muscles that stabilize each joint to act as shock absorbers, which dissipate much of the force of impact. By the time that shock wave hits your hips, the impact has been dissipated to about one-sixth its origi-

RUNNING TIPS

• If you haven't run before, don't try to run hard or far the first time you go out. Begin by alternating five minutes of slow jogging and five minutes of brisk walking. Otherwise, your muscles, tendons and ligaments will become sore and stiff. Alternate walking and jogging for the first three or four weeks, gradually increasing the jogging segments until you can comfortably run for the entire session. Avoid hard surfaces and excessive downhill running.

• As you improve, don't be tempted to run too quickly: This is more likely to lead to injury than to fitness. Stay well within your target heart rate zone. If you are running at a good pace and still have enough breath to carry on a conversation, you are probably training at the proper intensity.

• Run for time, not mileage. If you aim to run three miles at each session, you will probably run the same course again and again, and you may also try to run it as fast as possible. If you run for a set period of time, however, you can be creative about your route and maintain a reasonable pace.

• Don't increase your running time by more than 10 percent each week. If your total running time for Week A is two hours, for instance, add only 12 minutes at most to your running time for Week B.

• A study at Tulane University found that all running shoes lose about 30 percent of their shock absorbability after 500 miles of use, regardless of the brand, price or construction. If worn shoes can't be repaired, you should replace them.

nal strength; when it reaches your head, it is less than one-tenth.

Despite the body's shock-absorbing capabilities, most runners are well aware that they are not immune to injury. In a survey of entrants to a 10-kilometer road race in New York City, researchers found that 47 percent of the respondents had sustained a running injury within the previous two years. Predictably, the researchers found that the injury rate increased with the number of miles run per week, the pace and the frequency of competitions entered. The injury rate, surprisingly, was not related to running surfaces, terrain or interval training, which entails spurts of fast running.

Fortunately, the recovery rate among runners was high: 76 percent of those who consulted a doctor reported a good or excellent recovery from their injuries. Moreover, most running injuries can be prevented, first and foremost by wearing a good pair of running shoes and by not pushing yourself too hard. (For a review of running injuries and tips on recovering from them, see pages 72-73.)

Some running surfaces are better than others. Concrete—the material for most sidewalks—is made of stone and cement, and it provides little shock absorption for a runner. Roads paved with asphalt offer a softer surface that is preferred by many runners. More resilient still are cinder tracks, which consist of loose layers of crushed stone. You can run safely even on concrete, however, by wearing a pair of shoes with good cushioning and stability.

If you have never run before, or if you are out of shape, begin your training program by alternating brisk walking with slow jogging for 20 minutes three times a week (see box, page 69). As your muscles and tendons adjust to the stress, gradually lengthen the time you run and shorten the walking time until you can sustain a run for the full 20 minutes. Injuries can occur because muscles are tight and joints are not prepared for the stress of running. So before running, be sure to warm up properly and to stretch, which is crucial because running tends to stiffen the muscles at the back of the leg. It's also important to cool down and stretch afterward.

As you build up your stamina, you can pay more attention to your running form, which will increase your efficiency by reducing bouncing motions. The techniques shown on pages 78-85 will make running more enjoyable and also help you minimize injury.

Ideally, running should be viewed not as a monotonous chore, but as a vacation, a retreat from life's daily demands. But while many people are perfectly happy performing a 20-minute meditative jog several times a week, others do become bored. If you are interested in adding variety and a sense of camaraderie to your running regimen, this chapter will present some options you can pursue, from training with a partner to entering "fun runs"—races in which winning is not a concern.

Studies show that runners who enter races and fun runs tend to become long-term fitness enthusiasts. The survey of Peachtree Road Race entrants determined that most of them appeared to be dedicated runners: Almost 90 percent of the men and 80 percent of the women were still running one year after the race. In addition to the motivation spur that competition provided for these runners, friends also worked as a support group, providing camaraderie.

Although you do not have to compete to be a good runner or to continue on a running program successfully, many people find that weekend races and fun runs provide motivation on many levels. Beginning runners, for instance, may be inspired to train well enough to complete a local three- or six-mile race. Objectives for more experienced runners may be to improve their time, complete a longer race or perhaps to finish before a friend or another runner who had been faster in a previous race.

Once you have entered some races, you may decide to train to improve your time. To be reasonably sure of completing a race, your minimum weekly mileage should be at least twice the distance of the race you plan to run. A weekly mileage base of 20 or more miles will not only prepare you to finish the race, but will probably help you run stronger and faster.

In addition to accumulating miles to improve your endurance, your strength and speed will also be dramatically enhanced by running on hills, by taking long runs alone or with a partner, and by performing a technique called "fartlek," or "speed play." Developed by the coach of the 1948 Swedish Olympic Team, fartlek workouts are usually run with at least one other person and often consist of alternating easy running with untimed sprints over varied terrain. While on a fartlek run, you can play games such as tag, toss a ball back and forth or challenge your partner to short races. Since it helps boost performance as well as add variety, fartlek training is used by many runners.

By making up games to play while you run, by giving yourself attainable goals and by entering fun runs and weekend races, you can make running an enjoyable activity rather than just a solitary ordeal.

Pace and Posture

Runners experience slight but significant posture differences as they increase speed, as shown by the two figures at right, which are silhouettes of an elite middle-distance runner filmed while running on a treadmill. At six miles per hour — the equivalent of a 10-minute-mile jogging pace — the runner is more upright, his body has an up-and-down motion and his stride rate is moderate. When he doubles his speed to 12 miles per hour — the pace of an elite marathon runner — his body slants forward and his stride length and rate increase.

As you increase your running speed, therefore, you use new muscles or the same ones in slightly different ways. Exercise physiologists believe that to prepare for competition, you must train at about the same pace at which you plan to race, replicating race conditions as closely as possible. In this way, your muscles can rehearse the movements and postures they will undergo during the competition.

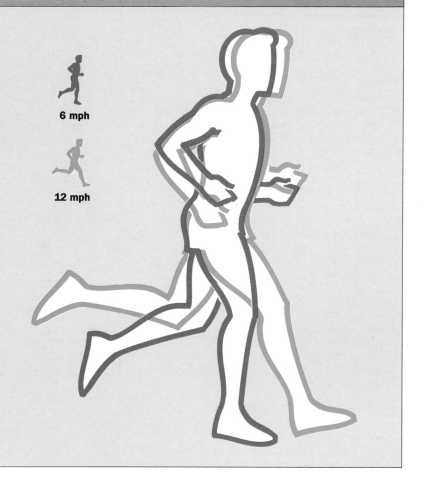

6 mph

12 mph

Common Running Complaints

Most runners (and some walkers) occasionally experience discomfort or pain due to injury. Often, the problems are stress, or overuse, injuries, which are the result of repeated microtrauma caused by exercise. If you experience any of the symptoms described below, cut back on your exercise training; if the pain is severe or persistent, stop altogether. In many instances, icing the affected area and elevating it will help reduce pain and swelling. If pain persists, or if you have any questions about your condition, consult a physician with a knowledge of sports medicine.

COMPLAINT/SYMPTOMS	RECOVERY AND PREVENTION TIPS
Achilles tendinitis Tightness or a burning sensation in the area from the lower calf to the heel, particularly when rising from bed	Massage with ice twice a day and try to avoid running or walking uphill. Be sure to warm up thoroughly and stretch frequently, as shown on pages 74-78. Strengthen your calves, as shown on page 40. if pain persists or is disabling, consult a physician.
Ankle sprain Acute pain—especially when standing or walking—and swelling of the ankle	Apply ice immediately, elevate the leg and use compression. Ice your ankle as often as possible for the first few days following your injury. If your ankle cannot bear weight, see a physician.
Black toenails A sometimes painful condition caused by pressure on the nails, which causes blood to collect underneath; can be acute or chronic	If you stub the toe and it turns black, have a physician puncture the toenail to release the blood, which will prevent loss of the toenail. A chronic black toenail, usually caused by tight shoes or running downhill, doesn't have to be drained. To avoid recurrences, make sure your shoes and socks have adequate room for your toes.
Blisters Most common in the summer when perspiration increases friction between your feet and shoes, irritating the skin	Clean the area around the blister carefully and puncture the skin with a sterile needle to drain the fluid. If the blister becomes infected, remove the top of the blister completely. To avoid blisters, rub petroleum jelly over the balls of your feet, your heels and other blister-prone spots.
Chafing Redness and discomfort of the skin, usually on the inner thighs or nipples	Friction between the skin and clothing or between skin rubbing against skin causes this problem. Rub petroleum jelly on troublesome areas, or wear soft, nonbinding clothing. Nylon fabric may also help.
Cubold bone displacement Pain or tenderness on the outside of the ankle that is difficult to pinpoint, resulting in an inability to push off the toes when running or walking	This is an acute injury that can occur suddenly, especially after running or walking over rugged terrain. If pain persists, consult an orthopedist or podiatrist.
Delayed muscle soreness Muscle soreness and stiffness a day or two after exercise, such as a race or excessive downhill running	Running or walking will help relieve the soreness, but be sure to exercise at a lower intensity. Warm up and stretch adequately before and after exercise.
Dizziness A feeling of faintness caused by a sudden drop in blood pressure, especially after standing up from a seated position	If you feel momentarily dizzy while running or walking on a warm day, you may be dehydrated. Stop immediately and drink plenty of cool water. But if you experience inexplicable dizziness or fainting during any vigorous exercise, you should immediately stop and seek medical evaluation.
Groin strain Pain or tightness on the inside of the thighs, resulting in a loss of stability and control as you swing your legs forward	Apply ice and elevate the injured area to reduce swelling. Perform gentle stretches for the adductor muscles, such as the exercise shown on page 77. Return to running gradually. Be sure to warm up sufficiently.

COMPLAINT/SYMPTOMS	RECOVERY AND PREVENTION TIPS
Hamstring pull Pain, tightness or swelling in the back of the thigh, forcing a shortened stride that is lacking in power	Ice is helpful, followed by rest. But the best approach is prevention: Be sure to warm up before exercising, and take extra time to stretch your hamstrings as well as your quadriceps (see pages 41-42 and 76).
Heel spur Pain and swelling just under the heel bone, sometimes accompanied by pain and tenderness along the bottom of the foot	Rest the heel by switching to an alternative activity such as swimming or biking. Ice massage also helps. Stretch and strengthen the calf muscles, as shown on pages 40-41 and 75. Make sure your shoes have adequate arch support.
Iliotiblal band pain Discomfort, tenderness or burning sensation on the outside of the knee, sometimes radiating up the side of the thigh	Reduce your mileage and workout intensity, and avoid hills and excessive running in one direction on graded roads. Make sure your shoes prevent excessive pronation (a term that refers to the feet and ankles turning inward toward each other).
Lower back pain Back muscle spasms or pain when bending or stretching your back	Rest is crucial. Perform exercises to condition your abdominal muscles and lower back (see Chapter 13). Make sure your shoes are adequately cushioned. Avoid excessive bouncing when you run.
Neuroma Numbness, tingling, pain or burning sensation between or under the toes	Make sure your shoes allow adequate toe room and have good forefoot cushioning. If pain persists, consult a podiatrist.
Runner's knee Pain behind or around the kneecap	Decrease running if it aggravates pain. Avoid sprinting and excessive hill workouts. Be sure your shoes prevent excessive pronation.
Sciatica Pain or cramping in the thighs and buttocks; tingling or numbness on the outside of the feet and toes	Avoid hill workouts. Be sure to perform hamstring and lower back stretches. If pain persists, consult a physician.
Shin splints Discomfort, tenderness or burning pain along the front or inner side of the shinbone	Ice massage is helpful. Reduce mileage and run or walk on soft surfaces. If pain is acute, stop altogether for a few days. Persistent pain be due to a stress fracture (see below); consult a physician.
Side stitch Muscle cramps, usually in the upper right abdomen, when running or walking	Stop and take deep breaths. Perform side stretches, as shown on page 74. If you are in a race and do not wish to stop, make sure your posture is erect, and take deep abdominal breaths.
Stress fracture Dull ache accompanied by local tenderness and swelling; pain returns even after resting a few days	Persistent shin splints are often a sign of stress fractures; pain is evident when you press on the site. Rest is essential. If you suspect a stress fracture, curtail your running or walking immediately and consult a physician.

Spread your feet and place your hands on your hips. Keeping your back straight, bend to the right, then forward, to the left and backward.

Stretches/1

Runners frequently rush through their preliminary stretches, or do not stretch at all. But stretching after warming up sufficiently is vital to your training because it increases joint range of motion and muscle suppleness, and thus helps minimize risk of injury.

Flexibility will help you avoid injury in three ways: First, supple muscles and tendons are less prone to tears and strains than stiff muscles; second, good joint range of motion reduces the chance of

sprains; and third, tissue elasticity places less strain on adjacent joints. A runner with tight hamstrings, for instance, is not only at a higher risk for leg muscle and tendon injuries, he may also injure his knees, lower back and hips.

Be sure to warm up your muscles before you stretch. You can stretch before or after a run, as long as you warm up by running in place or taking a short jog first. Warming up increases the blood flow to the muscles and helps make them loose.

Do not bounce when you stretch; this "ballistic" stretching may actually injure the muscles you are trying to protect. Instead, perform relaxed and deliberate stretches. Never push yourself to the point of pain, although the final stage of a stretch should be slightly uncomfortable.

Hold each of these stretches for 20 seconds and relax. You may repeat the stretch if you wish. If you perform a stretch on one side of your body, be sure to repeat the stretch on the opposite side.

Hold your arms out to the sides, parallel to the ground with your feet spread, then bend at the waist and reach your right hand toward your left toes.

Place your hands against a fence. Bend your right knee and extend your left leg, easing your heel toward the ground until you feel a stretch in your calf *(above)*.

Squat on the ground, supporting yourself with your hands. Extend your left leg, drawing your right leg to your chest.

Lie on your back, bend your left knee, grasp it with both hands and draw it toward your chest *(top)*. Then extend your arms to the sides to stabilize your upper body, and cross your left leg over your right. Keeping both shoulders on the ground, extend your left foot toward your right hand *(above)*.

Sit on the ground, extend your left leg and draw your right foot to your left thigh. With both hands, slowly reach toward your extended foot *(left)*.

Sit on the ground and draw the soles of both feet together. Hold your feet and move your knees toward the ground as far as you can to stretch your adductor muscles *(left)*.

Running Stride/1

Many runners mistakenly think of running as a bouncing motion rather than as a continuous movement, and you may notice that the heads of inexperienced runners often bounce. In fact, one researcher has calculated that an inexperienced marathoner may bounce so much that he runs the equivalent of a mile vertically.

In a truly efficient stride, such as the one shown here and on the following two pages, the runner's head barely moves up and down during any portion of the stride.

When you run, try to think of propelling yourself forward. If you do not bounce, your body will have a lower center of gravity, thus giving you a longer and more powerful drive. In addition, your knees and ankles will be more flexed, helping them to absorb road shock.

You can also use your arms to improve your running technique. Do not hold them limply at your sides when you run; pump them as if you were punching to improve your speed and power. The faster your arms move, the faster your legs move. Never let your hands swing away from your hips or across the middle of your chest. Allow your elbows to stick out slightly to counterbalance the rotation your feet make with each stride.

PUSH-OFF Extend your rear leg to propel yourself forward, not upward. Meanwhile, lift your front knee so that it pulls forward while the rear knee is extended. The calf muscles of your rear leg draw you up on your toes to push you forward.

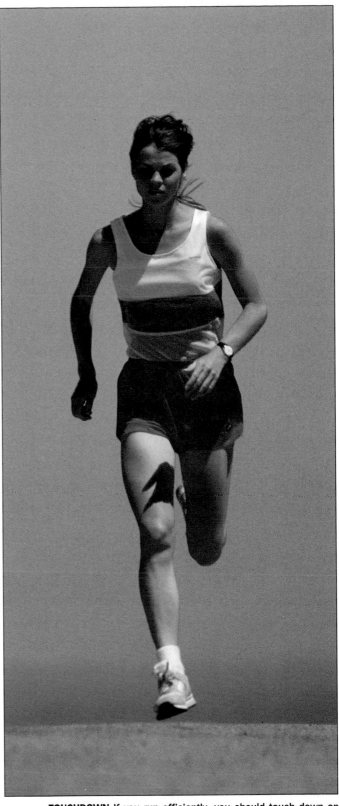

FLOAT After the push-off phase, your body becomes airborne. The float phase extends your stride so that you can move faster when you run than when you walk. Look ahead; looking down will shorten your stride.

TOUCHDOWN If you run efficiently, you should touch down on the outside rear of your foot, rather than on the heel, which allows greater weight distribution. You should feel more of a quick slap than a hard impact on the ground.

2

Running Stride/2

To maintain a relaxed stride, keep your shoulders back, chest
out and buttocks in *(1)*. During the float phase, do not over-
extend your stride; allow your legs to extend naturally *(2)*. As
your hands swing back and forth, they should occasionally
brush lightly against your shorts *(3)*. If you feel tension in your
shoulders, hands or jaw, remind yourself to relax; unclench
your jaw, loosen your hands and drop your shoulders *(4)*.

3

4

Learn to "fall" uphill by leaning forward; use a short stride and push from your toes. Pretend you are using your arms to pull yourself up a rope *(opposite)*. Do not sprint down a hill; stay relaxed and allow yourself to "fall" so that you can catch your breath, yet still maintain speed. Lean forward and land on the balls of your feet. Instead of pumping your arms, keep them low to maintain balance *(left)*.

Hills

Running uphill is taxing. However, nothing can help you build leg power better or condition you faster than hill work. In addition, it sharpens your mental toughness and builds the physical stamina required to race.

The technique of running uphill is fairly simple, although problems you have running on a flat surface are magnified once you go up a slope. Practice your technique by running hard up a quarter- to half-mile hill with a 10-15 percent grade. Do not stop at the crest; continue to run hard over the top. Then turn around and run downhill quickly, but at a relaxed pace so that you can regain your breath. Once you are on level ground, turn around to climb the hill again. Training in this manner is called running repeat hills. You may run repeat hills once or twice a week, but never on consecutive days, so that you give your body a chance to fully recover.

Although running down a hill takes about two-thirds the amount of energy as running up the same hill, downhill runs are more jarring to your body and are more likely to cause injury. Also, downhill runs are more likely to leave you with sore muscles a day or two later, because your muscles will be unaccustomed to resisting the forward momentum. This soreness will diminish with continued downhill training, however. If possible, train on grass at first; you can become accustomed to running down a slope while keeping the impact to a minimum.

Common Running Mistakes

Running technique can be idiosyncratic and still be effective. And you would never be disqualified from a race for bad running form. However, many runners — especially beginners — make wasteful movements that detract from their performance and contribute to fatigue and injury.

If you watch a top-ranked long-distance runner during a marathon, you may think that he is running at a relaxed and leisurely pace. However, if you clock his pace, you may find that the leading contenders are running five-minute miles. The key to this seemingly effortless movement is running efficiency: There is not a single wasted movement, and no sign of strain. Running five-minute miles for more than 26 miles is certainly not a leisurely pace; it only appears so because most elite runners maintain their form effectively.

You can improve your pace by eliminating wasteful movements that can drain your energy. These two pages illustrate the six most common mistakes that people make and suggest ways to correct them.

OVERSTRIDING *(right)* Do not lunge forward with your feet, but allow a natural stride. Focus on a short, fast arm swing.

LOSING DOWNHILL CONTROL *(left)* This may cause injury or the fear of it. Drop your hands, shorten your stride and run with a more erect posture.

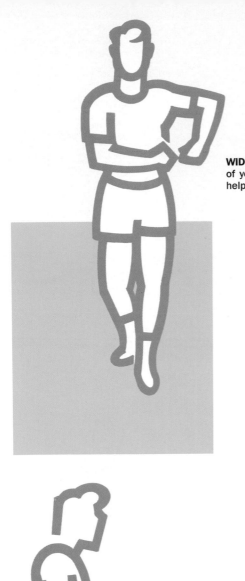

WIDE ARM SWINGS *(left)* Keep the palms of your hands turned in and slightly up to help keep your elbows near your sides.

HUNCHED SHOULDERS *(right)* This indicates tension. Shake your shoulders and hands to loosen up and relax.

LANDING ON YOUR HEELS *(left)* Shorten your stride and increase your lean slightly, landing toward the balls of your feet.

RUNNING ON YOUR TOES *(left)* This indicates you are bouncing too high. Lean forward and lengthen your stride.

Conditioning Routines

Some runners can enhance their performance with strengthening exercises that exaggerate running form. Two of these techniques are called bounding and prancing. When you practice bounding, you leap in the air and pump your arms powerfully to create as much lift as possible. This is an exhausting exercise, but one that will strengthen your shoulders, thighs and calves.

Prancing is not quite so tiring, but requires good balance and strong abdominal muscles to perform well. Although this is an exercise to improve your running, it is actually a walk, since you always have at least one foot on the ground. To do this, rise up on your toes and walk by lifting your knees high. Land only on your toes. This exercise teaches you to keep your knees high and your legs and arms moving quickly. It also helps you to move up onto your toes when sprinting.

Use these strengthening exercises to break up your regular running routine. Start by bounding and prancing on a 30-yard stretch of grass or dirt. When you get stronger, you can progress to 100 yards. Perform these drills no more than twice a week, and never on consecutive days.

To bound, leap as high as you can with each stride *(top right)*. Pump your arms powerfully to give yourself as much lift as possible *(top center)*, and extend your legs fully, landing on your forefoot *(top, far right)*.

To prance, rise up on your toes and lift your opposite knee until your thigh is parallel to the ground *(bottom right)*. Pause briefly and then step down, again rising up on your toes *(bottom center)*. Continue walking in this manner, making sure your heels do not touch the ground *(bottom, far right)*.

Partner Running/1

Although many distance runners enjoy the solitude of their pursuit, others like company on their runs, finding that the time and the miles move quickly with a friend. Indeed, sports psychologists at Louisiana State University and the University of North Carolina found that at light and moderate levels of intensity, exercisers perceived their exertion levels to be easier when they exercised with a partner.

In addition to the psychological benefits of running with a friend, a partner can improve your motivation through friendly competition and give pointers on your technique.

Running with a partner can make fartlek running more enjoyable. Fartlek is a loosely structured form of training during which you alternately run fast or easy, depending on your mood or the terrain. While running with a partner, for instance, you can challenge each other to short races, play tag or invent other games. Fartlek runs ease your sense of exertion and increase your feelings of exhilaration and fun.

Most people find training partners entirely by happenstance; for example, you may notice someone running in a park who appears to be at your level, or perhaps a neighbor suggests that you both work out together. You can also seek training partners actively by appearing at running clubs or races and talking with other runners. However you find a partner, you can ensure the greatest benefit by choosing someone whose ability is closely matched to your own — and by following the tips presented on the next six pages.

Partner Running/2

To minimize the level of exertion you perceive and still maintain a high-quality workout, do not race your partner; take turns leading. Drop a step or two behind your partner and "ride" her shoulder *(far left)*. If you look at a spot on her shoulder and match her stride, you can be "pulled" along. Trade places periodically by surging around your partner *(center)* and take the lead so that she can ride your shoulder *(left)*.

Partner Running/3

You can intensify the leading and riding technique shown on pages 84 and 85 by placing a series of cones, rocks or other markers at varying intervals along a course or around a field. Ride your partner's shoulder as he runs the course at a fast pace *(left)*. As you approach one of the cones, surge ahead so that you pass your partner when you reach the cone *(above left)*. Do not race your partner, but keep your pace strong as he rides your shoulder. Your partner should surge ahead at the next cone *(above right)*.

Occasionally play games with your partner to increase your enjoyment, prevent boredom and help you look forward to your next run. For instance, bring a ball with you that you can toss back and forth while you run *(below)*.

A game of tag is not only fun; it will help improve your ability to surge and sustain a sprint, either to pass someone in a race or to hold off another runner who wants to pass you *(above)*.

The Long Run

A weekly long run is the backbone of any endurance-running program; it is important for strengthening your heart and improving oxygen delivery to your working muscles. Long runs also teach your body not to rely exclusively on the glycogen stored in your muscles as an energy source: They require that you use body fat for energy, so that you not only spare some glycogen, but you burn off body fat.

Long runs also give you a psychological advantage for shorter races: If you complete a 10-mile run once a week in addition to your usual shorter runs, then completing a five-mile race will seem relatively easy.

Many runners perform a long run about once a week. In runs that may last an hour or two, many prefer to run in groups to help the time and the miles pass more quickly. Running clubs often sponsor after-work or weekend group runs of 10 to 20 miles, and runners frequently look forward to these events as social gatherings as well as endurance training. If the group is large, runners may break up into units, each one proceeding at its own pace.

Your long run should not be more than about one-third of your total weekly mileage. Plan your run in advance so that you can drink water along the route, especially in hot weather. Some runners carry water bottles with them; others prefer to carry money so they can stop to buy bottled water along the way.

CHAPTER 4

Swimming

An excellent all-around exercise for the least fit and the fittest

The rhythmic movements of swimming place a demand not only on the heart and lungs, but on virtually all the body's major muscle groups, thereby helping to build muscle endurance and strength along with cardiorespiratory endurance. And swimming conditions the body with less stress on tendons, ligaments and joints than running and other endurance activities.

Swimming is particularly effective at developing the upper body. A swimmer's leg muscles are used mainly to keep the body level in the water, not for propulsion; therefore, the more a swimmer relies on arm power, the more efficiently he or she will move through the water. Studies show that among competitive swimmers, about 80 percent of the forward motion comes from the arms and shoulders. And because of controlled breathing, swimming further conditions the res-

piratory muscles and improves forced vital capacity, a measure of breathing ability.

The low injury rate among swimmers is due in part to the buoyancy of water, which holds the body up and relieves it of weight-bearing stresses. Since swimming does not place a great burden on the spine, hips, knees and other joints, it is especially beneficial for people who are overweight and for those with knee or lower back problems. Because of the reduced stress, these people can work out longer and harder while swimming than while performing virtually any other type of exercise. Swimming is also effective for maintaining the aerobic capacity of injured runners and other exercisers who might not otherwise be able to stay active.

As to whether or not swimming will help you lose weight, research in this area has produced inconsistent results. Some studies have found that swimmers lost weight (and body fat); other studies showed no change in weight, while in others the subjects actually gained a few pounds—though often, when swimmers gained weight, it was lean body mass (muscle), not fat. Many overweight people don't swim fast enough or long enough to reduce body fat. You should swim as fast as your skill and conditioning allow, keeping in mind that there is a trade-off between swimming speed and calories used per minute: A person swimming 50 yards per minute expends twice the calories as he does swimming 25 yards per minute. Hence, if you are a slow swimmer, you need to compensate for a lack of speed by swimming for a longer period of time than a faster swimmer does to use the same number of calories. It is the *total distance* you swim that is the key for energy use. And of course, if your main reason for swimming is to lose weight, you should also try to cut down on the calories you consume.

To begin a swimming program, you must first find a suitable pool. In the United States, there are more than 2.5 million public and private swimming pools. Although competitive swimmers like to train in Olympic-size pools, many beginning swimmers find the 50-meter length of these pools daunting. In any case, most pools—even some advertised as Olympic-size—are a more manageable 25 meters (or 25 yards). Pools shorter than 20 yards have the disadvantage of making you turn frequently, which tends to reduce the intensity of the exercise.

The pool should have gutters and lane buoys to cut down on wave action and painted lines on the bottom to help guide you. The ideal water temperature for a workout is around 80° F; in warmer water, you expend too much energy throwing off the body heat generated by swimming exercise.

You can get a satisfactory exercise session simply by swimming continuous laps in a pool. But many people lose interest or fail to improve substantially if they repeat the same workout week after week. One way to vary a swimming pro-gram is with "broken swims," a training technique suitable for swimmers at all levels. This entails resting between each lap or set of laps, usually for a minute or less, so that you can partially recover oxygen without your heart rate falling below its target zone. By changing the length and frequency of these rest periods, you can control your progress, as described in the box opposite. During the rest periods between laps, you can monitor your heart rate if you wish. As with all endurance exercises, your goal is to reach a level of exertion that causes your heart to pump at your target heart rate for a sustained 20 to 30-minute period.

Since water is constantly washing over you and cooling you as you swim, you can sweat a great deal and not know it. Be sure to replenish lost fluid by drinking a cup or two of water before you go in the water, every 20 to 30 minutes as you swim, and again when you have finished.

You can also eat before you swim, though it should be in moderation. It is a common belief that eating before swimming will cause severe stomach cramps, yet no research has ever proved this. In one study, swimmers ate a meal at intervals of a half hour to three hours before undertaking a strenuous swim. None of the swimmers reported nausea or stomach cramps during or after the workout.

Swimmers are subject to some minor vexations. Chlorine will make your hair dry and brittle. Wearing a swim cap and shampooing hair after swimming will eliminate most hair problems. (There are special shampoos that convert chlorine into water-soluble chloride, which washes easily out of hair.) Both chlorine and salt (if you swim in the ocean) dry out the skin. To prevent or treat dry skin, shower with soap immediately after swimming to remove chlorine (or salt) residue, then apply moisturizer to damp skin, which seals in the skin's natural oils. Infection of the ear canal is another common problem. This can sometimes be prevented by the use of alcohol or glycerin drops after a swim. If problems persist, consult your physician.

- If your level of fitness is low but you have reasonable swimming skills, start by swimming 100 meters (four laps in a 25-meter pool) with a one-minute rest period between each lap. As you gain confidence and swimming ability, gradually increase the number of laps you can do continuously. For example, a session in the second or third week might consist of swimming 50 meters with a one-minute rest, then two 25-meter laps with a 30-second rest after each and finally another 50-meter swim. (The sequence can be written in shorthand as 1 x 50, 2 x 25, 1 x 50.)

- To build endurance, shorten the rest period and increase the length of your continuous swim. For example, you might swim a sequence of 1 x 25, 1 x 50, 1 x 75 with 30-second rest periods, then repeat the sequence, for each session during one week. The following week, do 1 x 50, 1 x 75, 1 x 100 per session, and shorten the rest periods to 20 seconds. As you build your aerobic base, take a particular distance—say 700 meters (28 lengths of a 25-meter pool)—and break it into segments. These can be of equal size, such as 7 x 100, or you could swim seven laps, then six laps, on down to one lap, with 15- to 30-second rest periods between segments.

- A more challenging variation is "pyramids," a series of laps in ascending and then descending number. You can swim a mile, for example, in a "pyramid eight": one lap followed by a rest period, then two laps, and so on up to eight—then back down. (In shorthand, just remember 1-2-3-4-5-6-7-8-7-6-5-4-3-2-1.) At the "height" of the pyramid, you should feel close to fatigue; as the numbers decrease, you will feel stronger and can even increase the pace of your swimming.

- You can build both endurance and speed with interval training, which consists of a timed swim alternating with a timed rest. For instance, if you are able to swim 50 meters in less than 1 minute, give yourself intervals of 1 minute, 15 seconds: Swim 50 meters as fast as you can, then rest for the remaining time. (If you swim the 50 meters in 50 seconds, you have 25 seconds to rest.)

- You can also string your intervals together for an interval set—for example, 4 x 50. The interval rest period encourages you to swim faster; yet the rest period is short enough so that your heart rate will not drop out of its target zone. Precede interval sets with a slow warm-up swim (15 to 25 percent of your total distance) and a cool-down (10 percent).

If you are a beginner, swimming lessons are worthwhile, and even intermediate swimmers can benefit from brushing up on their technique. Paying attention to your technique is especially important because minor lapses in swimming form are common, even among experienced swimmers, and such mistakes can be more costly than faults in running or cycling technique, since the resistance of water is so much greater than wind resistance. The following pages not only demonstrate the most efficient form for performing the freestyle (front crawl) swimming stroke—the stroke most often used for endurance swimming—but also show you mistakes that swimmers are most likely to make. You will also find drills to help you perfect your form. Work on some aspect of your form at every workout; this helps to make the exercise more challenging, and will reward you with small but steady improvements.

A note about target heart rate: Studies have shown that people have a lower maximum heart rate when swimming than when exercising on land. The reasons may primarily be due to an enhancement in the volume of blood pumped per beat during swimming, and more favorable conditions for regulating body temperature. This difference—averaging 13 beats per minute—must be subtracted from the age-related maximum heart rate (220 minus your age). Thus, a 40-year-old swimmer would subtract 40 plus 13 from 220 and get a maximum rate of 167, and then take 60 to 90 percent of that to get a training range while swimming of 100 to 150.

Streamlining

The hydrodynamics of swimming are based on principles similar to the aerodynamics of flying: An object that is flatter and more streamlined will move through either water or air faster than an angled object, which catches more resistance. A flat, streamlined swimming position creates relatively little disruption of the water. This means you will encounter less resistance — called drag — to hold you back, and require less energy for forward momentum.

Proper body alignment, shown on these two pages, is probably the most essential element of good swimming form, since effective stroke mechanics, kicking form and breathing techniques all stem from it. Your body should be streamlined both horizontally and laterally. Horizontal streamlining will keep you flat and shallow in the water so that you encounter minimum resistance to forward motion. Aligning your body laterally will keep it in a straight line so that it does not fishtail from side to side, which increases resistance by presenting a greater body area to the water. (In this chapter, common mistakes in body position, stroking and other aspects of form are shown in black-and-white photographs.)

For lateral streamlining, your head, shoulders, hips and feet should be aligned *(above)*. When stroking, your body should twist as a unit; avoid side-to-side swaying. Kicking helps to counterbalance the rolling caused by your arm stroke.

To streamline your body horizontally, keep it as flat as possible in the water. Your head should be lowered so it breaks the water at about your hairline, your back level and your feet and legs near the water's surface *(above)*.

WRONG Inclining your body at a diagonal to the water's surface *(right)* leads to inefficient swimming. Your hips and legs are sunken at a downward angle, while your head is high, which increases lateral resistance as you swim.

Stroking Mechanics

Most of the momentum of swimming comes from your stroke. Here and on the following 10 pages, the front crawl, or freestyle, stroke—the most frequently used stroke of both fitness and competitive swimmers—is broken into its component parts and accompanied by typical errors and corrective drills. Taking time to learn the elements of your stroke and to analyze it will improve your swimming efficiency markedly.

The freestyle stroke can be divided into three phases, starting with the *entry phase*—the beginning of the stroke in which the hand first enters the water. This phase concludes with the *catch*, when the hand, now under the water, first applies pressure to the water. The *power phase*, which includes the pull, push and finish (shown on pages 108-111), actually moves the water backward to provide the stroke's forward momentum. Finally, in the *recovery phase* (pages 114-115), the hand and arm leave the water behind you and then circle forward through the air to prepare for the next stroke cycle.

Although the three stroke phases are shown independently, it is important to remember that they are interrelated: Effective stroking depends on both a proper entry and recovery. You will best enhance your swimming by perfecting all the phases of stroking.

ENTRY The point at which your hand enters the water should be in line with your ear and between nine inches to a foot in front of your head. While your hand is still out of the water, hold your elbow high and bent at almost a 90-degree angle. Keep your palm pitched, or tilted, outward at a 45-degree angle so that your thumb enters the water first *(above)*.

As this underwater view of the entry shows, your hand should lead, with your bent elbow following *(top)*. In a correct entry, the pitch of the hand will allow a minimum of drag-creating bubbles. To prepare for the catch of the entry *(above),* as you enter the water, extend your elbow and press your hand forward, elevating your shoulder girdle as you push downward gradually to about a foot below the water's surface.

Entry Errors and Drills

WRONG A typical entry mistake is to extend your arm before it enters the water *(right)*. This not only strains the muscles of the shoulder and the back, but also traps air bubbles, creates more drag and can hinder proper torso rotation.

WRONG Reaching past the body's center line *(left)* disrupts your lateral alignment by causing your hips and shoulders to turn from side to side excessively. Your arm should not cross in front of your head on entry.

DRILL Exaggerating the point of entry will allow you to both feel and visualize the difference between proper entry and either overextending or overreaching. Instead of entering with your arm about a foot in front of your head, bend your elbow more sharply and push your hand downward into the water like a piston right next to your ear *(above)*. Alternate one lap of drill swimming with one lap of regular swimming for five-to-10 25-yard laps.

The Power Phase/1

During this part of the stroke, your arm sweeps from the catch position in front of your body to the finish behind you. The force of the power phase is determined largely by the roll of your shoulders and torso, which should rotate upward about 45 degrees as your arm moves past.

The power phase of the stroke starts with the pull *(top)*, during which you push your hand downward, turning it in toward the center line of your body, and start to bend your elbow. As the pull continues *(second)*, flex your wrist and continue bending your elbow until it reaches a maximum angle of about 90 degrees when your arm is beneath your chest. At this point, begin the push phase *(third)*, by rotating your hand to face almost directly behind you as it pushes the water away. Finally, at the finish *(bottom)*, begin to straighten your elbow as it leaves the water, rotating your palm in toward your thigh as your hand continues to push backward. Your pinky should lead as your hand begins to leave the water. When performing the power phase correctly, you should feel constant pressure on your palms.

The Power Phase/2

The correct elbow bend during the power phase *(right)* is crucial if you are to achieve maximum propulsion while swimming. Ideally, you should start bending your elbow immediately after the catch, and it should reach a maximum bend of 90 degrees when it is directly beneath your body. This angle should gradually increase as you continue to push backward.

WRONG The dropped elbow *(right)* is the most serious of all stroking flaws: The elbow is prematurely bent so that it is lower than the hand when entering the water. This wastes energy, since the lowered elbow and shoulder are not in a maximum power position and so cannot move the water effectively. In addition, this incorrect position can lead to shoulder injuries.

WRONG Powering your stroke with a straight elbow *(right)* is also ineffective, since it relies strictly on arm strength for power, and does not allow you to utilize the larger and stronger muscles of your back. Additionally, this stroking flaw can decrease torso rotation and lead to shoulder injuries.

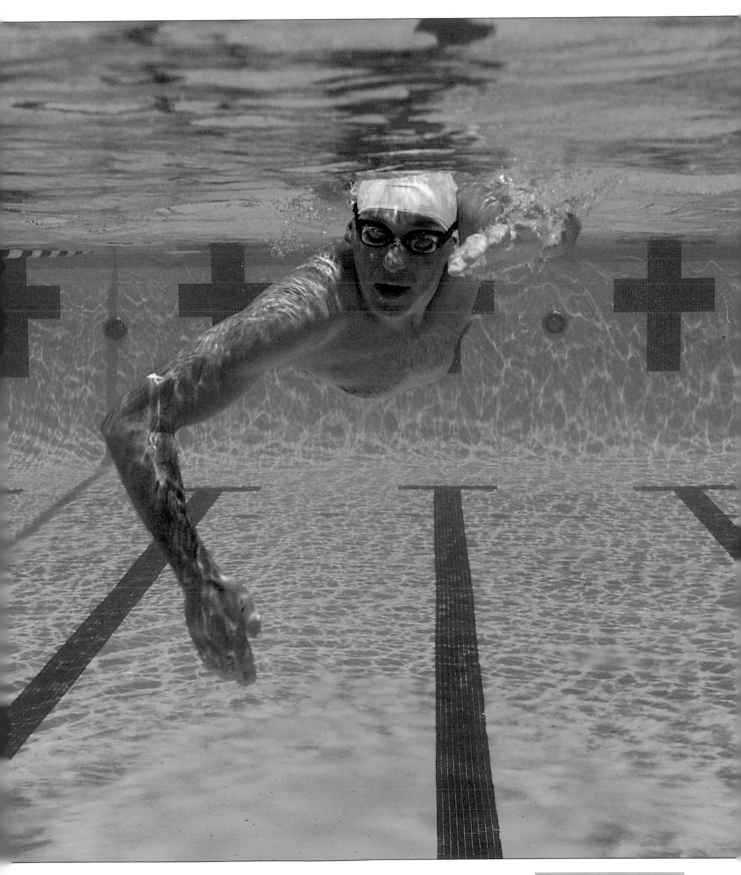

Power Drills

Swimming on your side is a good way to practice the correct rotation of your torso, which will enhance the power phase of your stroke. After completing a normal left-arm stroke cycle, turn onto your right side, extending your right arm underneath your body, and kick 10 times *(right)*. Return to a horizontal position and complete another full stroke cycle, then turn onto your left side and repeat *(bottom)*. Perform this for 25 yards.

A pulling set that works on the propulsive power of your stroke should comprise 10 to 20 percent of your workout. Use flotation devices to keep your legs suspended at the proper height *(above)*, so that all of your momentum comes from your upper body. Insert a pull-buoy between your upper thighs and, optionally, secure your ankles inside a small inner tube.

Recovery

A good recovery provides your arm with a restful transition between the more propulsive entry and power phases. Your elbow should emerge from the water first, with your forearm perpendicular to it *(above)*. Increase your elbow bend as you bring your hand fully out of the water and up along your side *(second)*. Start to extend your forearm, bringing your hand forward in front of your head *(third)*. Finally, swing your whole arm forward as you prepare for another entry phase into the water *(fourth)*.

WRONG A wide recovery is a common stroking error in which the arm stays straight and swings outward in a wide arc *(right)*. This can disrupt lateral streamlining, causing you to lose energy. Be sure that your elbow exits the water before your hand, and that it stays bent through the entire recovery.

WRONG The palm of your hand should not show during the recovery *(right)*. The recovery phase should give your arm a chance to relax, and rotating your hand outward creates stress that can cause shoulder injuries.

The Flutter Kick

While the forward momentum of swimming comes almost entirely from the stroking action of your arms, the kick has a crucial function: It prevents your lower body from sinking, helping to maintain streamlining.

The two most typical kick styles are the two-beat and six-beat kicks. In a two-beat kick, the swimmer kicks once with each arm stroke; in the six-beat kick, three times per arm stroke. Generally two-beat kicks plunge a little deeper than the more rapid six-beat kick. There are also less common kick variations, such as the four-beat kick — two kicks per arm stroke — and the two-beat crossover in which the feet actually scissor across each other. Ideally, you will develop your own kicking rhythm after you have perfected your stroke. The kick you use is largely — and best — determined by your particular body mechanics and stroking style.

Whichever beat kick you use, your form should be the same. Keep your toes pointed and your knees almost straight. The kicking action should come from your hips. Your feet should be about a foot apart at the widest point. Do not actually bring your upper foot out of the water completely; rather, your heel should just break the water's surface (above).

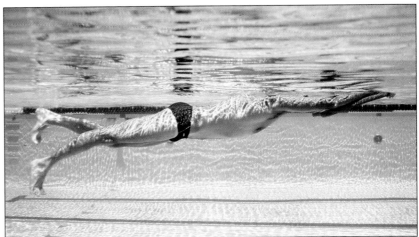

WRONG The hooked foot *(above),* with ankles flexed and toes pointed straight downward, decreases the effectiveness of your kick. Because it is less streamlined, this kicking flaw drags your lower body downward and wastes energy.

Kicking Drills

Using a kickboard is one of the best ways to perfect your kick as well as to condition your leg muscles. Stretch the board in front of you fully and grasp it on either side just where it begins to round *(left)*. Keep your body aligned, with your shoulders low and your hips near the surface of the water. Spend 10 to 15 percent of your workout on kicking drills.

Another way to practice kicking is on your side. Your lower arm should be fully extended to keep your body up. Power the kick from your hips. Perform this for 25 yards on your left side; repeat the drill on your right side.

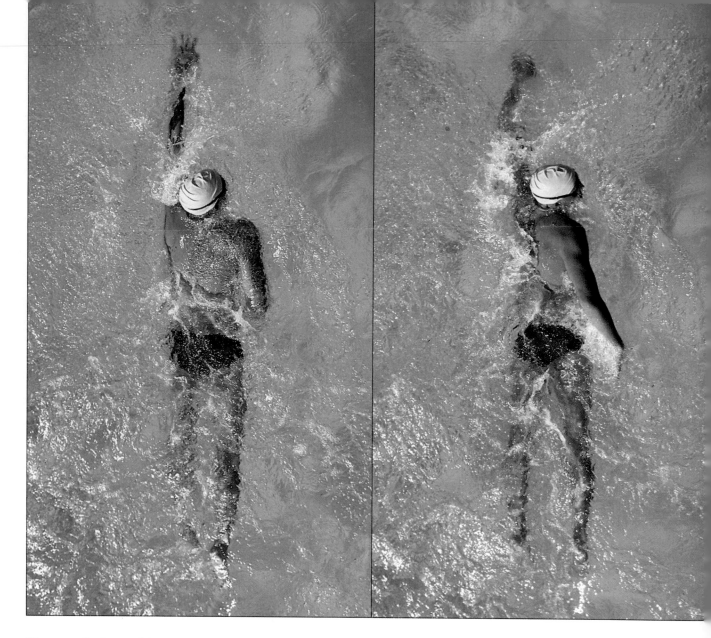

Breathing/1

Rhythmic, relaxed breathing is essential to swimming, as it prevents fatigue and aids in stroke mechanics. It should require no more thought than breathing while you are doing any other physical activity. You should exhale completely through both your mouth and nose while your face is underwater, and inhale through your mouth when your arm begins its recovery and your head rotates. One breath intake per stroke cycle—a right and left arm stroke—is usually adequate for most swimmers.

Determining which side to breathe on is a matter of personal preference. Actually, many experts believe that swimmers should be able to breathe bilaterally, as shown above. Whichever side you breathe on, turn your head into the trough of water, or bow wave, created by your forward momentum. The gap created by the bow wave will allow you more time to inhale.

When breathing bilaterally, take a breath every third arm stroke: As your right arm begins its recovery, take advantage of your body's rolling movement and start turning your neck to the right *(far left)*. When your right arm first leaves the water, turn your head fully to inhale *(second)*. Roll your head back to the center line of your body and exhale as your right arm completes its recovery *(third)*. Keep your head submerged and exhale gradually during a complete left- and right-stroke cycle, then inhale to your left as you begin your recovery *(fourth)*.

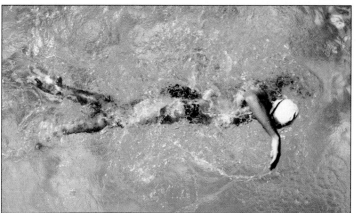

WRONG Breathing late in the recovery, or turning your head too far underneath your arm, causes your torso to twist out of lateral alignment, reducing stroke efficiency *(above)*. Avoid this by starting to turn your head when your arm is just beginning its recovery.

Breathing/2

The correct head position assists in breathing and also ensures that optimal streamlining is maintained. When exhaling, your head should be half submerged and your eyes focused downward at about a 45-degree angle *(left)*. As your arm completes its pull and begins its recovery, turn your head to follow the natural roll of your body *(below)*, but continue rotating your neck to allow your mouth and nose to emerge from the water for inhaling.

CHAPTER 5

Cycling

*Outdoor conditioning
on varied terrain*

I f you have had experience cycling, you are probably aware of some of the benefits. In terms of developing aerobic capacity, cycling gives the heart and circulatory system an outstanding aerobic workout, and can help you expend between 400 and 700 calories per hour. In one study that compared running and cycling during a 20-week training program, cycling was at least as effective as running for developing cardiorespiratory fitness. Yet cycling develops and maintains aerobic capacity and exercises the leg muscles while imposing far less stress on joints than running. And on the average, competitive cyclists have better-proportioned upper body builds than distance runners—presumably because cyclists use their upper bodies to transmit extra drive to their legs as they pedal.

You can choose to ride indoors on a stationary exercise bike (see page 31 for tips on choosing one.) But riding outdoors offers considerably more variety and mobility than any other form of exercise. It's true that cyclists are far more dependent on equipment than are runners or swimmers. Yet you can cover sweeping distances and varied terrain, and do so in a variety of circumstances—cycling on scenic tours alone or with a group, commuting to work, unwinding with a ride at the end of the day.

The introduction of mountain bikes—also called all-terrain bikes, or ATBs—has extended the enjoyment of biking by letting cyclists traverse routes that were once inaccessible to them. Indeed, ATBs have become so popular that they now make up half or more of bicycle sales in some parts of the country. Because these bikes allow better maneuverability and a more upright position than touring or racing bicycles, many cyclists have adopted ATBs for city riding as well.

For optimal cycling efficiency and comfort, it is crucial that your bike be fitted properly to your body proportions; otherwise, you may suffer discomfort and even injury. If you purchase a new bike at a reputable cycle shop, the sales personnel will help you make the proper measurements and adjustments. Here are some tips to help you select the right bike or alter the one you already own. (The pictures on pages 128-129 identify the parts of a bicycle that are referred to below.)

• Your first consideration is the *frame size,* which cannot be adjusted. A bicycle with a top tube is best; it is sturdier than one with no top tube and is likely to have a more efficient braking system. To find the right frame size, straddle the bike over the top tube and stand flat-footed in front of the seat, or saddle. With a touring or race bike, there should be a one- to two-inch clearance between the top tube and your crotch. Because a smaller frame size is preferable on an all-terrain or mountain bike, you should allow a clearance of at least three to five inches on these bikes.

• On a touring bike, *drop handlebars* should be about as wide as your shoulders or slightly narrower. The handlebars should be at the same level as the seat or slightly lower. Some cyclists with neck or back problems may prefer upright handlebars, which are also standard on all-terrain bikes. While you can easily rotate the handlebars, the length of the stem—which connects the handlebars to the frame—can be changed only by replacing the stem. To check stem length, stand alongside the bike, put your elbow at the tip of the saddle, and reach for the handlebars. Your fingertips should just reach them or come within half an inch. If not, the handlebar stem is too long.

• To determine the appropriate *seat height,* have someone hold the bike steady while you sit in a comfortable riding position with your hands on the handlebars. Pedal backwards so that one of your feet is at the bottom of the down stroke; in that position, your knee should be slightly bent, while the thigh of your other leg should be about parallel to the top tube.

Cycling does have a few drawbacks. While it is inexpensive in the long run, the start-up costs can be high: At the very least you need to buy a good bicycle and a well-made bike helmet. You also need to consider your location. Cycling for fitness in stop-and-go traffic is difficult, while cycling over hilly terrain in the country may be too strenuous at first. Rain can hamper your cycling by limiting both your vision and the effectiveness of your brakes; ice and snow, obviously, make cycling even more hazardous. Fortunately, you can cycle indoors on a stationary bike when conditions outdoors aren't optimal.

The information on pages 128-129 highlights the major differences between a 10- or 12-speed racing or touring bike and an ATB. Just as important as choosing a bike is fitting it to your dimensions (see box, above). Women below average height may have to make an extra effort to get the right bike, since most models are built to accommodate an average man's dimensions.

Having a bike fit properly is the first step toward feeling comfortable on it; learning to handle it is the next. Indeed, cyclists training for Olympic competition are so relaxed that they can graze one another without falling when they are in the middle of a pack moving at 25 miles per hour. The point of such mastery is not simply to avoid spills, but also to feel at ease so that your energy for forward propulsion is conserved. The riding techniques on the following pages are designed to help keep your upper body movement to a minimum and let your legs do the work. You will also ride more safely.

Because a bicycle is such an efficient machine, it is possible to ride it and never reach your target heart rate. If your cardiorespiratory system is already well conditioned from another aerobic activity, familiarize yourself with cycling by riding on relatively flat terrain for 20 to 30 minutes three times a week for at least two weeks. Begin each ride pedaling in a low gear at 55 to 60 revolutions per minute to warm up; after 10 minutes, increase your cadence to 70 to 80 rpms and shift to a higher gear that pushes your heart rate into its target training zone.

Perhaps the most common mistake that novice cyclists make is to pedal in too high a gear, which is not only tiring, but puts undue strain on your knees. Use this initial period to concentrate on high-rpm, low-gear riding and to improve your bike-handling skills. Save high gears for riding downhill or with a good tail wind.

Over the next two to four weeks, add a fourth cycling day per week, and climb some modest hills twice weekly. Try to accomplish a minimum of three rides of 45 to 60 minutes; use weekends for at least one longer, relatively easy ride of 20 to 30 miles. After five or six weeks, your technique should improve considerably and your cadence should be a steady 75 to 90 rpms.

With this conditioning as a base, you should reach the point in your third month of training when you can ride 30 to 40 miles at a time, and be able to increase your weekly mileage by 8 to 10 percent. Add variety to your cycling program by climbing steeper hills or by interval training, in which you alternate high-intensity periods, or intervals, of exercise with low-intensity periods. You should aim to increase your heart rate to 80 to 90 percent of its maximum for three- to five-minute intervals, followed by pedaling easily in a low gear for five-minute periods. Repeat this sequence four or five times. Vary the length and intensity of riding intervals, but do not overdo them; experienced cyclists generally limit bouts of interval training to twice a week. Mountain biking over uneven trails also provides an ideal opportunity for intervals of intense riding.

Be sure you are properly outfitted. A cycling helmet is essential. Wearing brightly colored reflective clothing is always sensible, but is vital when you cycle at night or when visibility is poor. Stiff-soled shoes help spread the pressure of the pedals across the length of your feet. Special cycling shoes also have grooves that grip the pedals like cleats (but are comfortable to walk in). And cycling gloves decrease pressure on hands and also reduce scrapes if you fall.

Finally, use road sense. Give hand signals to drivers and other cyclists, watch out for railroad tracks, storm drains and the like, and, unless you are in an organized event, avoid riding side by side with another cyclist.

CHOOSING A HELMET

Helmets keep getting lighter. Models with a hard outer shell and an energy-absorbing interior made of polystyrene foam weigh a pound or less; new ultralight models weight as little as 8 ounces. Made of very dense foam, they are cool and comfortable, but such helmets may be less able to withstand daily wear and tear over the years than helmets with hard outer shells. Whichever style you choose, check for an American National Standards Institute (ANSI) sticker, which signifies that the helmet meets reasonable safety standards for absorbing severe blows in laboratory tests.

Also look for these features: The helmet's liner should be at least half an inch thick and made from crushable expanded polystyrene (the foam used for picnic coolers). Sponge-rubber or fabric pads should hold the helmet firmly in place, and slits or holes in the shell should allow for good air flow. A snug-fitting chin strap will keep the helmet from flying off.

Because the plastics used in helmets will deteriorate over time, you should replace your helmet every five years—sooner if you have an accident. (Some manufacturers will replace damaged helmets free of charge.)

The Right Bike

SADDLE

SEATPOST

SEATPOST BINDER BOLT

REAR BRAKE

SEAT TUBE

FREEWHEEL

REAR
DERAILLEUR

DROP HANDLEBARS

HEAD TUBE

BRAKE HOOD

BRAKE LEVER

FRONT BRAKE

FORK

QUICK RELEASE

RIM

BRAKE CABLE

STEM

SHIFT LEVER

DOWN TUBE

TOP TUBE

PEDAL

TOE CLIP

CRANKARM

CHAINRING

FRONT DERAILLEUR

CHAINSTAY

R O A D   B I K E

CANTILEVER BRAKE

UPRIGHT HANDLEBARS

THUMB SHIFTER

KNOBBY TIRE

NUTTED OR
QUICK-RELEASE
AXLE

A L L - T E R R A I N   B I K E

LARGE-DIAMETER TUBING

SMALLER FRAME SIZE
THAN COMPARABLE
ROAD BIKES

WIDER SADDLE

SEATPOST QUICK RELEASE

PEDAL WITH
SOLE GRIPS

LONGER
CRANKARM

TRIPLE CHAINRING

U-BRAKE OR
ROLLER CAM

VARIABLE-LENGTH
CHAINSTAY

WIDE-RANGE
FREEWHEEL

LONG-CAGE DERAILLEUR

B uying a good bicycle is an investment. To choose wisely,
you should be familiar with
bike parts and the differences between road or touring and all-terrain
bicycles (*above*).

The most apparent differences
between these two popular types of

bicycles are the smaller, heavier
frame sizes, upright handlebars and
wider, knobby tires of the ATBs.
While these features increase your
riding stability and comfort, they
also result in less speed potential.
Likewise, the cantilever brakes, U-
brakes or roller cams found on ATBs

are bigger and more powerful than
the brakes on road bikes.

ATBs also provide up to 18 gears,
which allow you more options and
control when climbing steep hills or
navigating over rough terrain. Such
features are not needed on a road
bike used for touring or racing.

The correct cycling posture shown here demonstrates the importance of streamlining. Lower your torso by bending forward at the waist, keeping your back parallel to the top tube *(right)*. Your head should be low, with your neck in line with your spine. Keep your elbows flexed slightly and tucked toward your knees.

Body Position

Your position on a bicycle can make a considerable difference in both the effectiveness and comfort of your riding. One study that examined the effects of several variables on speed showed that improved riding position accounted for a greater benefit than any other variable.

Proper riding posture begins with an accurate fit of the bike to your body, as described on page 126. Only after such mechanical adjustments are made can you evaluate your actual riding posture.

To achieve an optimal cycling position, consider two dynamics. First, distribute your body weight between the handlebars and the saddle. Weight distribution is dictated by terrain, and can be adjusted by changing your hand positions, as shown on pages 132-133. You can also redistribute weight by sliding backward or forward on the saddle. Secondly, minimize wind resistance: Research has shown that 90 percent of your cycling energy is expended in pushing air away from you. Thus, the more you streamline your body position by keeping your torso as horizontal as possible, the more effective your riding will be. Not only will you meet much less resistance when you ride against the wind, you will pick up more speed when riding with it.

Hand Positions

Hold the handlebars near the stem when hill climbing from a seated position or for a rapid, smooth descent with no braking required to slow down.

Resting your hands on the handlebars above the brake levers is ideal for cruising, since it allows you to assume a slightly more upright, relaxed posture.

Grasping the brake hoods provides easy access to the brakes for riding downhill. In this position, you can feather the brakes off and on with your first two fingers.

Wrap your hands around the tops of the brake levers to shift your body weight to the front of the bike for out-of-the-saddle uphill climbs.

Place your hands in the dropped part of the handlebars below the brake hoods, which allows easy access to the brake levers, for rapid descents that might require braking.

You will frequently need to ride with one hand on the handlebars, whether to change gears or to grab something to eat from your shirt pocket. Stabilize the bike by moving both hands close to the handlebar stem; then you can steer safely with one hand without losing your balance.

Maintaining a straight line while turning to look behind you is a simple — but necessary — skill, especially when riding in traffic. Keeping your hands close to the handlebar stem, maintain a straight line by turning your head only, with your body weight centered forward.

For efficient pedaling, both legs should be in constant motion of equal effort, with your knees tucked in close to the bike *(above)*. When one foot is at the 12-o'clock position to begin the downstroke, the other is about to begin the upstroke from the 6-o'clock position *(top left)*. The 12-to-6 o'clock downstroke utilizes your quadriceps and calves; the 6-to-12 o'clock upstroke works the hamstrings and shins.

Pedaling

Skillful pedaling is probably the most important component of cycling. Novice cyclists often think of pedaling as an up-and-down motion, which is an ineffective way to ride, since it overdevelops some muscles of the leg while underutilizing others. Instead, pedal in a smooth, circular pattern to better distribute the workload throughout the leg muscles. This depends as much on pulling upward on the pedals as it does on pushing downward.

To perform smooth rotations, and make sure that your upward and downward force on the pedals is equal, it is essential that your bike be equipped with toe clips, or that you have cleated shoes that lock into the pedals. Practice inserting your feet in and out of the toe clips so you are prepared to disengage them if you need to stop.

For maximum cycling speed and endurance, your cadence, or pedaling rhythm, should be constant. Cadence is measured in revolutions per minute, or rpms. Strive to pedal between 80 to 90 rpms; with practice, this cadence will become second nature. To determine your cadence, count the complete pedal strokes of one foot for 15 seconds and multiply this number by four.

One-legged pedaling will isolate the pedaling action to strengthen your hip flexors, and thus improve your upstroke. To perform this exercise, put your bike on a windloader, or home trainer, such as the one shown at right. This valuable training aid — available at most bike shops or sporting-goods stores — holds your rear wheel upright and stationary, allowing you to pedal at a particular resistance or rpm. Pedal for 10 minutes for each leg, extending your resting leg to the side.

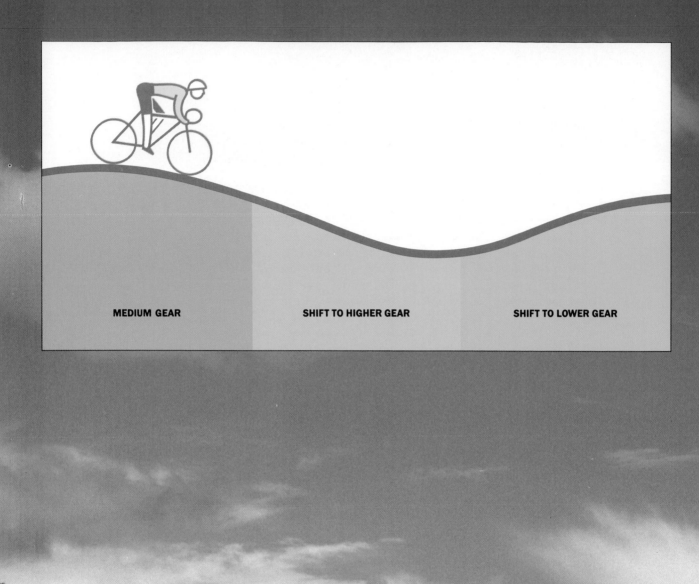

MEDIUM GEAR   SHIFT TO HIGHER GEAR   SHIFT TO LOWER GEAR

Gearing

Gearing is a necessary element of efficient pedaling, since it allows you to maintain a constant cadence over variable terrain. Efficient gearing depends on the incline and condition of the road. Adjust your gears whenever your cadence drops or increases for more than a few pedal rotations. If it drops, downshift to a lower gear; conversely, if it increases, shift into a higher gear.

Usually, you will need to adjust your gears only for hills. Proper gearing requires anticipation, as demonstrated in the illustration at left. You should shift gears as soon as you lose forward momentum; it might be necessary to shift several times in the course of an uphill run. When pedaling downhill, you should generally shift into a higher gear before you start spinning the pedals. Downhill momentum will allow you to maintain your cadence part of the way up the next grade — usually for 15 to 50 feet.

When starting up a hill, be sure to downshift before your cadence drops precipitously. For the derailleur to function, the chainwheel must spin evenly. If you shift too late and exert too much pressure on the pedals, the derailleur might not respond. In that case, you will have to slow your cadence for a few pedal rotations to allow the gearing mechanism to click in properly.

In standard derailleur systems, moving the shift levers changes gears by skipping the chain from one cog and chainwheel to another. Bicycle derailleur/chainring systems vary, so you will have to learn yours to know just how far the shift levers must be moved to change gears. Allow several seconds for the derailleur to make the shift. Index derailleur systems avoid some of the guesswork by clicking immediately into gear.

Braking

Effective braking is a vital bicycle-handling skill. However, proper braking technique is not only a safety factor, it also increases your riding efficiency by allowing you to decelerate appropriately as required.

Most of the stopping force comes from the front brake; while the rear brake does exert some braking power, its main function is balance. Get in the habit of applying both brakes simultaneously, since operating just the front brake could lock the front wheel and send you tumbling over the bike. Shifting your weight backward on the saddle will also help you to stop more quickly.

Braking on wet or slippery roads requires special attention, because the brake pads slip on the rims. It may take three times as long to stop in wet conditions, and you are at a greater risk of skidding. Anticipate slow-downs, and apply the brakes gently, allowing plenty of time to stop.

To slow or stop your bike gradually with your hands on the brake hoods, use your first two fingers of each hand to operate the levers *(right).* If you are slowing, apply greater pressure to the front brake than the rear, and shift your weight backward slightly. To be prepared to make an abrupt halt, you should practice the emergency stopping technique *(inset).* Apply both brakes, putting more pressure on the front brake. Simultaneously slide your weight all the way back behind the saddle to increase the pressure on the rear wheel. Your arms should be straight.

Riding a Line

Riding a straight line, and choosing a path around objects in the road as well as corners, sounds easier than it is. And following a line is an important skill that you must be able to maintain at all times. Not only does it make your movement predictable to cars and other riders, it also conserves energy otherwise wasted in unnecessary side-to-side adjustments.

Ideally you should follow a straight line about six inches from the shoulder of the road. Practice riding on a white line in an empty parking lot or a deserted stretch of road with no cars around. Then work on following the same line while you look over your shoulder.

Like most riding techniques, setting your line requires an awareness of the terrain and anticipation of what lies ahead. You want to veer from your line as little as possible: Plan ahead for maneuvers such as swerving around objects in your way or negotiating corners.

Riding a line is a function of two elements: choosing the correct focal point and body position. Experts recommend focusing about 20 feet ahead of you when riding 10 to 15 miles per hour; add one foot for each additional mile per hour. This distance allows you to see obstacles ahead and to make subtle adjustments. Your wrists and elbows should be relaxed as you grip the handlebars (above).

To avoid an obstacle in the road, use your hips to steer around it, leaning your body weight to the side as necessary. This will keep the front and rear tires in alignment and conserve your energy *(left)*. Relying on your focal point will allow you to anticipate the correct line to follow around an obstacle on the basis of the road and traffic conditions *(below)*.

Cornering

Successful cornering is accomplished by shifts in body weight. You should never steer with the handlebars while actually in a turn; rather, you should position the bike to follow a wide arc that will also allow you to coast through it. Prior to encountering the turn, flick your brakes to slow slightly, then lower your body and use a slight movement of your hips to lean in the direction of the turn *(left)*. Stop pedaling just before you enter the turn. Hold your pedals in the 12 o'clock/six o'clock position, with your weight completely on the outside pedal and your leg extended, and your inside knee bent *(above)*. You should be able to lean more than 30 degrees in a turn and still stay upright. Never brake abruptly while in a turn.

Hill Riding/1

Practice climbing short, gentle hills while seated *(above left)*. Place your hands midway on the handlebars, and slide backward slightly in the saddle to give you better leverage on the pedals. Use your arms to pull up slightly on the handlebars, rocking your upper body forward rhythmically to increase your momentum. It is easier to climb steeper hills while standing on the pedals *(above right)*. With your hands widely spaced on the brake hoods, shift your body weight over the front of the bike.

All your bicycle-handling skills come into play when tackling hills. Pedaling technique, gearing, braking, choosing a line and even cornering are included in successful hill navigation. Hill climbing can also take a considerable amount of strength in your upper body, as pulling on the handlebars allows you to increase the force that you apply on the pedals.

Gear selection for both uphill and downhill riding should be based on staying as close as possible to your optimal cadence over level terrain. The correct gear to select depends on your fitness level, your climbing style and the grade and length of the hill. In general, if you climb while standing on the pedals, you will ride in a higher gear than if you climb while sitting. However, it is essential that you anticipate gear shifts before you crank too hard at the pedals on the uphill, which makes it difficult to change gears, or spin the pedals too quickly on the downhill.

Avoid coasting after a long climb, even if you encounter a downhill immediately. It is better to keep your legs turning to speed recovery of your muscles.

Leveraging is an effective way to utilize your upper-body strength when climbing from a standing position *(left)*. With your hands in a wide grip on the brake hoods, shift your body weight forward over the handlebars. As you perform each pedal downstroke, lean your body toward that leg to increase your pedaling force, alternating left and right *(below)*. This will create the sensation that you are throwing your bike back and forth. Your front and rear tires should stay in alignment.

Hill Riding/2

Maximizing both speed and safety is the goal of skillful descents. The primary danger in downhill riding is losing control on a curve. Prepare for curves by keeping your hands on the brake hoods, ready to use the brakes to reduce speed before you enter the curve *(right)*. Raising your upper body to increase wind resistance will also help slow the bike. Remember not to brake while actually cornering, and to steer the bike by leaning. The tucked position *(inset)* optimizes speed on a downhill straightaway: Center your body weight over the back of the saddle, keep your knees close together, place your hands next to the stem, and lower your body and head as close to the top tube as possible. To increase your balance, place your pedals in the three o'clock/ nine o'clock position.

Group Riding

Group riding, called riding the paceline, or drafting, is more than social cycling. It is a time-honored training technique that allows riders to benefit by protecting one another from the effects of wind resistance.

A paceline is a closely packed formation of riders, one behind the other. The lead rider is said to be pulling the rest, as they benefit from the draft created behind him or her. Indeed, studies have shown that paceline riding can save 20 to 25 percent of a cyclist's energy. The paceline changes constantly, with a new rider assuming the lead position at a predetermined interval. Riding a paceline demands excellent bike-handling skills, since only a few inches separate you from the other riders.

When riding a single paceline, all cyclists should follow about 12 inches behind the wheel of the preceding rider. The lead rider's pull lasts between one and 10 minutes. He then eases off to one side, allowing his speed to slow so he falls back to position 1. As the last rider passes him, he starts to accelerate and swings back into line behind him at position 2. The formation rotates continually, as the other riders maintain speed, and the second rider assumes his pull at the front.

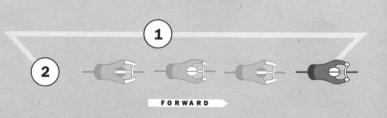

An echelon is a paceline that is adjusted diagonally to minimize the effects of a crosswind. In an echelon, the riders are angled downwind from the leader, with the front wheel of each bicycle approximately aligned with the rear wheel of the preceding bike.

The lead rider might pull for less than a minute. He then eases his pace, falling back to position 1 as he allows the second rider to pass him and assume the lead. After the last rider passes him, he accelerates and slips behind him into position 2.

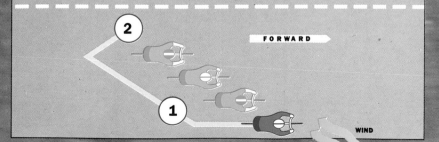

2

FORWARD

1

WIND

All-Terrain Biking/1

The excitement and variety offered by all-terrain biking have made it the fastest-growing kind of cycling. Combining racing technology with the off-road capabilities of the popular children's BMX (bicycle motocross) stunt bikes, all-terrain bicycles — also called mountain bikes — can tackle steep, uneven trails. They have made accessible many areas formerly off-limits to the rider and, because of the special handling skills required, have presented new challenges even to experienced cyclists. Indeed, the added element of rough terrain makes good bike-handling skills even more crucial to safe and efficient riding.

Even though ATBs are ideally suited for rugged terrain, one of the more popular uses of off-road bicycles is for urban riding. The knobby tires that improve traction on uneven mountain trails do the same on potholed city roads. So, while its heavier frame means you will not be able to achieve the same on-road speeds with an ATB, it is perfectly appropriate as your only bicycle — unless you intend to get involved in road racing.

The off-road techniques on the following six pages demonstrate specific handling skills for mountain bikes and show how they vary from those of traditional racing.

The upright posture is not as essential when riding your ATB on a relatively smooth road, so bend your elbows to try to lower yourself slightly into a more standard, aerodynamic cycling position *(above)*.

A more upright posture and wider arm position *(left)* are the primary variations between mountain and road bicycles. This difference allows you to distribute your weight over a wider area, thus increasing stability. When riding, focus on the path ahead to prepare for upcoming rocks, roots or gullies.

All-Terrain Biking/2

Rising out of the saddle is usually the easiest way to go uphill on an ATB *(above)*. Bring your weight well forward over the handlebars, keeping your arms widely spaced to balance the front wheel.

Controlling the bike is significantly more difficult as the terrain becomes more pitted and uneven *(above)*. Use your upper-body strength to control the front wheel, while maintaining your pedaling momentum as long as possible. If pedaling slows so much as to become ineffective, walk your bike through the area to save your energy *(right)*. Stabilize the bike by holding it at both the handlebar and the saddle.

All-Terrain Biking/3

Controlling your speed downhill on an ATB is essential, since hazards in the terrain can appear with little warning. Keep your weight as low as possible to increase your stopping power. If you have a quick-release saddle, lower it just as you start down the hill. Shift your body backward and plant your feet in the three o'clock/nine o'clock position *(right)*. Flick the brakes off and on, making sure not to hold the front brake too long, since it can lock the wheel. On steeper downhills *(inset)*, shift your weight to the rear of the saddle, with your arms outstretched, to stabilize the rear of the bike.

CHAPTER 6

Aerobic Movement

The key: combining arms and legs

Combining choreographed rhythmic exercise with music, aerobic movement mixes running, "stepping" and calisthenics for an exercise that is varied and lively, whether you perform it in a class or at home. Although initially perceived as a woman's activity, aerobic movement has made significant inroads with men. Professional athletes, including boxers and baseball players, were among the first to take it up, and it has since gained popularity with other men looking for an enjoyable way to improve fitness levels.

Aerobic movement works the entire body with a variety of exercises that involve muscles in your arms, legs and torso. Many of the movements are drawn from other aerobic activities; yet aerobic movement does not restrict you to repeating a single motion. Your muscles and joints move through their full range of motion, building mus-cle endurance and enhancing flexibility in a way not usually found in activities like running and cycling. And many people also find that the music heightens their enjoyment and their motivation to exercise. Rock, folk, musical comedy, jazz and other types of music can all supply a tempo and a rhythm that will inspire you to move.

Not only is aerobic movement enjoyable, but it can also exercise your heart on a par with bicycling, running and swimming. However, the variety of movements and the intensity of jumping can expose people who do this type of exercise frequently to stress injuries. Most complaints are similar to those of runners—shin splints, runner's knee, calf muscle stress and lower back pain (see pages 70-71). Many of these injuries can be prevented by proper stretching and warming up and cooling down, as well as wearing shoes designed for aerobic movement.

Bench aerobics, also called step aerobics, bench stepping or step training, adds a new wrinkle to aerobic dance with a small platform about the height of a stair step. Working to music, you step onto and off the bench in a routine that gives you a cardiovascular workout while it tones your legs and buttocks. And it's low in impact, since one foot is always on the floor or step.

Two recent studies looked at the benefits of step training. At San Diego State University, researchers found that working at a rate of 120 steps per minute while pumping the arms was as exerting as running at seven miles per hour, but that impact was low—similar to that created by walking at three miles per hour. In a University of Pittsburgh study, subjects working at 80 steps per minute expended almost 300 calories in 30 minutes. The calorie expenditure increased 19 percent when one-pound hand weights and a pumping arm motion were added.

Step aerobics classes, using sturdy, adjustable platforms, are proliferating at health clubs across the country. If you plan to purchase a bench and work out at home, take a few classes to learn the necessary coordination and technique.

Here are some tips to keep in mind:
• Beginners should use a 4-inch step, increasing the height eventually to 8 to 12 inches. (Your knee should not flex beyond 90° as you step up, or you risk strain and possible injury.)
• Commercially available benches, made of high-impact plastic or wood, are about 42 inches long and 14 inches wide, with adjustable height and non-skid top surfaces. Anyone with basic carpentry skills can build a solid box-shaped bench to these basic specifications; you can also perform a modified routine on the bottom step of a staircase. But don't try this with a lightweight household step-stool or other makeshift equipment: a fall is almost guaranteed.
• Always place your sole (not your toes or the ball of your foot) flat on the center of the platform, and keep your knee slightly bent. Land on the floor with the ball of your foot, then bring your heel down smoothly, bending your knee as you do so to absorb the impact. You may have to look down at your feet to start, but with experience you'll be able to look straight ahead most of the time. As with any aerobic exercise, be sure to warm up and stretch beforehand and cool down afterward.

But increasingly, a popular and effective option is low-impact aerobic dance, in which one foot always remains in contact with the floor. One strategy for reducing the jumping and bouncing that are inherent in high-impact aerobic dance—and at the root of most dance-related injuries—is step aerobics (see box, above). In other low-impact routines, high-impact movements are replaced by walking, marching, side-stepping and lunging. Because performing arm movements can help boost your heart rate, an increase in upper-body work compensates for the reduced demands on the lower body. Hence, whereas boosting your heart rate in high-impact aerobics relies on jumping, the aerobic benefits of low-impact routines come from carefully choreographed combinations of arm and leg work. These routines must be performed vigor-ously, and yet with precision, to achieve cardiorespiratory benefits, so low-impact routines require greater concentration and coordination than high-impact ones do.

Research thus far indicates that, as is the case with walking, when participants in low-impact dance programs exercise vigorously, they can reach and maintain their target heart rates for at least 20 minutes—the amount of time it takes to receive cardiorespiratory benefits from exercise. One study compared the results of a group of 25 subjects who performed both high-impact and low-impact aerobic dance routines. Although the subjects' oxygen consumption rose 28 percent during the high-impact session, the heart-rate response during both sessions was nearly the same—the pulses recorded during the high-impact session averaged only 8 percent higher than those in the low-impact session. The researchers concluded that while the high-impact routine provided a more intense workout, the low-impact routine also provided an aerobic training stimulus—and that in fact it met the aerobic exercise guidelines set by the American College of Sports Medicine.

To allow for the more deliberate coordination of low-impact dance, the music you use to pace yourself should be slightly slower—between 125 and 145 beats per minute—than it is for high-impact routines. If you are incorporating weights into your routine, choose music with a tempo of 120 to 140 beats per minute. Counting to the beat of the music will keep you working at the proper intensity as well as help you coordinate your movements.

Reducing the impact lessens the stress on the lower body, but the increased lateral floor movements and arm use in low-impact routines can result in injuries to the back, shoulder, arms or knees. Taking a few precautions during your workout will minimize the risks. Maintain proper posture: abdominal muscles contracted, buttocks tucked under and knees slightly bent. When lunging, make sure that your bent knees never extend beyond your toes to avoid excess stress on ankle and knee ligaments; your knee should also always be pointed in the same direction as your lower leg. Be careful not to arch your back when working the upper body: Keeping your pelvis tilted forward and your knees relaxed will avoid this. Arm movements should be smooth and controlled; jerky arm movements can hyperextend and possibly injure the shoulder and elbow joints, forearms and wrists.

A suitable surface is also important to cushion the impact as your feet land. You can make any floor suitable by exercising on a dense rubber pad. The best surface is a hardwood floor suspended over a cushion of air. Though generally difficult to find, this type of surface is used in most good dance studios. Bare concrete or concrete covered only by a carpet is the worst surface for exercising.

Make yourself a tape of music to fit the length of your routine. Choose music with a steady beat that inspires you to move. The music should have an eight-beat rhythm—like most popular and country music—without irregular beats or sudden shifts in tempo. Fit the tempo to the exercise: Warm-up music should be slower than the aerobic phase, and music for the cool-down and stretching should have a leisurely beat. To choreograph your routine like a professional, choose a new piece of music for each exercise.

As your aerobic fitness increases, you will find that it becomes increasingly difficult for you to reach your target heart rate. This indicates that your heart muscle has adapted to the workload and become more efficient. Increasing movements that cross the floor and doing more arm work at shoulder level or higher will increase cardiovascular demands. You can further intensify your workouts by incorporating light hand-held or wrist weights. Adding weights, when combined with arm swinging, has been shown to increase oxygen consumption, heart rate and calories burned during exercise. Excluding warm-ups and cool-downs, you can use weights with any of the aerobic dance routines on the following pages.

Part of the fun of aerobic movement can come from performing it with a group. When you enroll in an exercise class, choose a level that is comfortable for you and check the instructor's qualifications. You can also take advantage of videotapes that present aerobic routines. But be aware of excessively prolonged repetitions, high jumping or repeated patterns on one foot, since these are among the movements that will increase your risk of injury.

Setting Your Routine

The following routine progresses from simple sequences that focus on arm work to more complicated steps requiring you to move across the floor. Begin the routine with the warm-ups on these two pages and the following two; they should be sustained for at least five minutes. The cool-downs on pages 184-185 should also be done for a minimum of five minutes.

Following the warm-ups is a series of exercises in which you lunge, march, roll up on your toes and use your arms but essentially stay in one place. These precede the more complicated moving-around steps, in which you move across the floor. Combination sequences couple the arm work of stationary sequences with the movement steps. Each sequence should be performed symmetrically, so that if you first move to your left, you should then reverse direction and repeat the exercise to your right. Repeat each sequence four times.

You will probably get the most benefit—and the most enjoyment—from your low-impact routine if you mix the steps in different combinations and move in different directions. You can combine sequences that use side-to-side movement with those that go forward and backward, interspersed with moving-in-place steps. Be sure to vary the height of your arm movements.

As your fitness level improves and you get stronger, you will find that it becomes more difficult to achieve your target heart rate. To make your dancing more demanding, do more knee bends, take longer steps and concentrate more on moving-around sequences. You can further intensify your workout by adding hand or wrist weights. Strengthening exercises that incorporate weights into your workout are demonstrated on pages 186-191. For the greatest benefit, you should perform the routines four to five times a week.

Warm-Ups/1

Stand up straight with your arms lifted slightly to the side and your right leg extended; point your toes *(far left)*. Bend your knees as you bring your feet together and swing your arms so that they cross in front of your chest *(center)*. Straighten your right leg as you repeat to your left side *(left)*.

After warming up, you can increase the intensity of the above routine by raising your arms on the extension phase. Start by bringing them to shoulder height *(left)*. When you can do this comfortably, raise them over your head *(below)*.

Warm-Ups/2

Stand with your feet shoulder-width apart, toes pointed outward and arms at your sides with your palms facing downward. Bend your knees and push off on your left foot, leaning to the right and lifting your shoulder *(left)*. Bend your knees again to recenter your weight *(center)*. Push off to your left, lifting your right shoulder and pointing your right foot.

Warm-Ups/3

Stand with your feet together and knees bent. Bring your elbows back to chest height, with your palms facing forward *(right)*. Simultaneously push your hands forward and thrust your right foot out, resting it on its heel *(below)*. Return to the starting position and switch legs.

From a standing position with your arms
at your sides, rotate your torso and swivel
your right foot to the right as you bend
your right knee. Push your hands down on
either side of your body *(left)*. Bring your
left foot in to your right, at the same
time raising your arms in front of your
chest *(center)*. Rotate to your left *(above)*
and return to the center. When bending
your knees, do not extend them farther
than your toes.

Moving in Place/1

Stand straight with your shoulders relaxed, your abdomen contracted and your buttocks tucked under. Vigorously march in place, bringing each knee high and keeping your foot positioned directly beneath it. Land on the ball of your foot and rock to the heel on impact. Pump with your arms, holding your elbows flexed at 90-degree angles. Continue for a minute or more. You can use this as a transition step between routines.

Stand with your feet together and your arms extended in front of you at shoulder height, your palms facing downward *(below)*. Tilt your pelvis forward and point the toes of your right foot as you make your hands into fists and forcefully pull your arms into your sides *(bottom)*. Repeat with your left leg.

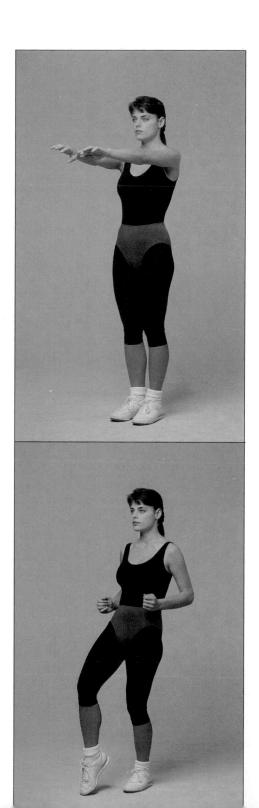

Moving in Place/2

Bend your left knee slightly as you bring your bent right leg behind you and rest on your toes. At the same time, cross your bent left arm in front of you and your bent right arm behind you *(left)*. Raise your arms to shoulder height as you extend your right leg to the side *(below)*. Shift your weight onto your right leg, dropping your heel and crossing your left leg and left arm behind you, your bent right arm in front of you *(bottom)*.

Bend your arms and hold them at
shoulder height. Roll them over each
other and rotate your torso slightly to the
left as you extend your right leg to the
side, pointing your toes *(above)*. Bend
your knees as you bring your right leg
back to your left *(right)*.

Moving in Place/3

Bend your right arm upward and touch your right elbow with your left hand. Lift your right hip as you move your right leg to the side *(below)*. Shift your weight onto your right foot and bring your left foot into your right *(center)*. Transfer your weight onto your left foot *(right)*, then back to your right.

Bend your arms so that your hands are behind your shoulders and touch your right toe in front of you *(top).* Take a small step forward onto your right foot as you swing your arms forward *(center).* Touch your left toe behind you, then swing your arms back up as you step back onto your left foot and point the toe of your right foot *(right).* Leading with your right foot, march in place for seven steps; then repeat the entire sequence, beginning with your left foot.

Stand up straight. Simultaneously step to the right onto the ball of your right foot and raise your right arm over your head *(far left)*. Then step to the left onto the ball of your left foot as you raise your left arm over your head *(left center)*. Bend your left knee as you step in with your right foot and bend your right elbow, pulling your arm into your chest *(right center)*. Bend both knees, bringing your left foot into your right and pulling your left arm into your chest *(above)*.

Moving Around/1

Bend your arms at the elbow, keeping
your fingers straight. Step forward onto
your right foot *(below)*. Rotate your arms
at the elbow in a locomotive-like motion
as you step forward onto your left foot
(left center), then forward onto your right
(right center). Touch your left foot to your
right instep *(far right)*. Step backward
onto your left foot. Continue backward
with two more steps, then touch your
right foot to your left instep.

Repeat the walking sequence shown at left but bring your arms to shoulder height, using an alternate punching motion with each step.

Moving Around/2

Clockwise from top left: Raise your arms to shoulder height and extend your right leg, pointing your toes. Shift your weight onto your right foot as you bend your left knee and bring your left foot behind your right, bending your elbows into your waist. Shift your weight back to your left foot and again extend your right leg to the side with your arms outstretched. Bring your elbows back into your waist as you shift onto your right foot and bring your left foot in next to your right instep.

Increase the arm work in the preceding sequence by clapping your hands over your head for the final step *(right)*. You can also cross your arms in front of you on the arm extensions, alternating the arm that is on top *(below)*.

Combinations/1

Bend your elbows and bring your arms to shoulder height. Leading with your left foot, take three steps forward, punching in front of you with alternate arms *(far left)*. On the fourth step, bring your right foot forward as far as your left instep *(left center)*. Step back with your right foot as you bring your right arm back to your chest *(right center)*. Kick your left foot forward and push out with your arms *(right)*. Bring your arms back into your chest and step backward with your left foot. Kick your right foot forward, extending your arms. Go back two more steps, kick, then lower your right foot next to your left.

Lift your arms up over your head and, turning to your left, bring your bent right leg up to hip height *(far left)*. Bend your elbows and drop your arms and leg; repeat, then pivot to your right and lift your arms upward again, this time lifting your left knee *(center left)*. Drop your leg and arms, repeat, then pivot back to your left, kicking your right foot forward and pushing back with your arms *(center right)*. Bring your arms and leg back, then repeat once. Pivot to your right and kick with your left leg twice *(above)*.

Combinations/3

Swing your arms and hips to the right as you lean into your right hip *(below)*, then swing to the left; repeat. On the final swing, bring your left foot behind your right *(center)*. Rise onto the toes of your left foot and step to the right with your right leg, swinging your arms back to the right. Touch the ball of your left foot to your right instep, then extend your leg back to the left as you clap your hands overhead *(right)*.

Cool-Downs

Stand with your feet about shoulder-width apart, your toes pointing outward. Bend your knees slightly as you rotate your right arm at the shoulder, bringing it downward in a crawl-like swimming motion *(left)*. Straighten your legs and bring your right shoulder back, then flex your knees again as you repeat with your left arm *(below)*.

From a standing position, raise your arms in front of you at shoulder level and bend your knees *(above)*. Start to swing your arms down and straighten your knees. Bring your arms behind you, bending your knees again *(center)*, then swing your arms up toward the ceiling. Straighten your body as you extend your arms overhead *(right)*.

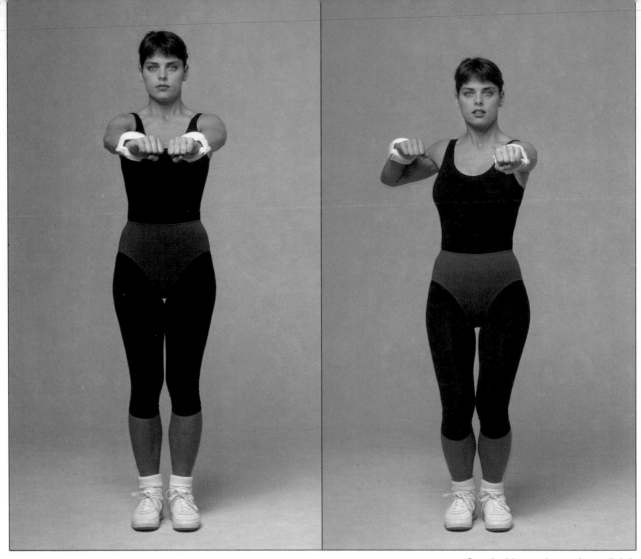

Stand with your knees bent slightly and your arms raised to shoulder level *(above left)*. Bend your knees, pulling your bent right arm backward so your fist is about level with your shoulder *(above)*. Straighten your legs as you return to the starting position, then repeat with your left arm.

Adding Weights/1

Weights help to intensify an aerobic dance program, but they should only be incorporated once you can easily perform your usual routine without reaching your target heart rate. An indication of the right time to add weights is when you can perform 16 repetitions of the same step without becoming fatigued. This is a sign that your body has adapted to a higher level of fitness. Adding additional weights will place more de-

mands on your cardiovascular system, boosting your heart rate back into its target range.

Begin with the lightest hand weights, usually a half-pound per hand. (Because of the stress they add to the shin, the Achilles tendon and the back, ankle weights are not recommended during aerobic exercise.) As your body adapts to this new load, you can increase the weights by half-pound intervals. Do not use weights heavier than three

pounds each when performing low-impact aerobics.

Hold the weights firmly but not tightly — the isometric pressure of tight gripping can impair blood flow in the arms and thus raise blood pressure. If you develop muscle pain or joint soreness, stop using weights until the pain disappears. Consult your physician if the pain persists. When you are ready to take up weights again, begin with a light load, and increase it gradually.

Stand with your knees slightly bent and your arms at your sides with your elbows bent *(right)*. Move both arms behind you as far as possible, keeping your elbows bent *(center)*. Return to the starting position.

Stand with your legs shoulder-width
apart and your arms outstretched at
shoulder height. Lunge to the left as you
extend your left arm and bend your right
elbow (above).

Adding Weights/2

From a standing position with your arms at your sides, step to your right, so your feet are shoulder-width apart and your knees are bent. Your arms should be at shoulder height with your elbows flexed *(below left).* Simultaneously pull your elbows into your sides and bring your right foot back to center *(center).* Repeat the arm motion as you step to your left. Vary the motion by raising your arms over your head when you step in *(below),* then pulling them down to shoulder height when you step out. Keep your elbows bent when you raise your arms over your head.

Adding Weights/3

Raise your bent arms to shoulder height.
As you lift your left knee to hip level
(right), pull your arms down to touch
slightly under your bent knee *(below)*,
then bring the arms back up as you put
your left leg down and raise your right.
Keep your back straight.

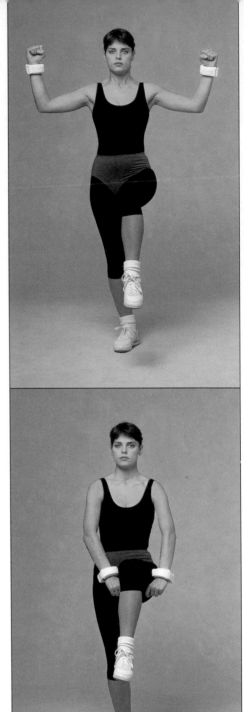

From a standing position, extend your arms directly in front of you. Push off on your left foot to lunge backward onto the ball of your right foot. Keep your back knee bent *(left)*. Return to the starting position by pushing off your back foot and bringing you arms into your chest.

STAYING FLEXIBLE

CHAPTER 7

The Benefits of Stretching

How the right stretches can provide greater agility, better posture and insurance against injury

B eing flexible means having the ability to use muscles and joints through their full range of motion. The natural structure of each joint and the direction in which it allows movement determines range of motion. Ball-and-socket joints, such as those in your hips and shoulders, afford greater range of motion than the hinge joints in your knees and elbows, the condyloid joints in your wrists, the pivot joints in your spinal column or the gliding joints in the metatarsals of your feet.

A joint is flexible when the muscles and connective tissues around it do not restrict its natural range of motion. You should, for example, be able to extend your arm straight at a 90-degree angle from your body and then flex your elbow joint enough to rest your hand comfortably on your shoulder. A flexible elbow joint allows full extension and flexion of your arm.

Why is staying flexible important?
For the active person, most experts believe that good flexibility reduces the chance of injury. Muscles that restrict the natural range of motion in the joints are more susceptible to pulls, tears and stress injuries than those that are flexible enough to allow a full range of motion.

Among athletes, a low degree of flexibility detracts from the grace of the gymnast, dancer and ice skater, may limit the muscular power of the golfer and tennis and baseball player, and may even lead to injury. Tight calf muscles, for instance, can place undue stress on the foot, leading to a variety of orthopedic problems, including painful Achilles tendinitis.

At the same time, being flexible is not just for athletes. It can help provide relief from everyday muscle tension and stiffness, and it is also crucial for proper posture.

What limits flexibility?

Resistance to movement from soft tissues is the major obstacle to a joint's full natural range of movement. For example, researchers have determined that, in extending and flexing your wrist, approximately 40 percent of the resistance comes from the stretched muscle and its connective tissue fascia; about 50 percent of the resistance comes from the joint capsule; the rest of the resistance is primarily from tendons and ligaments. In addition, voluntary or involuntary contraction of muscles that oppose the desired movement will also limit your range of motion.

Are some people naturally more flexible than others?

Yes, but there is no ideal or standard for flexibility. The only standards available are based on norms that indicate how hundreds of individuals of both sexes and various age groups have performed on average. Generally speaking, tests have shown that children are more flexible than adults and that women are more flexible than men. Two studies, for instance, tested the flexibility of 510 males aged 18 to 71 and 407 females aged 18 to 74. These studies found that, for the average man tested, flexibility was greatest for most muscle groups and joints between the ages of 23 and 24; among women, it was greatest between the ages of 25 and 29.

Although it is commonly thought that "muscle-bound" people are inflexible, studies show that strength-training exercises, when performed properly, do not limit flexibility. It is important during strength training that you move through the full range of motion for the joints involved in each exercise. Bodybuilders who are conscientious about this, and who regularly stretch their muscles, have better-than-average flexibility.

Another study measured the flexibility of 300 randomly selected girls between the ages of 6 and 18. In most of the 12 flexibility measurements the researchers took, the girls' flexibility increased from age 6 to age 12 and then showed a decline. But the results were inconsistent: In terms of shoulder, knee and hip flexibility, there was a decrease between the ages of 6 and 18; yet 18 year olds were more flexible in their trunk and wrist muscles and had better flexibility in the muscles along the outside of their thighs than younger girls.

Because flexibility is such an individual and joint-specific characteristic, it is prudent to use your own current degree of flexibility as a yardstick. If you want to improve flexibility in a specific joint, it's important to monitor your progress against your own previous level of flexibility, not against someone else's.

Can lack of flexibility cause health problems?

A lack of flexibility can create poor posture, resulting in mechanical imbalances in the back, hip and neck. These imbalances pull body segments out of line, causing stress, strain and even worse posture. The resulting muscular tension, joint strain and ligament and cartilage damage can produce deformity. Inflexible joints and weak muscles in the shoulder and chest, for instance, can cause rounded shoulders, which can lead to kyphosis (humpbacked spine), a sunken chest and impaired respiratory capacity.

Tight hip-flexor muscles, hamstrings and back muscles can rotate the pelvis forward, resulting in lordosis (excessive curvature of the lower back), chronic lower back pain and sciatica (a radiating pain in the thighs or buttocks along the sciatic nerve). Drooping your head forward may produce headache, dizziness and chronic strain on the muscles along the back of the neck, resulting in neck and shoulder pain.

How can you increase flexibility?

Simply using your muscles will help. For instance, you are usually the least flexible when you get out of bed in the morning. Then, just by engaging in your normal routine and using your muscles to walk, sit and stand, you gradually gain flexibility throughout the day. Exercise also helps. In general, athletes and people who work out regularly are more flexible than nonathletes and sedentary persons.

Warming the tissues involved in movement around a joint can also enhance flexibility—though the temperatures reached in most studies are not ones you would typically encounter. One study showed that deep-tissue warming to 113° F can increase the range of motion in a joint by as much as 20 percent. Cooling the joint to 65° F reduces flexibility by 10 to 20 percent. The preferred method of enhancing flexibility is through a stretching program.

What occurs during a stretch?

In some respects, muscles are like ropes—they exert force by pulling, not pushing. Most muscles attach to bones and cross over one or more joints; when the muscles contract and shorten, they cause a limb or body part to move in a particular direction. To stretch a muscle requires an external force to move the limb or body part in the opposite direction. The external force can be applied by gravity, by the contraction of an opposing muscle, or by a stretching partner. Each of the exercises in the following three chapters uses these forces to achieve a stretch.

How much stretching is required to make a muscle more flexible?

To increase a muscle's length, studies show, you must regularly pull it about 10 percent beyond its normal length: That is the point where your muscle feels stretched enough to be slightly uncomfortable but not enough to cause pain. Typically, you should hold this position for 10 to 30 seconds, relax, and then repeat the stretch three to five times.

How often should you stretch?

The approach in a progressive stretching program to increase flexibility is related to the overload principle used to build muscle strength. To increase muscle strength, you must regularly contract the muscle against progressively more resistance with a slightly greater force than it is used to. In time, the muscle responds to the overload by becoming stronger. Similarly, to increase flexibility, you must regularly stretch the muscle slightly beyond its normal length. It will adapt to this overload and reward you with a greater range of joint motion. Studies show that you should stretch three to seven days a week to increase your flexibility. For maintaining flexibility, three days a week is probably adequate.

What are some of the immediate benefits of stretching?

Stretching is a natural, relaxing sensation. It helps relieve tension and the feeling of stiffness. Many people stretch in one way or another after getting out of bed in the morning. Most people also stretch intermittently while sitting for long periods. These simple routines do not increase general or long-term flexibility—they are simply pleasurable movements.

Studies show that stretching can help relieve delayed muscle soreness after strenuous exercise. And evidence now suggests that stretching can at least reduce and sometimes prevent dysmenorrhea, or painful menstruation. If you suffer from dysmenorrhea that is not the result of a disease, you can probably relieve your symptoms by regularly performing stretching exercises of the muscles in the pelvic region.

Stretching is not only pleasurable, it can also alleviate pain. For example, since one common cause of lower back pain is tight hip-extensor muscles, a stretching program aimed at hamstring flexibility may reduce the risk of lower back pain. Some experts think that stretching can help prevent or alleviate about 80 percent of all cases of lower back pain; that 80 percent is caused by tightness and spasms in the musculature of the back and pelvis.

You can also stretch to reduce muscle soreness associated with stress injuries, which result from overdoing sports and exercise. According to one theory, this type of soreness is produced by a cycle of muscle tension, soreness and increased neural reflex activity, which results in more muscle tension and soreness. Slow, deliberate stretching reduces the neural activity in the muscles, breaking the cycle and reducing the pain.

Will warm-up stretches improve flexibility?

A flexibility warm-up is a group of stretches performed just before engaging in exercise or sports and is designed to temporarily elongate the muscles directly involved in that activity. For instance, stretching out for running would involve working primarily on the gluteals, quadriceps, hamstrings and calves. Stretching exercises as part of a sports warm-up have been shown to increase a joint's range of motion by 4 to 18 percent for 90 minutes or more. But there is no evidence to suggest that sporadic flexibility warm-ups can result in long-term gains in joint range of motion.

To improve general flexibility, you need to regularly perform a set of exercises that work on muscle groups all over the body, concentrating on the tighter muscles. These stretches should be performed apart from or following other exercise sessions.

Can you become too flexible?

Too much flexibility without muscle strength can cause instability in the joints, leading to a risk of dislocations and other traumas. Victims of poliomyelitis and other diseases or injuries of the neuromuscular system may suffer from this condition. However, it is unlikely that you can ever become so flexible from a stretching program that you will have this problem. Nor will you become "double-jointed," a congenital condition that results in unusually flexible joints and permits contortions of limbs and torso.

Overly flexible or loose joints can result from stretching ligaments, the connective tissue that binds joints together. Ligaments, unlike muscles, are not elastic, and remain lengthened when stretched repeatedly. Weight-bearing joints such as the knee or ankle may become unstable and susceptible to dislocation or abnormal twisting. It is widely accepted among athletes that loose joints can lead to injury. Many athletes therefore tape joints to increase stability, and many who have loose joints also strengthen supporting muscles to improve control over their joint flexibility. Their concern may be unwarranted, however, since studies do not show a direct correlation between loose joints and frequency of athletic injuries.

Do some muscles need to be stretched more frequently than others?

Since flexibility is specific, you can increase a joint's flexibility only by stretching muscles and other soft tissues associated with that joint. The need, then, is to identify the muscles and joints that are tight and spend the bulk of your stretching time working on them, not on joints that are already sufficiently flexible.

Generally speaking, the muscles most in need of stretching are the ones on which you place the greatest demands. Most reasonably active people should routinely stretch the following muscles: calves (to increase the range of motion in ankles and to prevent calf pain and Achilles tendinitis), hamstrings, gluteals and lower back (to prevent running-related injuries and lower back pain), inner thighs (to reduce the chance of groin pulls), quadriceps and hip flexors (to prevent knee stiffness), and upper back, chest and shoulders (to prevent rounded shoulders and restricted range of motion).

Is it hard for older people to become flexible?

One of the most obvious signs usually associated with advancing age is reduced flexibility. In far too many cases, range of motion becomes so severely restricted that an elderly person may be afraid of getting injured simply by walking or climbing stairs.

Luckily, inflexibility can be reversed, even among the elderly. In a study that compared the joint stiffness between 20 young men (aged 15 to 19) and 20 elderly men (aged 63 to 88), it was found that both groups could reverse joint stiffness with equal ease. A number of other studies have shown that virtually anyone, regardless of age, can improve flexibility by stretching.

Is there a simple way to test flexibility?

Flexibility used to be thought of as a general characteristic of the body: You were either flexible or you were not. However, researchers have now determined that flexibility is not equally apparent in all joints of the body. Just as there is a great range of flexibility among individuals in the same age and sex group, studies show that flexibility can even change drastically from one muscle group to another. You can have tight hamstrings and supple shoulder muscles, or tight hip flexors but flexible trunk muscles. You can even have bilateral differences in flexibility—your right quadriceps, for example, can be less flexible than your left.

Touching your toes without bending your knees has been the timeworn test for flexibility. But in fact, touching your toes tells little more than how flexible you are in the hamstrings and lower back. Some experts also believe that the standing toe touch may be dangerous under certain circumstances because it can place stress on the lower back. For a better test of your ability to stretch, see the next page.

Flexibility also changes according to the direction in which the joint allows movement. You can be quite flexible when you bend your arm in one direction, for example, but less flexible when you use different muscles to rotate your arm in another direction. Also, the relation of one joint to another may influence the range of motion in one or both joints. For instance, if you are like most people, you can easily flex your fingers and tuck them into the palm of your hand so long as your wrist is extended. But if you flex your wrist, you will significantly reduce the range of motion in your finger joints, and you may not be able to tuck your fingers into your palm.

Clearly, flexibility is highly specific, making it difficult to provide an overall measurement without testing virtually every joint in the body. But you can get a general idea of your level of flexibility by taking several key measurements. The tests on pages 200-201 will help you define your own level of flexibility.

Measuring Your Flexibility

Everyone has a different degree of flexibility that varies from joint to joint, from day to day, sometimes even from hour to hour. No single test can give you a sense of your overall flexibility. However, you can get a general assessment by testing the range of motion you can achieve in the major joints of your body. Furthermore, by taking a number of tests that measure specific muscles and muscles groups, you can determine where to concentrate the most effort. Perhaps the greatest benefit of a flexibility test is to establish a personal baseline. You will then have a gauge by which to measure your progress.

The five simple tests on these two pages measure flexibility in the lower back, hamstrings, hip flexibility in the lower back, hamstrings, hip flexors, shoulders and calves—areas where flexibility is particularly important among active people. All you need are a yardstick or ruler and a box or step about eight inches high.

Ask a friend to help you take the measurements; perform each test three times and record the best result. Take the tests about once a month to chart your progress.

Before taking these tests, perform a general 5-minute aerobic warm-up by running lightly in place, then perform some specific flexibility warm-ups such as a seated toe touch, triceps stretches (page 229), and stretches for hamstrings (page 210-211) and calves (pages 226-227)).

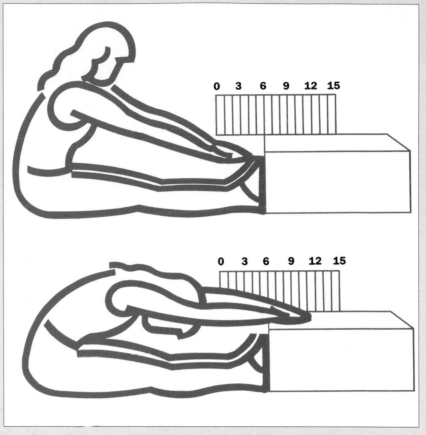

Two of the muscle groups important to your overall flexibility are the lower back and hamstring muscles. To test their flexibility, sit with the soles of your feet against a box or step and your arms outstretched *(top)*. Reach as far forward as you can toward the edge of the box without bending your knees. At first, you may not be able to reach the box, but once you've begun a program of regular stretching, your results will improve. Have a partner record how far your fingertips reach on a yardstick extended six inches in front of the edge of the box. Find your flexibility rating using the chart below.

How Far Can You Reach?
(in inches)*

	Men	Women
High	14+	15+
Above Average	11-13	12-14
Average	7-10	7-11
Below Average	4-6	4-6
Low	3 or less	3 or less

*These norms are for persons in their 20s. Values will decrease by 1 inch for every decade beyond. For example, a 62-year-old woman would have excellent flexibility with 11+ inches.

Sit on a box or a straight-backed chair, holding your back erect. Rest one leg on the floor while extending the other. If your hamstrings are adequately flexible, you will be able to extend the leg fully without moving your other leg or altering your upright seated position.

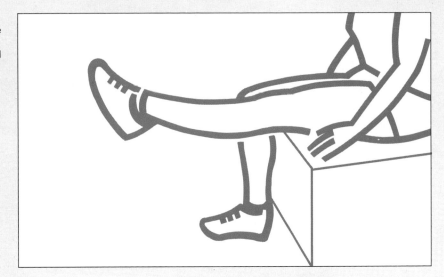

While lying prone with one leg bent, have your partner grasp your knee with one hand and, pushing down on your pelvis with the other, raise your leg. If your quadriceps and hip flexors are flexible, your partner will be able to raise your knee several inches without causing you undue discomfort.

Raise your right elbow and reach behind your back (near right). Place your left hand in the small of your back and slide it upward. If you can touch your hands behind your back and overlap your fingers, your arms and shoulders are adequately flexible. To test your calf muscles, stand about three feet from a wall with your feet spread shoulder-width apart (far right). Place your hands on the wall and bend forward until your chin touches the wall. You should be able to do this while keeping your body straight and your feet flat on the floor.

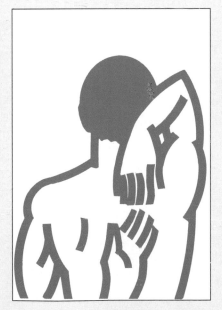 

Common Mistakes

Relax When You Stretch

Contracted Muscle

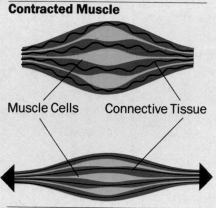

Muscle Cells   Connective Tissue

Relaxed Muscle

When you try to stretch a contracted muscle *(top)*, as in performing ballistic stretches, proportionately more of the external force is placed on the muscle fiber than on the connective tissue. This may result in microscopic tears. When you stretch a relaxed muscle *(above)*, you stretch the connective tissue, which helps prevent injury.

A growing body of research suggests that some people who stretch to avoid injury when they work out or play sports can get injured from the stretches themselves. In one survey of 4,000 running injuries, stretching exercises were found to be a major cause of injury. The study also determined that those who were injured performed certain exercises that placed excessive stress on joints, ligaments and muscles. The most common of these are shown opposite. If you avoid these stressful stretches and observe the following precautions, you will be able to design a safe stretching program.

Perform slow static stretches, not bouncing or ballistic stretches such as leg kicks. Although studies show that ballistic stretches are as effective as static stretches for increasing flexibility, there is a possibility you will rupture ligaments and cause microscopic tears in your muscles. One reason for this is that bouncing causes the muscle to contract at the same time you are forcing it to stretch. Also, ballistic stretches are not as deliberate as static stretches, and the uncontrolled momentum of your limb may overload a joint and force it to move beyond its natural range of motion, very likely damaging the connective tissue.

Stretch your muscles only about 10 percent beyond their normal length. When a muscle is stretched to this limit, you should feel a comfortable tightness in the center of the muscle. Do not stretch any farther; if you feel discomfort at the muscle's end attachments, you are stretching too far and subjecting the tendon to too much tension. Never stretch to the point of pain. And remember that improving your flexibility is progressive — it cannot be done in one session. Forcing your muscles to stretch beyond their capability will cause injury and also loss of elasticity.

Always work within a joint's natural range of motion. If you force a joint to move beyond its natural range of motion, you may rupture or overstretch the ligaments. This can occur with certain dangerous stretches that place most of your body weight on one particular joint. Both the "plow" and the "hurdler's stretch" shown opposite can place excessive stress on certain joints. Deep knee bends can overstretch ligaments in the knees. Also, the ballet barre stretch can place a great deal of force on the extended knee, possibly damaging the cartilage and ligaments. This stretch can also compress the sciatic nerve, causing pain to radiate down the back of the legs from the buttocks.

Stretch before and after a strenuous workout session. A single stretching session will significantly improve flexibility and joint range of motion for at least 90 minutes. Stretching beforehand may reduce your chance of injury and improve your athletic performance. However, some athletic activities may tighten your muscles or cause delayed soreness. By stretching afterward, you can regain flexibility and prevent soreness.

If you do happen to become injured from overstretching, treat the injury like any other stress injury. Reduce the intensity of your exercises and apply ice packs to the affected area. Ice will lessen the discomfort and reduce the swelling. Of course, if you experience severe pain or if the discomfort of an injury lasts for several days, consult a physician.

The plow *(left)* is a popular but dangerous stretch for the hamstring and back muscles. It places tremendous pressure on the back of the neck, which must support your entire body weight.

Toe touching with locked knees *(below)* is all too common as a stretch of the lower back and hamstrings. These muscles must contract to support your body at the same time you are trying to stretch them. Not only is toe touching inefficient as a stretch, but it can also result in injury.

Ballistic stretching, such as kicking your leg with the knee locked *(above)*, will stretch your muscles. But it will also induce the stretch reflex. This type of stretching often causes delayed localized muscle soreness.

The hurdler's stretch *(left)* should not be performed by anyone except very flexible athletes. The awkward twisting can cause strain and torn ligaments in the bent knee.

Increasing Your Flexibility

Training your muscles to stretch farther is similar in concept to training them for strength: You must use the progressive overload principle. Just as the only way to strengthen muscles is to exercise them slightly beyond their normal capacity and then progressively increase the workload, you can only increase flexibility by following a progressive stretching program.

As you advance in a flexibility program, you will not see steady improvement from one day to the next. Muscle soreness, motivation, ability to relax, room temperature and warm-up preparation are among the factors that influence your range of motion. But regardless of your flexibility at any particular time, by following the guidelines here, you should notice an improvement in a month.

HOW HARD

Studies show that you should stretch a muscle about 10 percent beyond its normal length in order to increase its flexibility. For most people, this will mean stretching to the point of tightness and discomfort, but without feeling pain. If you do feel pain in muscles or joints, consider it a warning to ease up on the stretch.

HOW LONG

Most experts agree that you should hold a stretch between 10 and 60 seconds to lengthen a muscle effectively. For the best results, however, you should stretch a muscle or muscle group for 10 to 30 seconds, pause and then repeat the stretch three to five times.

HOW OFTEN

You should stretch at least three days a week in order to obtain minimum benefits. For optimal results, though, you should stretch four to seven days a week.

Special Situations

If you spend long periods sitting or standing, or if you are so busy during the day that you do not have time for a full stretching routine, you can benefit from the following exercises.

SITTING

When you sit a lot, tension builds up in your lower back, shoulders and neck. Sitting for extended periods of time can also shorten your hamstrings and hip flexors and cause soreness in your buttocks. This set of exercises will counteract tension and discomfort in these areas. Half of the exercises can be done while you are sitting.
• Hamstring stretch on a stool, page 211.
• Buttocks, pages 212-213.
• Hip-flexor stretch on a stool, page 223.
• Seated back stretch, page 215.
• Seated chest, back and shoulder stretches, page 229.
• Neck stretches, pages 232-233.

STANDING

The strain of prolonged standing is usually felt in the muscles of your feet, calves, hips and lower back. These exercises are performed standing upright, and you can do them anytime, anywhere.
• Foot and shin stretches, pages 230-231.
• Calf stretches, page 227.
• Hamstring stretch on a stool, page 211.
• Hip-flexor stretch, page 222.
• Chest stretch against a wall, page 228.

BRIEF STRETCHING

If your time is limited, doing only a few stretches is better than doing none or trying to hurry through a full routine. Here is a round-up of stretches that you can complete in a few minutes.
• Calf stretches, page 227.
• Hamstring stretch on a stool, page 211.
• Hip-flexor stretch against a wall, page 223.
• Upper back and shoulders, pages 250-251.

Ten Guidelines for Stretching

1. **CHOOSE THE BEST TIME OF DAY.** Find a period when you are not likely to be interrupted by phone calls or other distractions. Proper stretching requires concentration and patience. Be sure that you do not rush through your routines. Also, do not work out immediately after a meal; a full feeling will make you uncomfortable.

2. **WEAR LOOSE-FITTING CLOTHING.** Special exercise outfits are not essential for a stretching program, but you should wear loose, comfortable clothing that does not restrict your movement. To achieve the best results, you should stretch on a carpeted floor in bare feet. For comfort's sake, do not wear a belt or jewelry.

3. **WARM UP.** Perform a 5- to 10-minute aerobic warm-up, such as jogging in place or stationary cycling, before you stretch. You will be adequately warmed up when you begin to sweat. Warming up helps increase the circulation and temperature in your muscles, which in turn increases their pliability. Stretching muscles that are cold is less effective than stretching them when they are warmed up.

4. **LISTEN TO YOUR BODY.** Remember that your flexibility changes from day to day and you may not be able to perform the same stretch on one day that you did the day before. Never try to force a stretch; instead, ease into it and take the muscle only to the point of slight discomfort. The stretch should always occur in the center of the muscle, not at the attachments, and should never cause pain.

5. **BREATHE EVENLY.** The key to stretching is to remain relaxed during your exercises. Breathing rapidly or irregularly or holding your breath may make you tense. Instead, go into a stretch as you are exhaling, then concentrate on breathing normally and slowly.

6. **BE SPECIFIC.** Flexibility does not diffuse itself throughout the body. Achieving flexibility in part of the body, or having stretched a particular muscle, does not mean that you will necessarily gain flexibility in another area. Be sure to pay special attention to those body areas that are the least flexible and stretch them more often.

7. **DO STRETCHES IN PAIRS.** Work for bilateral flexibility—that is, equal flexibility on both sides of your body. When stretching one side of the body, be sure to follow with the same stretches on the other side.

8. **PROGRESS AT YOUR OWN SPEED.** Do not attempt to force your muscles into flexibility. Begin slowly and gradually work toward your goals. Never try to compete with another person by seeing who can stretch farther. Flexibility is an individual matter.

9. **TAKE EXTRA TIME IF NECESSARY.** If you have been inactive for a while and your muscles are unaccustomed to being stretched, then you should start slowly. The same is true if you have muscle soreness as the result of a stress injury from overdoing a sport or exercise. However, never stretch muscles that are torn or strained; you will only worsen the condition.

10. **KEEP TRACK OF YOUR PROGRESS.** Test your general flexibility (pages 200-201) at the beginning of your training program to establish your flexibility baseline. Then retest your suppleness monthly as you progress. Once you have achieved the flexibility you want, continue stretching about three times a week to maintain your level.

CHAPTER 8

Basic Stretching

A whole-body routine for greater flexibility and better posture

Static stretching, also known as sustained or passive stretching, is by far the most popular technique for improving flexibility. It is safe, effective, convenient and pain-free. You can perform static stretches whenever and wherever you want. You can do them standing up, sitting or lying down. And you do not need a coach, a trainer, exotic exercise equipment or a health club. All that is required for most static stretches is loose, comfortable clothing, a wall or another solid surface to lean against, a carpeted floor or exercise mat and, occasionally, a chair or bench to support you.

One of the great advantages of static stretching is that it helps you become better acquainted with the interrelationships of your body's muscles and tendons. Its slow, deliberate movement teaches you to feel how your muscles work in groups. You will become more aware of muscle

tension, contraction and relaxation; and you will be able to isolate particular muscle groups to determine which are tighter or less flexible than others. By recognizing the limits of your muscles' flexibility, you can avoid overstretching and injury; furthermore, you will be better able to gauge the improvement in your flexibility.

Static stretching involves a slow pull that extends a muscle just beyond its normal length. Continued pressure holds the muscle in a stretched position for a sustained period. To benefit from static stretching, you must hold the stretch for at least six seconds. However, to get the best results, you should hold a stretch from 10 to 30 seconds and then repeat the exercise three to five times. The stretching must be forceful enough to enhance flexibility but not so rigorous as to cause injury to the muscles or tendons. Most experts agree that you should perform stat-

ic stretches to the point of mild discomfort but never stretch so far that you feel acute pain. While stretching can help alleviate muscle soreness, it can also cause soreness when overdone. If you are just starting a stretching program, therefore, you should be especially careful that you do not overstretch a muscle.

Because a static stretch is gentle and prolonged, the technique reduces the muscle-spindle stretch reflex, which would normally cause the muscle to contract when it is stretched (see box, page 197). For this reason, mild static stretches are superior to forceful ballistic stretches, in which a person bounces or swings part of his or her body to gain momentum and force a stretch. Ballistic stretching causes the muscle spindles to induce a reflexive contraction in the very muscle you are trying to stretch. As long as your stretch is slow and deliberate, however, you can safely lengthen a muscle beyond its normal reach as you develop flexibility.

Static stretching is most effective when you can apply an external force to aid your stretch. As the stretching exercises on the following pages show, there are a number of ways to do this. For example, you can induce a static stretch of your chest muscle simply by drawing your arm as far back as possible and holding it there. But that stretch is limited by the flexibility of your chest muscle and by the strength of the opposing muscles on the other side of the shoulder joint pulling your arm back. The weaker those muscles, the less effective the stretch. You can get a much better stretch of the chest muscle by bracing your hand against a wall and twisting your body away from the wall. Then you do not have to rely on the strength of your chest's opposing muscles; instead, your leg and trunk muscles are able to apply greater force by using the wall for leverage. You will be able to hold the stretch for a longer time without the opposing muscle becoming fatigued.

Another way to introduce an external force to enhance static stretching is to apply the leverage of one or more limbs against that of another. You can, for instance, support yourself against a wall or lie face down on the ground and grasp your ankle, pulling it toward your buttocks. This technique will stretch your quadriceps on the front of your thigh far more effectively than if you tried to stretch them by contracting your opposing hamstring muscles and lifting your foot without external assistance.

Gravity, too, can play a role in stretching. When you lean into a wall with one or both legs extended backward, gravity pulls your body down and applies a measure of force to the musculature of your lower leg, thereby stretching your calf muscles. If you happen to have an exercise partner, this person can apply the external force that is needed to perform many stretching exercises.

When you embark on a static stretching program, give yourself plenty of time to stretch. Do not hurry through it. Be sure you are properly supported so that you do not lose your balance. Too often, for instance, people try to perform a quadriceps stretch by pulling their heel back to their buttocks while trying to balance on one foot. Stretching in this manner not only causes undue muscular tension in the supporting leg, but the unsteady stance can diminish the effectiveness of the stretch.

At the beginning of your stretching program, you may notice inappropriate contractions, chiefly in the opposing muscles. For instance, while stretching your hamstrings you might feel a tense quivering or tightening of the quadriceps. These muscle contractions are normal. Some people embarking on a stretching program also report a temporary numbness in some muscles while they stretch them. As you gain experience and develop better flexibility and control, both the contractions and sensations of numbness should disappear; your muscles should feel a warm tightness as they are being stretched and a pleasant looseness afterward.

Note: In the photographed sequences that follow, the people performing the stretches possess a high degree of flexibility. As you start out, you probably won't be able to stretch to the same extent. Think of these pictures as a guide to the positions you can ultimately aspire to. Keep in mind that flexibility varies among individuals, and that some of your joints are capable of greater flexibility than others. Above all, remember never to force a stretch: You should feel slight discomfort, but the stretching motion should never cause pain in muscles or joints.

Hamstrings

A group of three large muscles in the back of the thigh, the hamstrings are among your body's most important muscles, since they act to straighten the hip and bend and rotate the knee. Virtually every sport and physical activity makes use of these muscles, and, as a result, they are frequently subject to tightness and stress injuries.

In the stretching routines that follow, many of the exercises are shown for only one side of the body: For example, in the hamstring stretch at right, the left leg is being stretched. When you do this or any other exercise that stretches muscles on either the right or the left, be sure to repeat the exercise for the other side of the body.

Sit on the floor with one leg extended and the other leg bent at the knee. Loop a towel around your foot and pull your leg. This is a good stretch if you have particularly tight hamstrings and calves.

Sit on the floor with one leg extended and the opposite knee bent. Keeping your back straight, lean forward slowly toward your toes. This will stretch your hamstrings, lower back and calf muscles.

Place your heel on a stool and loop a towel around your foot. With your standing knee bent, pull your leg into the stretch. Be sure to keep your back straight.

Lie on your back with one foot on the floor and the other leg extended in the air. Loop a towel around the foot of your extended leg and draw it toward you as far as you can.

Buttocks

The buttocks region is composed of nine major muscles. They include the gluteals, which straighten the hip, rotate the thigh and take part in straightening the knee. Because the buttocks muscles stabilize the pelvis, they are particularly active while you walk. They can become strained with overuse, and they can tighten with inactivity. To prevent inflexibility in the buttocks muscles, you should perform at least one of the exercises on these two pages regularly.

Extend your left leg and cross your right leg over it *(above)*. Draw your right knee back with your left arm. For a greater stretch, tuck your left foot under your right thigh *(below)*.

Stretch the muscles in your right buttocks by lying face up on the floor, resting your right ankle just above your left knee and drawing your knee toward your chest by pulling with both hands *(above)*. Then stretch the hamstrings as well as the buttocks by extending your left leg *(above right)*.

Lying on your back with your arms outstretched, twist your hips to the left and tuck your right calf under your left knee *(above)*. The weight of your left leg will help stretch the right buttocks muscles. For a hamstring stretch *(above right)*, straighten your left leg and extend the right leg; try to bring your toes to your left hand.

Lower Back

Sit on the floor with your legs crossed, then twist to the right and lean forward on your hands, stretching the lower back *(above)*. To stretch the lower back and buttocks, lean forward and bring your forearms toward the floor *(below)*.

The muscles and connective tissues of the lower back support your upper body. Like the rigging on a ship's mast, the deepest layers of muscles anchored in the lower back rope up the entire spine and attach to the vertebrae. The latissimus dorsi — the muscle you use when you pull your elbow back — also attaches to the lower back region. No wonder, then, that the lower back is frequently the site of muscle and connective-tissue stress. Poor posture, of course, can exacerbate lower back pain. To relieve pain and reduce stress to the region, perform these stretches.

Sit on a stool or a chair with a high seat. Gently drop your body toward your lap, letting your hands dangle to the floor and your head drop between your legs.

Lie on the floor and raise your legs with your knees bent. Hold on to your feet and pull your knees toward your chest to stretch your lower back and hamstrings. For an easier stretch, grasp behind your thighs to bring your knees to your chest.

Kneel down and place your hands on the floor with your elbows extended and your back straight. Curl up like a cat by arching your back.

Inner Thighs/1

The muscles of the inner thigh and groin area are called the adductors, since they adduct the thigh, or move it in toward the opposing leg. The adductors are connected to the lower portion of the pubic bone and run down the inside of the thighbone, where they attach along a tendinous strip. Many people who exercise regularly ignore their inner thigh muscles, allowing them to become tight. These muscles can then be easily injured, resulting in what are commonly called groin pulls. To reduce the chance of injury and to extend the range of motion in your legs, you should routinely stretch your inner thigh muscles with the exercises on these two pages and the two pages that follow.

Lie on your back with your knees bent outward and spread as far apart as comfortable. Prop your feet on a wall for support and press down on your knees.

While lying on your back, extend your feet in the air and spread your legs as far apart as you can. Press down on your inner thighs with your arms.

Draw one knee up and support it with your hand as you straighten your other leg, where you will feel a concentrated stretch.

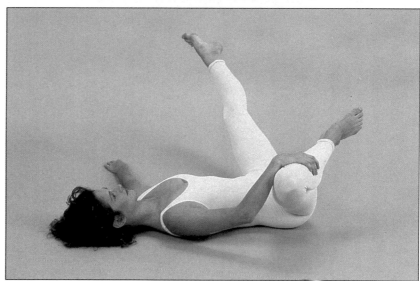

Bring the soles of your feet together and grasp your feet with your hands. Pull your feet toward you to stretch the inner thigh muscles closest to your groin area.

Inner Thighs/2

With your legs stretched in front of you, straighten your knees and spread your legs as wide as you can. To stretch both the inner thigh muscles and the hamstrings, lean forward and rest on your elbows *(near right)*. To concentrate on the musculature in your right leg, rotate your torso to the right and reach toward your foot with your left hand *(far right)*. Then lean to the left and raise your right hand toward the ceiling to stretch the abdominals, obliques and other side muscles *(below)*.

Sit on the floor with the soles of your feet together. Grasp your feet and lean forward, pressing your forearms on your shins.

While still sitting, spread your legs as far apart as you comfortably can, keeping your knees bent. Lean forward from the waist and place your hands on the floor. Press against your knees with your elbows.

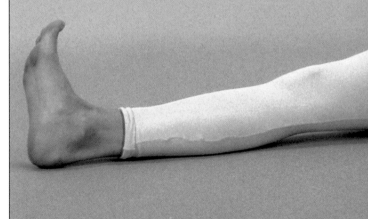

Quadriceps and Hip Flexors/1

The quadriceps are four thigh muscles that begin on the hipbone and the thighbone and become united on a single tendon that is attached to the knee-cap. These muscles work together primarily to straighten the knee. The hip flexors are a group of muscles, including one of the quadriceps, that lift your thigh. Tight quadriceps and hip flexors can limit your ability to run and jump. In addition, tight hip flexors can tilt your pelvis forward and lead to lordosis, or excessive curvature of the lower back.

Lie on your stomach and grasp your right foot with your right hand. Pull your heel toward your buttocks to stretch the quadriceps *(above)*. To stretch the hip flexors, pull your knee off the floor *(below)*.

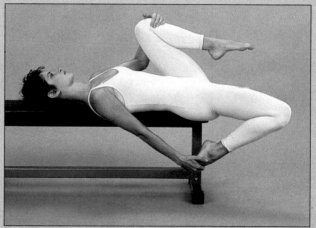

Lie on your left side and grasp your right foot with your right hand *(above left)*. Pull back on your foot until you feel a stretch of the quadriceps and hip flexors. Lie face up on an exercise table with your left leg tucked toward your chest, grasping the knee with your left hand *(above right)*. Extend your right leg over the edge of the table. Pull on your foot with your right hand. To stretch the hip flexors and shin muscles, stand facing away from a stool. Using a wall for balance, rest the top of your right foot on the seat *(right)*. Bend your left knee until you feel the stretch.

Quadriceps and Hip Flexors/2

Take an exaggerated step forward with your right foot. Brace yourself on your right knee and extend your left leg backward to stretch the hip flexors.

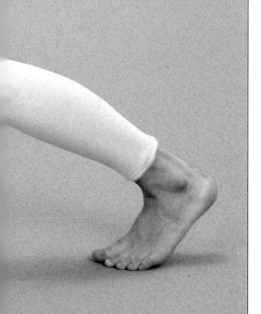

Kneel on your left leg with your right foot flat on the ground, turned out at the same angle as your right shoulder. To increase the stretch and include the right inner thigh, lean farther over your right foot.

Perform a lunge stretch by using a wall for balance. Place your palms against the wall and extend your right leg behind you to stretch the hip flexors.

Place your right foot on the seat of a stool for a lunge variation. The higher the stool, the greater the stretch you can achieve. Grasp your shin and lean forward to lengthen the hip flexors in your left leg.

Kneel and lean backward on your hands *(above)*. Be sure to keep your body straight and do not drop your pelvis. You will feel this stretch in all the muscles in the front of your thighs. Extend your right hand toward the ceiling *(below)* to add an abdominal stretch.

With your hands on the floor for balance, extend your left foot behind you while keeping your right foot on the floor; lower your chest toward your right knee *(above)*. This is a difficult stretch if you do not have flexibility in your hip flexors.

Kneel on your right knee and place your left foot flat on the floor. Balancing on your right hand, twist around to hold your right foot with your left hand *(above)*. Pull your foot upward to stretch the quadriceps as well as the hip flexors.

Calves

Your calf muscle is composed of two distinct parts, the gastrocnemius and the soleus. The gastrocnemius is the large bulging muscle of the calf. It is connected to the Achilles tendon and is principally involved with lifting the heel off the ground and pushing off for walking, running and jumping. The soleus extends underneath the gastrocnemius and also connects to the Achilles tendon. Not as powerful as the gastrocnemius, the soleus pulls on the ankle joint when you stand on your toes.

Many people, especially those who run, have inflexible calf muscles. Tight calves can result in Achilles tendinitis, pronation, or inward roll of the foot, and plantar fascitis, an inflammation of the connective tissue in the sole of the foot.

Stand with your legs slightly apart. Bend forward from the hips and place both hands on the floor, stretching the calves. Your heels may rise slightly.

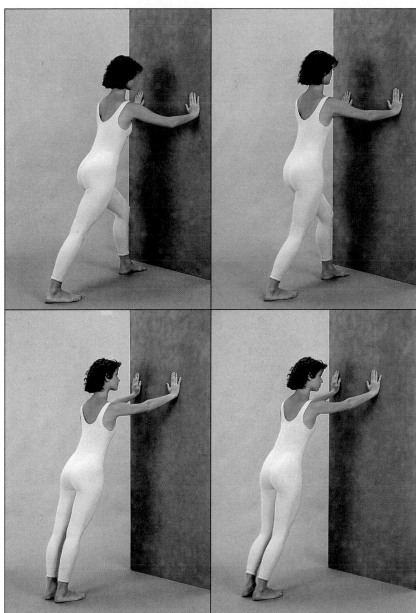

Place your palms against a wall; draw your left knee forward and extend your right leg behind with the foot turned slightly inward. Keeping your right knee locked and your heel on the ground, lean forward slightly to stretch the gastrocnemius *(top left)*. To stretch the soleus, flex your right knee slightly *(top right)*. Lean into the wall with both feet extended behind you and both knees locked to stretch your left and right gastrocnemius muscles *(above left)*. Flex your knees slightly to include a soleus stretch in both legs *(directly above)*.

Upper Body

Stretching exercises for the upper body are important not only to protect you from muscle strain, but also to improve your posture and general appearance. Tight or weak chest and shoulder muscles, for instance, may result in rounded shoulders and bad posture, which are aggravated by sitting hunched over a desk all day. The upper body stretches on these two pages will help alleviate muscle tension in your chest and shoulders. You can perform the stretches on the opposite page while sitting at a desk.

Stand erect with your feet together. Grasp the ends of a towel with both hands and hold the towel behind your head *(right)*. This is a general stretch of the chest, shoulders and upper arms.

Face a wall and bend from the hips so that the top of your head points to the wall. Place your palms against the wall for a stretch of the shoulders and arms.

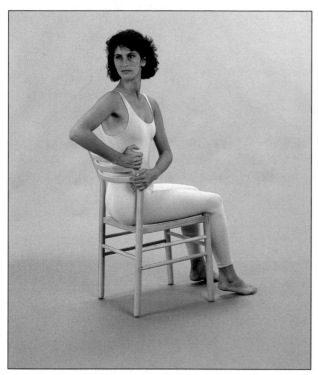

Sit upright in a straight-backed chair. Twist to the right and hold onto the chair frame. Pull back with your left arm and hold tight with your right to stretch your upper and middle back muscles.

Sit on a stool with your legs spread apart. Grasp your left calf with your left hand. Stretch your right hand toward the ceiling to elongate your chest and upper and middle back muscles.

Sit upright with the palm of your right hand behind your neck. Grasp your right elbow with your left hand and pull it toward the back of your head, stretching the right shoulder and triceps.

Sit on a stool and swing your right arm leftward across your chest. To enhance a stretch of the right triceps and shoulder, place your arm in the bend of your left elbow and pull up with your left arm.

Feet

The foot is an amazingly complex structure that not only provides the strength to support your entire body, but also imposes subtle yet significant changes in pitch and direction to control your posture and gait. A well-functioning foot routinely absorbs tremendous force. Walking, for instance, subjects the foot to a force of up to 120 percent of your body weight with each step. Running subjects the foot to even greater loads — up to about five and a half times your body weight.

For all that the foot must do, it requires remarkably little care. Shoes that provide support and shock absorption are all that your feet normally need. In addition, stretching your feet helps increase circulation and relax the musculature.

Sit comfortably in a chair with your foot off the floor and follow this sequence: First, extend your toes as far as you can, feeling the stretch from your ankle to your toes along the top of your foot *(right)*. Then turn your foot in *(far right)* to stretch the muscles along the outside of your foot. Pull your toes back toward your shin so that you feel tightness along the sole *(below left)*. Finally, turn out to lengthen the inside muscles *(below right)*.

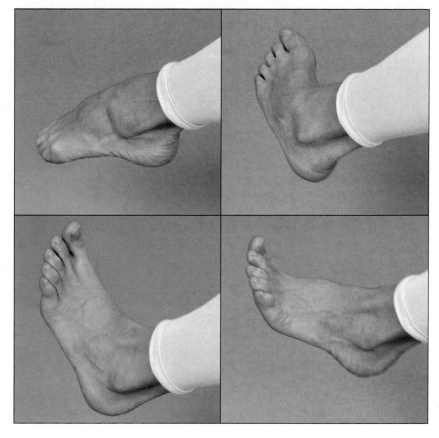

Kneel on the floor. Lift your right knee and draw it forward slightly *(opposite)*. Press the top of your right foot to the floor. This stretches the muscles of the metatarsal region, your ankle and shin.

Neck

Not counting the larynx, your neck contains more than 30 muscles that act to rotate your head and to flex forward, backward and side to side. In addition to giving you this mobility, your neck must also protect your spinal cord and support your head. In daily living, these functions can sometimes be at odds, resulting in neck strain and stiffness. Regular exercise that requires extensive neck movements, such as cycling or swimming, can also cause neck strain. You can help prevent this problem by performing the exercises on these two pages.

Note: If you hear or feel popping or rubbing in your neck while you are performing any of these movements, discontinue the exercise.

Drop your head backward to extend your neck. Do not force your neck back, but let your head drop naturally to lengthen the muscles along the front of your neck.

Grasp the back of your head with your right hand, and pull it forward and to the right to stretch the trapezius.

Place your right hand over your left ear, and pull your head to the right. This will stretch the mastoid muscle.

Interlace your fingers behind your head. Gently pull your head forward and down toward your chest to length-en muscles in the back of your neck.

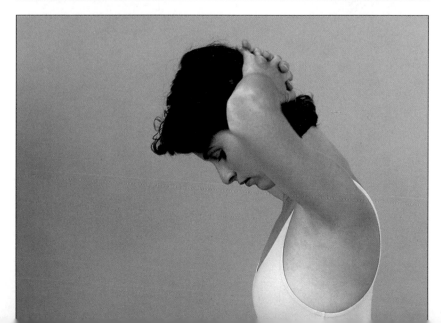

CHAPTER 9

Partner Stretching

*Not only fun,
but more effective*

Partner, or assisted, stretches involve two people: One person stretches and the other person helps to achieve the stretch. Assisted stretches can increase your range of motion farther than static, single-person stretches. The reason is simple: For most of the static stretches covered in Chapter 8, the muscle-stretching force is provided by body weight—applying the force of one limb on another or grasping an immovable object for leverage and then pulling. All these forces are limited by gravity or by your own strength.

More effort and leverage can be applied to your limbs by a partner, increasing the length and duration of a stretch. Of course, your partner needs to be cautious and not exert too much external force, which could lead to an injury. But with the proper technique, partner stretching not only permits a longer static stretch, but also

allows you to perform a type of stretch called contract-relax. To carry out a contract-relax stretch, you must first perform a static stretch. Your partner holds the stretched limb in place while you push as hard as you can against the stretch with an isometric contraction. Then you release the contraction while your partner pushes your limb to a new point of tightness. You will find that this stretch is greater than what you can normally achieve. Although the contract-relax technique can sound complicated in theory, it is actually quite simple in practice.

The contract-relax method of stretching has consistently proved more effective for increasing range of motion than traditional techniques. In one study, Swedish researchers asked two groups of subjects to stretch three times a week. One group used the ballistic method and the other the contract-relax technique. After 30 days, the

The Contract-Relax Method

To perform a contract-relax stretch, the basis for most of the routines in this chapter, your partner first guides you into a conventional static stretch. As you begin to feel the stretch, you reverse the motion and push against your partner as hard as you can. This is the contract phase, which is shown at top right for a stretch of the hamstring muscles. When you push against your partner, who provides immovable resistance, be sure to use only the muscles you are going to stretch. For example, in the hamstring stretch, you push with your thigh — which requires keeping your leg straight — not with your calf.

After five or six seconds, relax your muscles completely. Your partner then pushes the muscles back into a stretch that extends them farther than before. The two of you hold this position, shown at bottom right, for 20 to 30 seconds.

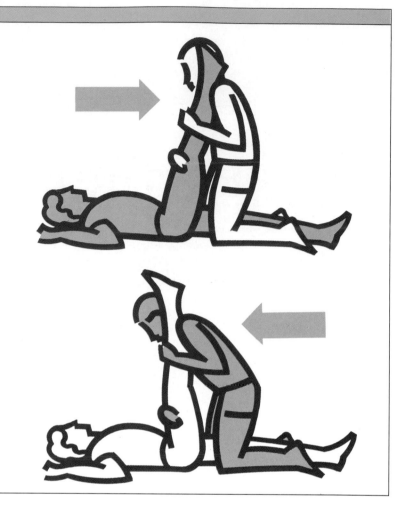

researchers found that the contract-relax group had improved its flexibility more than twice as much as the ballistic-method group. The improvement in joint range of motion by those using the ballistic method averaged between 1.4 and 3.5 degrees, while improvement among those using the contract-relax technique averaged between 6.0 and 10.5 degrees.

In an American study comparing the contract-relax method with both ballistic and static stretching, subjects were randomly assigned to one of four groups: ballistic, static, contract-relax or control (no stretching at all). After a six-week, three-times-a-week flexibility training program, the subjects were tested for flexibility of their shoulder, trunk and hamstring muscles. The results confirmed the Swedish tests, indicating that contract-relax techniques are superior to other stretching methods for improving flexibility.

Physiologists developed the contract-relax method as one of a group of therapies for paralyzed individuals. The doctors called this group of therapies proprioceptive neuromuscular facilitation, or PNF. Although a number of studies have documented the effectiveness of PNF techniques for increasing the range of motion, researchers do not agree on why this is so.

One theory concerns the Golgi tendon organs, which are nerve fibers that sense tension in muscle tendons. During the contraction phase of the PNF routine, the tension caused by the strong pull of the isometric muscle contraction induces the Golgi tendon organs to send signals to the central nervous system. These signals, called inhibitory impulses, are part of a protective reflex response to prevent muscle and tendon tears. The inhibitory impulses override any signals to contract the muscle further. Then, when the muscle is stretching during the relax phase, the inhibitory impulses dampen the stretch-reflex response of the muscle spindles. Although the neuromuscular process is complicated, the simple result is that you can stretch farther.

An added benefit of the contract-relax method is that it increases strength. According to one recent study, PNF stretching can be superior to weight training for improving athletic performance. Researchers randomly assigned 30 college women to one of three groups—a PNF group, a weight-training group and a control group. After training the women three times a week for eight weeks, the scientists found that the PNF group performed significantly better than either the weight-trained or the control group in both throwing and jumping abilities. Those women who trained with PNF exercises improved their throwing distance by 25 percent and their vertical jump ability by 16 percent,

while the weight-trained group had increases of only 13 and 10 percent, respectively. Many athletic coaches consider contract-relax routines an important component of their training programs.

Some contract-relax exercises can be performed without a partner. You can, for instance, stretch your inner thigh muscles by sitting cross-legged on the ground, pushing upward with your knees against the palms of your hands for the contract phase, then relaxing your inner thigh muscles and continuing to push down with your hands. But most PNF routines require another person to provide external force during the first stretching phase, followed by resistance to your isometric contraction, and then strength to push you into the new stretch.

The following pages offer a number of partner-assisted stretches, most of which involve the contract-relax method. Be sure to choose a partner who is sensitive to your needs and aware of your level of flexibility. He or she should stretch your muscles gently, until the stretch becomes slightly uncomfortable but not so far as to cause pain in muscles or joints.

Hamstrings and Calves

Your hamstrings, among the longest and strongest muscles in your body, are likely to become tight and inflexible if you do not stretch them regularly. This is also true of your calves, which form part of a biomechanical pulley system with the Achilles tendon, the heel and the plantar fascia along the bottom of the foot. The contract-relax method of stretching can be the most effective way to loosen the hamstrings and the calves. You can perform either the contract-relax stretch or a simple static stretch with your back on the ground, on a cushioned massage table or even on top of your kitchen table, putting a towel underneath you for comfort.

As in the previous chapter, any stretch that works muscles on one side of your body should be repeated for muscles on the other side.

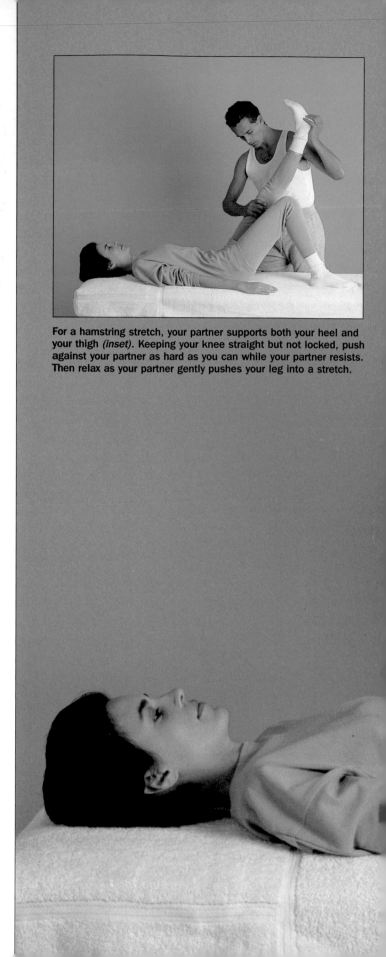

For a hamstring stretch, your partner supports both your heel and your thigh *(inset)*. Keeping your knee straight but not locked, push against your partner as hard as you can while your partner resists. Then relax as your partner gently pushes your leg into a stretch.

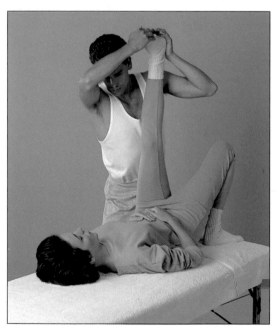

Lie down, knees flexed. Straighten one leg as your partner supports your heel and applies pressure to the ball of your foot, stretching your calf. Contract your calf muscles—point your toes—as your partner resists; then relax as your partner eases your leg into a new stretch.

Hamstrings and Lower Back

Since the hamstrings attach to the lower part of the pelvis, they frequently influence the lower back region. Tight hamstrings can tilt the pelvis and lead to an inflexible lower back. It makes sense, then, to stretch not only the hamstrings but also the lower back region. The partner-assisted stretches here will help ease tightness in your lower back as well as increase the flexibility of your hamstrings.

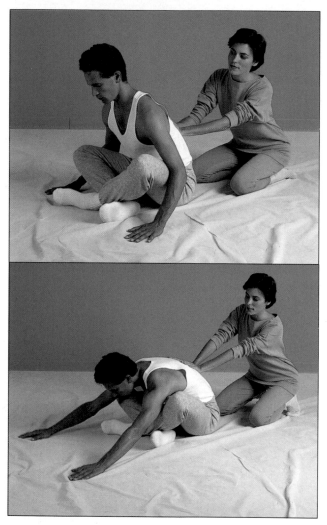

Sit cross-legged, hands at sides. Your partner kneels behind you and places her hands on your back *(top)*. Push against her as she resists. Then reach forward with her assistance to stretch your lower back and some buttocks muscles *(above)*.

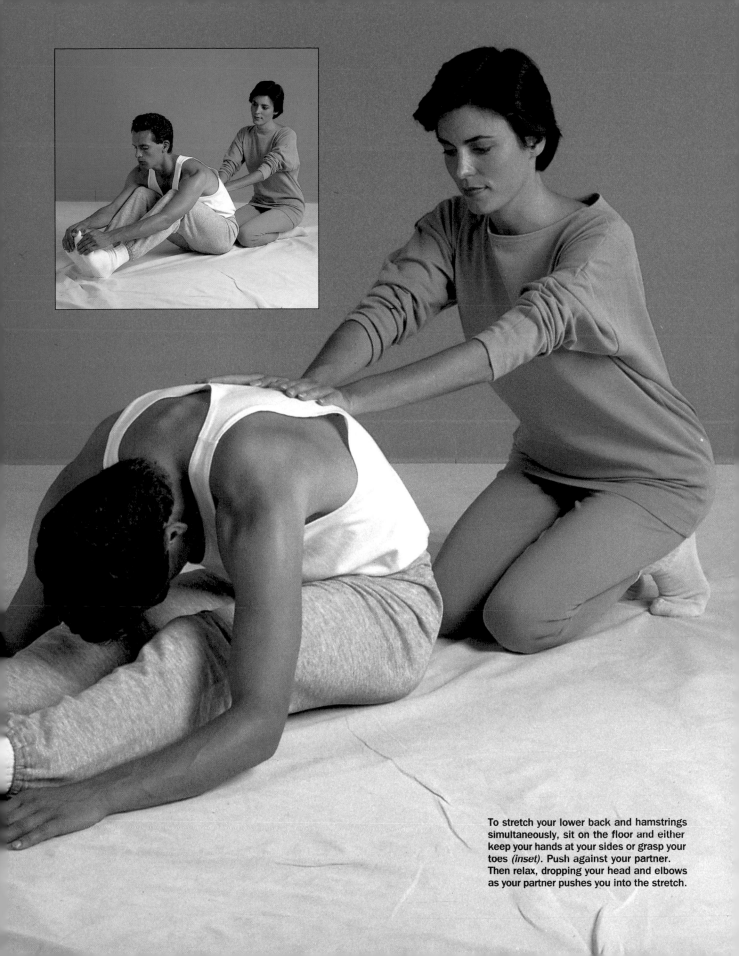

To stretch your lower back and hamstrings simultaneously, sit on the floor and either keep your hands at your sides or grasp your toes *(inset)*. Push against your partner. Then relax, dropping your head and elbows as your partner pushes you into the stretch.

Inner Thighs

Many people — especially men — have tight inner thigh muscles, which can be particularly troublesome for those who are active. Recreational runners, for instance, frequently report pulled groin muscles. The inner thigh muscles, like the hamstrings and those of the lower back, are attached to the pelvis.

Sit cross-legged with the bottoms of your feet together. Your partner places her hands atop your knees while you attempt to push your knees upward. As you relax, your partner presses your knees toward the floor for the stretch *(above)*.

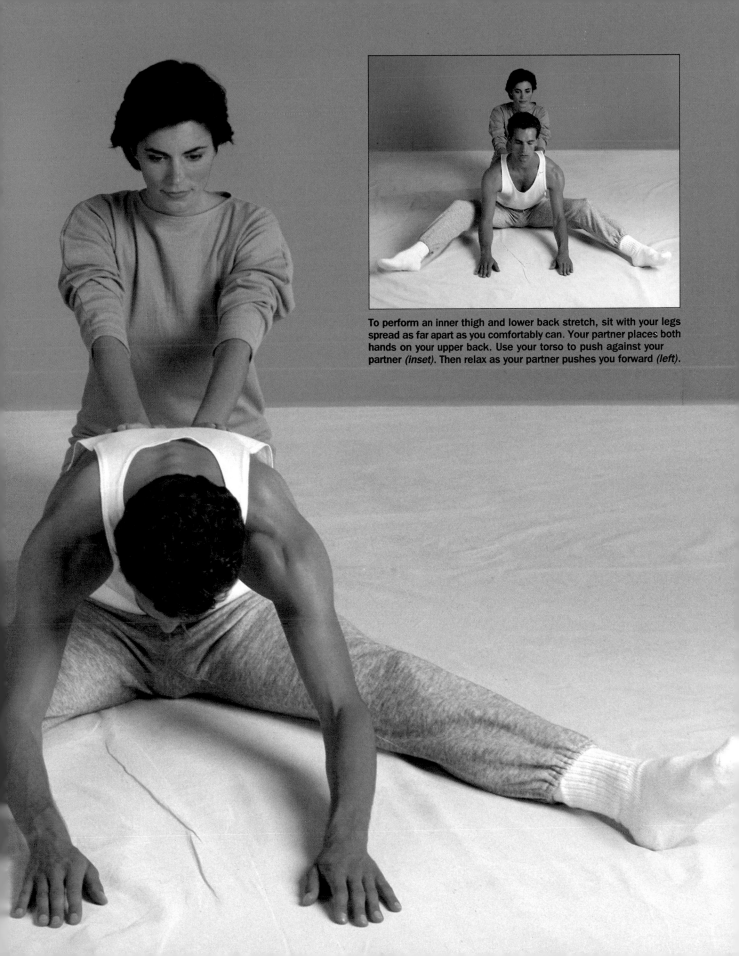

To perform an inner thigh and lower back stretch, sit with your legs spread as far apart as you comfortably can. Your partner places both hands on your upper back. Use your torso to push against your partner *(inset)*. Then relax as your partner pushes you forward *(left)*.

Quadriceps and Hip Flexors/1

The quadriceps and hip flexors are the primary muscles along the front of your thigh. They are extremely powerful and therefore lend themselves particularly well to partner-assisted routines, since your partner can use your leg as leverage.

If you run, cycle or climb stairs frequently, you should also stretch the iliotibial band, a strip of connective tissue that runs from one of the hip flexors on the outside of your hip all the way down to the outside of your knee. The iliotibial band can become tight from these activities and cause a burning sensation around the knee. The stretch on pages 246-247 is designed to loosen the iliotibial band.

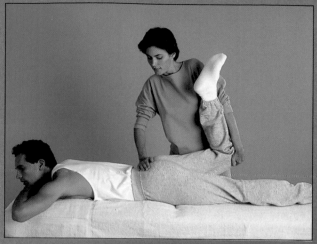

To isolate your hip flexors, lie face down on a table as your partner presses one hand against your right pelvis, grasps your right leg just above the knee and lifts it into a stretch.

To perform a quadriceps stretch, lie face down on the floor or a massage table. Your partner stabilizes your pelvis with one hand and bends your leg with the other. Attempt to straighten your knee by pushing against her hand, then relax as she bends your leg to a new point of tightness.

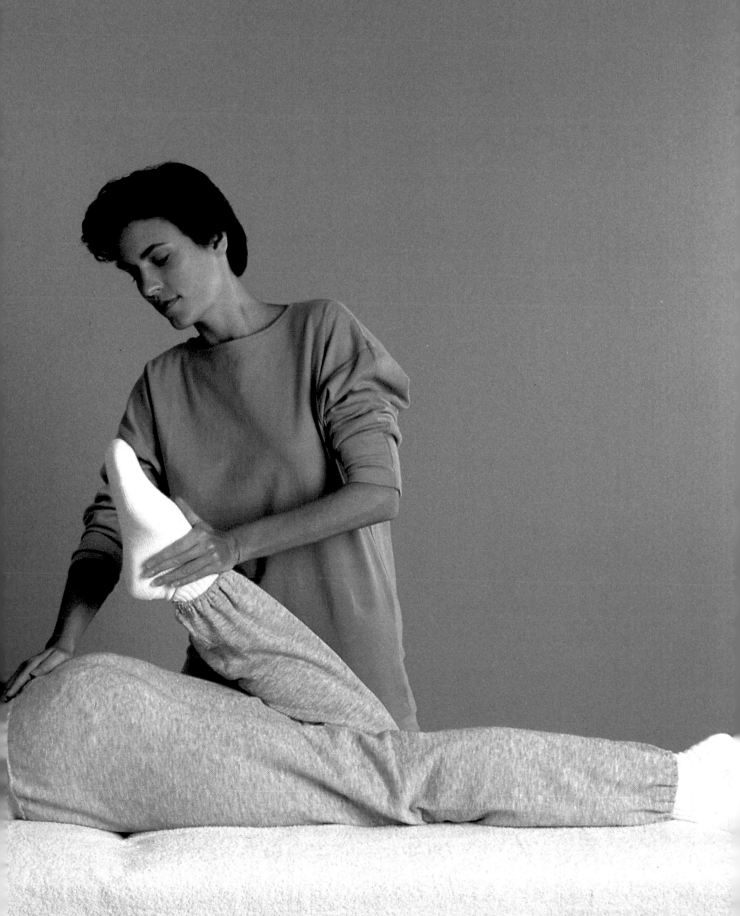

Quadriceps and Hip Flexors/2

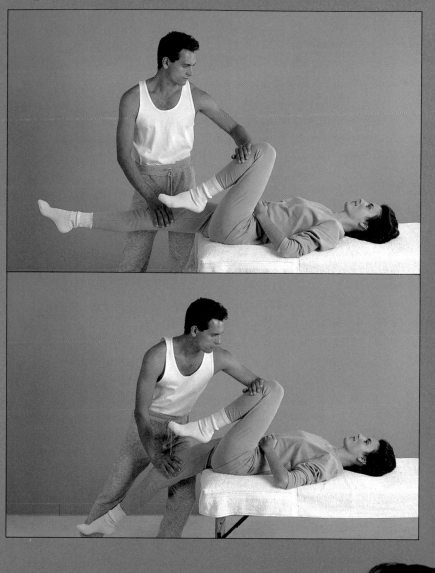

For an additional hip-flexor stretch, lie on your back with your buttocks near the end of a table. Stretch your right leg out and draw your left leg up *(top left)*. Your partner helps hold your left leg in place as you extend your right leg. Relax as your partner pushes your right leg down and your left knee toward your chest *(bottom left)*.

To loosen the iliotibial band, lie on your side at the end of a table. Bend the bottom leg to support your pelvis but keep your other leg straight. Your partner uses one hand to hold your pelvis and the other hand to press down lightly on your knee *(right)*.

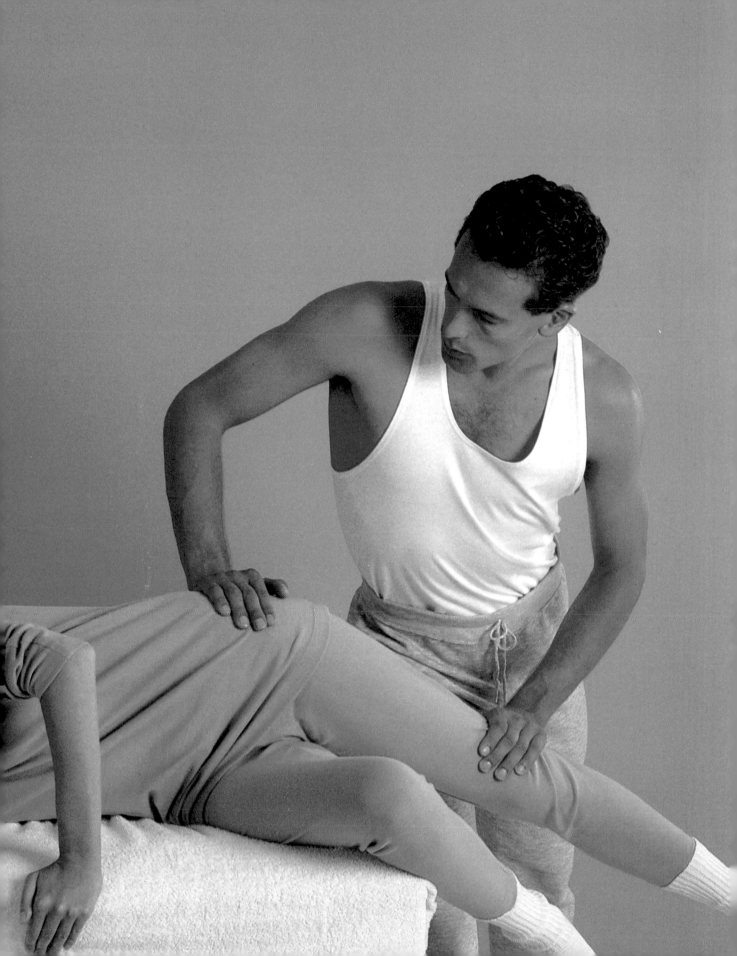

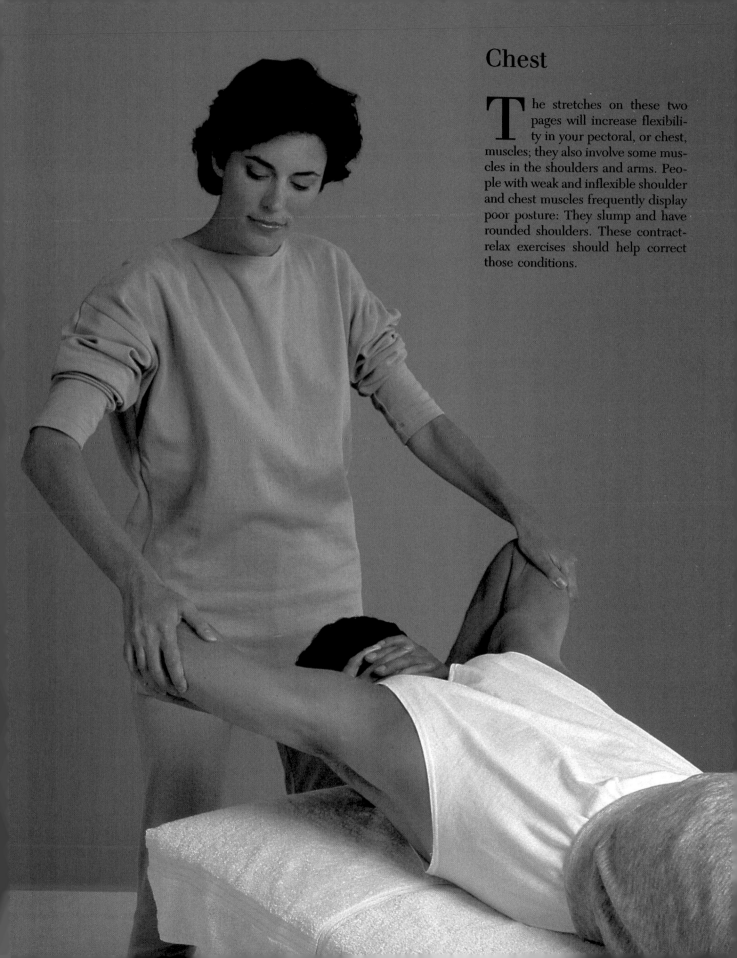

Chest

The stretches on these two pages will increase flexibility in your pectoral, or chest, muscles; they also involve some muscles in the shoulders and arms. People with weak and inflexible shoulder and chest muscles frequently display poor posture: They slump and have rounded shoulders. These contract-relax exercises should help correct those conditions.

Lie face down on a table. As your partner draws your arms up by the wrists, the force of your body weight stretches your chest muscles. Keep your elbows loose.

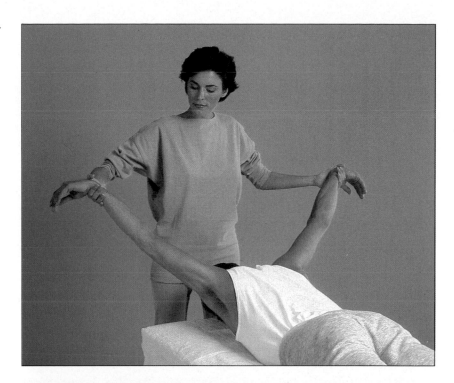

Sit cross-legged with your back supported by your partner's leg. Interlace your fingers behind your head. Your partner pulls your elbows back.

Lie face down on a table with your hands clasped behind your head *(opposite)*. Your partner grasps your elbows and draws them up. You will feel a stretch of the pectorals of the chest and the biceps and triceps of the upper arm.

Back

Your back contains dozens of muscles in five crisscrossing layers. The outer layer consists of the latissimus dorsi and the trapezius, both of which influence shoulder movement. Most of the inner layers of back muscles are anchored on your pelvis and are connected to your vertebrae and ribs. These muscles hold your spinal column erect and permit your spine to move in all directions; they allow you to rotate around and arch backward, forward and sideways. Despite their importance, these muscles are often too short and easily strained, causing backache. Partner-assisted back stretches help provide gentle traction and stretch these deep spinal muscles.

To stretch the muscles of the upper back and chest, kneel and extend your hands in front of you while pressing your chest downward. Your partner overlaps her hands and presses gently on your spine.

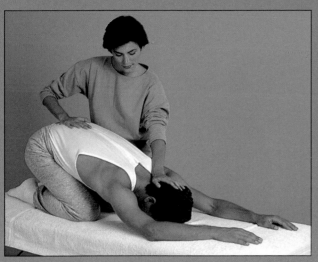

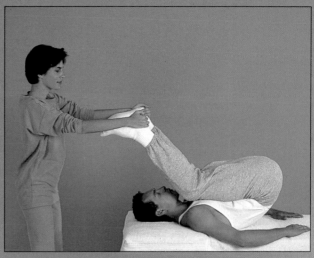

To stretch the entire spine, assume a kneeling position, lean over and sit back on your heels. Your partner places her hands on your head and lower back. Without moving her hands, she exerts pressure gently but firmly in opposite directions *(above)*.

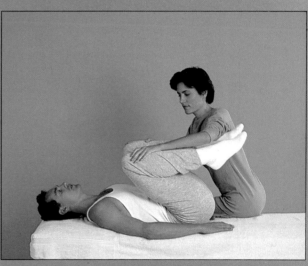

To stretch the lower back, buttocks and hamstrings, lie on your back and draw your legs up *(top)*. Your partner grasps your ankles and pulls them over your head. To stretch just the lower back and buttocks *(above)*, your partner pushes your knees to your chest. *(In the top position, keep your shoulders and upper back in contact with the table; be certain not to roll up on your neck.)*

CHAPTER 10

Stretching for Sports

*Better performance,
fewer injuries*

To most athletes, the benefits of stretching and good flexibility are obvious. A full range of motion in certain joints is necessary for the successful performance of many sports. Dance, figure skating and gymnastics, for example, require extensive muscular flexibility and a good range of motion in virtually all body joints. Contact sports like football, hockey, basketball and soccer also require a better-than-average range of motion in the joints, as well as flexibility in the muscles of the thigh, hip flexors, trunk, arms, shoulders and neck. For most noncontact sports like track and field, swimming, golf and baseball or softball, you need varying degrees of flexibility specific to the particular sport. For example, swimmers who perform the front crawl will especially benefit from improved flexibility in the rotator cuff muscles of the shoulders. Without it, they may

experience limitations in their stroking ability and possibly develop a stress injury called swimmer's shoulder.

Flexibility is also related to power. Experiments have shown that muscles can store elastic energy and then release that energy in a powerful burst. The more a muscle can stretch, the greater its potential for energy release during contraction. Thus, muscle elasticity plays an important role in sports that require forceful stretch and contraction, such as jumping and throwing.

Baseball pitchers, for instance, need to be especially flexible in the chest. Like the string of a bow, the major chest muscle is pulled taut as the arm swings back to pitch a ball; like an arrow, the farther the ball is drawn back, the more force can be applied to it and the greater its velocity when released. Runners, too, may be able to im-

Hand Stretches

Your hands are crucial tools for playing almost any sport. First, they translate muscle power from your body into the motion of a racquet, ball or club. They must also control that motion, giving a precise arc to a basketball, for instance, or the right angle and velocity to a tennis shot. In addition, your hands may have to support your body, such as during a long cycling trip.

   Use the four simple exercises at right to stretch your hands for power and flexibility. The top two are for your thumbs, the bottom two for your fingers. Before you perform them, shake your hands vigorously to increase circulation.

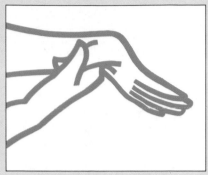

Firmly but gently stretch your thumb toward your wrist. Do not force it.

Stretch your thumb in the opposite direction by pulling back on it.

Stretch your palm by pulling back on all your fingers at the same time.

Spread your fingers and pull them back one at a time.

prove their performance by increasing their flexibility. According to a U.S. Olympic track coach, tight muscles present internal resistance to movement. Runners with loose, pliant leg muscles, therefore, may be able to move their legs faster and longer than those with tighter muscles. And by adding just an inch to your stride length through stretching, you can gain about seven yards per quarter mile. For such distance events as a 10,000-meter run or a 26.2-mile marathon, even a minuscule increase in stride length can make the difference between a top performance and simply finishing the race.

   Coaches and athletes alike generally accept the importance of stretching and flexibility for the enhancement of sports performance. Although few studies have been conducted in the area of flexibility and performance, there is some evidence that increased flexibility can improve performance in certain specific activities such as long jumping, ball hitting, throwing and sprinting. No studies have established minimum norms of flexibility necessary for each sports activity, however; nor has research determined how general sports performance may change in response to a progressive stretching program.

   While it is clear that some level of flexibility is essential for the successful performance of any sport, once you have reached that level, you may not be able to improve your performance further by continuing to increase flexibility. For example, slight variations in flexibility among a group of top gymnasts will not determine who will rank highest in competition. However, gymnasts and other athletes must stretch to achieve the level of flexibility required by their sport and continue stretching to maintain that flexibility.

Some studies suggest that stretching can also help prevent injuries. A study of Swedish soccer players showed that athletes with muscle tightness and restricted range of motion have a higher-than-average incidence of injuries. Muscle strains occurred in 31 percent of the players with muscle tightness, but in only 18 percent of the players with normal flexibility. Studies of soccer players in the United States show that those players with tight or inflexible hamstring muscles may develop lower back and knee injuries.

The reason for this is that muscles adapt to exercise in the range of motion habitually used in the exercise. And vigorous exercise places greater loads on inflexible muscles, leading to chronic stress injuries. A tight gastrocnemius muscle in the calf, for instance, may result in pronation, or inward rotation of the foot, which is the most common cause of stress injuries to the foot and can lead to ankle and leg injuries and even a stress fracture.

If you do get an injury, stretching may help you recover more easily: It has been shown to reduce muscle soreness, and many athletes believe that it also speeds recovery. In addition, muscle injury often results in the formation of scar tissue, which is inelastic and acts to reduce a muscle's pliability. Thus, stretching can help restore flexibility to an injured muscle. However, the use of stretching to rehabilitate injured muscles should only be carried out under the direction of a certified specialist who is knowledgeable in sports medicine, such as an orthopedist, a registered physical therapist, or an athletic trainer.

Since flexibility is joint-specific—that is, you become more flexible only in the muscles and joints you stretch—and each activity places its own pattern of stress on joints and other body parts, your stretching routine must vary according to which sports you engage in. The following 14 pages offer stretching routines for seven of the most often played recreational sports. (Stretches for running are covered in Chapter 3.) These routines will not necessarily make you a better player (though they might), but they can help you from getting injured and enhance your enjoyment of the game. In performing the stretches, be sure to repeat them on both sides of your body.

Baseball

Almost everyone, whatever his level of conditioning, can enjoy a good game of baseball. Nevertheless, it helps if you have agility and coordination and can muster explosive bursts of strength and speed for pitching, batting and running. To prepare for such bursts and to protect yourself from possible injury, you should stretch out frequently, particularly if you play baseball often.

Perform the lunge at right to stretch the hip flexors of the straight leg and the buttocks muscles of the bent leg. Feel the stretch in the shoulders, the upper back and the latissimus dorsi. Assume a sitting position with arms extended *(inset)* to stretch your inner thighs and lower back.

Grasp your elbows over your head and pull to one side to stretch your latissimus dorsi, chest, obliques and side muscles.

Extend one arm and grasp it above the elbow. Pull it toward your chest to stretch your shoulder and middle back muscles.

Sit on the floor and bend your left leg so that your left sole is against your right inner thigh. Bend forward from the hips, using a basketball for support. This stretches the inner thighs and lower back.

To stretch your calf muscles, keep your toes straight and your heels on the ground as you lean forward.

Basketball

Basketball is a sport that requires not only coordination and agility, but a great deal of stamina, jumping ability and speed. Basketball is a fast, stop-and-start sport that involves twisting and turning and sudden dashes and leaps on a hard court surface. In addition, basketball unavoidably involves occasional collisions.

Basketball players need strength and flexibility, particularly in their hips, thighs, calves and trunk. These two pages present six basic stretches that will help loosen you up to play basketball. These stretches focus particular attention on the hip region, which is where most of the stress of basketball's demanding twists and turns occurs.

While sitting, draw one knee up. Extend your arms and lean forward from the hips to stretch the hamstrings of the straight leg.

Remain seated and cross your legs, pulling your right knee toward your chest. You will feel the stretch in your right buttocks.

Lie on your right side and extend your right arm. Pull your left foot toward your buttocks but keep your knee in line with your hip to stretch your quadriceps.

Lie on your back with your arms outstretched. Twist your legs to the right. Cross your right leg over your left to stretch the outer hip, thigh and lower back.

Bicycling

Bicycling is an endurance activity that requires as much effort and stamina as long-distance running. As in running, the large muscles of the thighs and calves provide most of the driving force needed to propel you forward. Cycling requires particular flexibility and strength in the hip flexors to draw the pedals up and, similarly, in the quadriceps and calves to push the pedals down. For this reason, good cyclists have unusually powerful and pliant leg muscles.

Because cycling places a demand on the musculature of the trunk as well as the legs, endurance riding all too often leads to muscle strain and pain in the lower back. These discomforts occur in novices and seasoned cyclists alike. In addition, cyclists often suffer from neck stiffness and sore wrists. For neck soreness, try the stretches on pages 232-233; otherwise, the five stretches on these two pages should be all you need to help you maintain flexibility for bicycling.

Lie on your back and extend your legs into the air, keeping your knees straight. Support your legs with your hands and separate them to stretch the inner thighs.

Lie on your right side with both arms extended as shown. Draw your left leg back until you feel a stretch in the hip flexors, outer thighs and latissimus dorsi.

Find an object just below waist level for support. Clasp your hands behind your head and place one foot on the object *(opposite)*. Keep your back straight and your heel on the ground to stretch the hip flexors, calf, Achilles tendon, chest and buttocks. Perform the stretch at right *(inset)* for the wrist flexors, shins and ankles. With your wrists reversed, lean forward as shown: Bending your right knee will stretch the ankle and shin in your left leg extending behind.

Lie on your back and draw your right knee toward your chest. Use your arms to pull the back of your knee. You should feel a stretch in the hip extensors and lower back.

139-153

Golf

Golf is a popular weekend sport; yet most people neglect the fitness aspects of the game. Golf requires a good deal more strength and endurance than most golfers realize, especially for those who carry their own golf clubs. Many weekend golfers also fail to appreciate the importance of fitness for improving their game and preventing injuries. A good golf swing involves a powerful twist of the arms, spine and shoulders in order to bring the head of the club around with sufficient force. In addition, the momentum of the club carries the golfer's arms into a wide arc, which may cause strains and even tears in the muscles of the shoulders, back, sides and wrists.

To minimize the chance of injury, and to give yourself the greatest range of motion in the joints of the shoulders and upper body, perform these four stretches.

Place your palms against a wall with your fingers pointing down. Move one leg forward while keeping the other leg straight. Lean into the wall. This not only stretches your calf, Achilles tendon and wrist flexors, but should also help you avoid golfer's elbow, an inflammation of the connective tissue in the elbow.

Turn sideways to a wall and support yourself with your left arm. Swing your right leg behind your left and lean on the outside of the foot, twisting your body to produce a stretch in your left chest. This will also stretch the outer muscles of the right leg.

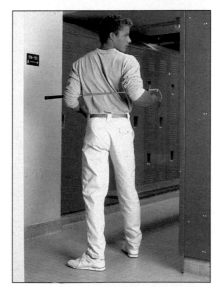

To improve flexibility in your spine, place your golf club behind your back and under the inside of your elbows. Then turn your head to the right and twist your body to the right from the waist up. Twist slowly and smoothly—do not bounce.

Extend one leg to the side and rest it on a bench or stool *(opposite)*. Grasping a golf club at each end and holding it above your head, bend sideways toward the extended foot. You will be stretching the latissimus dorsi, the obliques and the inner thigh of the elevated leg.

Racquet Sports

Racquet sports, which include badminton, squash, racquetball and tennis, are excellent all-around conditioners. However, these sports are performed most frequently by recreational players who pay little attention to the fitness aspects of the activities. Most players launch right into their games with little or no warm-up, play intensely for a short period of time and then stop playing abruptly, only to resume days or weeks later. The consequence is almost inevitably injury. Few realize how physically demanding these sports can be, nor how much their game could improve if they simply took a little time to get into better condition. One of the best ways to improve your condition and to avoid unnecessary injuries is to improve your flexibility.

Racquet sports require speed and agility, particularly for quick lateral movements. Thus, players with tight muscles may experience frequent groin muscle pulls. And since returning a ball in play often calls for sudden lunges and stretches, pulls in the back, sides, wrist, ankles and shoulders are also common. These two pages offer five stretches to help you improve your racquet game.

Sit on the floor with your knees straight but not locked and your feet as wide apart as comfortably possible. Hold your racquet on the floor in front of you for support; lean forward from the waist. You should feel a stretch of your inner thighs, lower back and upper back.

To stretch your chest muscles, stand at arm's length from a wall and place one palm on the wall as shown. Turn your body slightly away from the wall but keep your hand in place.

Grasp both ends of your racquet and hold it over your head. Spread your feet apart and arc your body to the left, bending your right knee slightly but keeping your left leg straight.

To stretch your shoulder muscles, your chest and spinal rotators, hold the racquet behind you and twist from the waist up.

Support yourself against a wall with the back of your hands, which will promote flexibility in the wrists. Keeping one leg straight will stretch the calf muscles as well.

To stretch your chest, hip flexors and
calves, face a wall with your arms extended
over your head. Bend one knee and press
your chest to the wall.

Swimming

Swimming is one of the most popular sports in the United States. Although you do not have to be particularly skillful or fit to enjoy swimming, this activity can place a tremendous demand on virtually all of your body's major muscle groups. Swimmers need strong arms, shoulders, chests and abdomens, since the muscles grouped in those areas provide most of your stroking power. Because swimming is a dynamic sport that requires full range of motion, particularly in the shoulders, you must stretch out frequently to avoid tight muscles. Perform the six stretches on these two pages at least once a day.

Lie on your stomach and extend your arms, keeping your hips on the floor. You will feel the stretch in your abdominals and hip flexors.

Stand with your arms above your head and grasp your left elbow with your right hand. Pull your arm to the right *(top left)* to stretch the latissimus dorsi and obliques. For your shoulders and biceps *(top right)*, grasp a towel behind your back and pull it up with both arms. You can then use the towel to stretch the shoulder's rotator cuff muscles *(near right)*. Hold it behind your back and pull down with one arm while the other arm is just behind your head *(far right)*. Then pull up with one hand over your head while the other is bent behind your back.

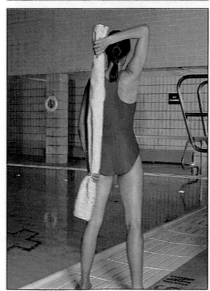

Volleyball

Volleyball is a game conducted at a fast pace. It requires frequent bursts of speed and the ability to jump high and hit hard. Volleyball players need flexible shoulders and calves for spiking — smashing a ball downward from the top of a jump. Supple hip flexors and inner thighs are also important so as not to pull a muscle when you drop down under the ball for a save.

Spread your feet apart, bend one knee and drop toward the floor. Grasp a railing behind you with both hands and pull forward to stretch your chest, shoulders and inner thighs.

Lie face up, keeping your back flat by raising your left knee. Pull back on your right ankle for a quadriceps stretch.

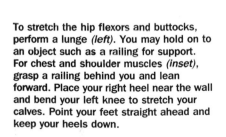

To stretch the hip flexors and buttocks, perform a lunge *(left)*. You may hold on to an object such as a railing for support. For chest and shoulder muscles *(inset)*, grasp a railing behind you and lean forward. Place your right heel near the wall and bend your left knee to stretch your calves. Point your feet straight ahead and keep your heels down.

Sit on an exercise bench with one leg extended flat along the bench to stretch the hamstrings. Be sure to keep your back straight.

PART 3

GETTING STRONGER

Strength Training for Everyone

The Lower Body

The Middle Body

The Upper Body

Exercising with Machines

CHAPTER 11

Strength Training for Everyone

*Toward firmer muscles
and greater strength—with the added
dividend of a better physique*

—

Until fairly recently, many people associated "exercise" with aerobic exercise—activities such as running and cycling that enhance cardiorespiratory fitness. Strengthening muscles was something that concerned only bodybuilders and was done out of vanity. But recently more and more fitness experts recommend strength training for fitness and health reasons—and for women as well as for men, the elderly as well as young people. The influential American College of Sports Medicine has altered its exercise guidelines to include a recommendation for a "well-rounded" program that includes strength training along with aerobic exercise training.

What are the benefits of getting stronger?
Many of the declines associated with aging are the consequence of inactivity. Many people start losing muscle tissue (and gaining body fat) in their thirties, particularly if they are inactive. Good muscle strength can have obvious benefits in your daily activities—when lifting grocery bags, gardening or shoveling snow, for example—and can give you increased stamina and self-confidence.

For people who are already active, an equally important benefit is injury prevention. Many musculoskeletal injuries, especially those related to routine exercise (such as runner's knee or shin splints), are due in part to muscle weakness and imbalances as well as joint instability, which strength training may correct. Exercise is especially crucial for maintaining a strong back and protecting it from injury. Lower back pain often results from weakness of back muscles and abdominal muscles. Poor posture and a lack of hip flexibility can also contribute to back problems, and strength training may help improve both these attributes.

In addition, like any exercise that puts stress on your bones, strength training may increase bone density and thus help delay or minimize the development of osteoporosis, the loss of bone mass that makes many older people (especially women) vulnerable to fractures.

Isn't aerobic fitness more important than strength?

Being aerobically fit—through activities like jogging, brisk walking, swimming, and cycling—is of first importance as far as fitness and good health is concerned. But it may not be enough. Studies have found that over time, people who only jog, for instance, typically lose muscle mass, especially in the upper body. An appropriate strength training program may counter this. And when it comes to athletic performance, strength is often as or more important than aerobic fitness—for example, strong muscles can help power your golf swing or tennis serve.

Muscles can only pull; they cannot push. Therefore, muscles typically act in pairs to move your body: Your arm moves upward when the biceps contracts and thickens, thereby flexing the elbow while the triceps relaxes. When the elbow is extended against a resistance, the triceps contracts; because of this arrangement, you must always work two opposing muscles in order to properly tone and strengthen any part of your body.

What happens to muscles when you start strength training?

When a muscle contracts against a resistance (usually a weight) with sufficient force, the muscle fibers adapt by increasing the synthesis of protein—and thus increasing in size and strength. With enough training, and with adequate rest between training sessions, the individual fibers that make up a muscle actually grow larger by means of a complex process that promotes the synthesis of new myofibrils—the structures within a muscle fiber that contract. This synthesis contributes to the enlargement of the muscle fibers and of the muscles themselves. You can also train in a way that helps improve muscle endurance—the ability to contract a muscle repeatedly. This produces little, if any, increase in muscle size, but can help you perform repetitive activities, as explained in the box on page 275.

Is strength training simply another term for bodybuilding?

Strength training doesn't necessarily mean lifting massive weights in order to build bulging muscles. Such "power lifting" has little to do with fitness and health—and, in fact, may be injurious. Building strength, as generally recommended, calls for working out against *moderate* resistance, whether you want to increase strength or muscle endurance. The resistance can be provided by free weights (dumbbells or barbells) or resistance machines—but also by thick elastic bands or even cans of tomatoes. You can also use your own body weight as resistance, as in calisthenics such as push-ups or pull-ups.

Still, aren't some men and women likely to gain muscle bulk as they get stronger?

Some men—and probably many more women—have neglected strength training because they thought it would make them look and feel muscle-bound. They needn't worry. For one thing, successful bodybuilders and competitive weight lifters very likely have genetic endowments that aid their prodigious development. Moreover, "bulking up" requires heavier weights and much more time—perhaps several hours a day of lifting weights in strenuous routines that leave muscles completely fatigued. And, regrettably, some bodybuilders have used illegal or unethical (and unhealthy) substances to promote dramatic gains in muscle mass.

However, women in particular, even female bodybuilders, don't develop the bulging muscles attainable by men for one simple reason: They

There are two basic components of muscular fitness—muscle endurance and strength. Most workouts build both to some degree, though you can emphasize one or the other, as follows:

Light resistance, many repetitions. Lifting light-to-moderate weights (50 to 75% of the maximum amount you can lift) for many repetitions primarily builds *muscle endurance*—that is, the ability to contract a muscle repeatedly in quick succession, as in lifting a suitcase 20 times in a minute or two. To a lesser extent, this also builds muscle strength and may increase muscle size. This type of training can actually enhance oxygen utilization by muscle cells and make muscles work more efficiently. It can thus help improve performance in endurance activities such as brisk walking or cycling.

Heavy resistance, few repetitions. Lifting a heavy weight (more than 75% of your maximal lift) only a few repetitions, in contrast, primarily increases *muscle strength* (and size). Strength is the force a muscle produces in one all-out effort—as when you swing a mallet to ring a carnival bell. This type of training can be useful—for instance, when preparing for an activity that requires explosive strength, such as a jump. However, anyone with high blood pressure or heart disease should avoid exercising with heavy resistance without the prior approval of their physician.

produce only a small fraction of the hormone testosterone that males do, and researchers believe that this hormone (among others) may promote the building of muscle mass. A moderate training program won't create obvious muscle bulk in men or women, but instead a firmer, trimmer physique.

It's a fallacy that you can lose fat at a specific site by exercising the muscles in that area. Strengthening certain parts of the body, like the abdomen, can ultimately improve your appearance, as the increased muscle tone makes the area look firmer. But even though the muscles may firm up, the fat will remain until you shift your overall energy balance so you use up more calories than you take in. The best type of exercise to accomplish that is an aerobic activity such as walking, jogging or cycling, which engages large muscles repeatedly for many minutes.

Isn't an activity like swimming, which works the whole body, better for getting stronger?
Swimming is a superb exercise, but you cannot use it to target specific muscles for development, as you can with the exercises in the follow-

ing four chapters. And you can do these strengthening exercises conveniently at home, away from the pool or beach, as a supplement to swimming or other activities.

What type of strength training is most effective?
The key to increasing strength is to start out by lifting a manageable amount of weight and, as you get stronger, progressively increasing the working load, or resistance, on muscles—a process known as progressive resistance training. A basic workout should consist of both calisthenic-type exercises, in which you lift the weight of your own body, and routines performed with adjustable amounts of resistance.

You can adjust the resistance with weights such as dumbbells and barbells, or with machines that use hydraulics or motors to move weights or to create "drag." In all cases, the chief advantage is that these devices allow you to precisely regulate the resistance you are working with, and to increase it by small increments as you progress. Calisthenic-type exercises don't allow for such precise control. However, you can still adjust the load of standard exercises like sit-ups by changing the angle of your body position or by shifting your center of gravity. You can also increase the demand of the exercise by performing it more rapidly. In addition, calisthenics may reach muscles that are difficult to exercise with weights—such as the abdominals—and they also engage muscles that help stabilize the body during the exercise. Weight training, by contrast, tends to pinpoint individual muscle groups, and there is less work by assisting muscles. You can also perform calisthenics virtually anywhere, and without equipment.

As to how weight machines compare with free weights, both types have advantages and disadvantages, as explained in the box below.

Can strength training help you lose weight?

It's a misconception that training causes fat to turn to muscle, and that when you stop training for a while the muscle turns back to fat. Muscle and fat cells are completely different, structurally and functionally. However, weight training can help you lose body fat by using up calories: A nonstop, intense half-hour workout uses about 200 calories. But you can expend calories more effectively with sustained aerobic activities like walking, jogging, cycling, or cross-country skiing. As you gain muscle through weight training, you may well lose body fat if you maintain your normal calorie intake, and this will make you look trimmer, whether or not you lose weight.

If you stop exercising, will your muscles turn into fat?

Fat and muscle are separate tissues, and nothing will directly change muscle to fat or fat to muscle. If you stop exercising and maintain the same caloric intake, your muscles will weaken and di-

FREE WEIGHTS VS. MACHINES

Are weight machines, such as those by Nautilus or Cybex, the best way to build strength? Or are free weights—barbells or dumbbells—more effective? Both types of weight training have advantages and disadvantages. Virtually any health club or Y has both types of equipment these days, as do sporting goods stores. For home use, most beginners purchase a basic set of free weights, since machines are so costly. But at a health club, you can start with weight machines, and eventually supplement them with free-weight exercises.

FREE WEIGHTS

Advantages
- Relatively inexpensive (as little as $100 for a basic set).
- Versatile—you can work out virtually any muscle from any angle.
- One exercise can work several muscle groups—for instance, lifting a weight over your head works muscles in your arms, shoulders and upper back.
- Can help improve balance and coordination.

Disadvantages
- Possible injury—weights can slip or be dropped.
- Adjusting weights can take time.
- Safely lifting heavy weights requires a training partner, or "spotter."

MACHINES

Advantages
- Safe—resistance comes from weights held in place in stacks or from springs or hydraulic devices.
- Easy to use—machines guide your movements, and you can easily adjust the resistance.
- Single muscle groups—for instance, biceps or quadriceps—are isolated more efficiently.
- Newer machines tax muscles consistently through their full range of motion.

Disadvantages
- Expensive and bulky; using them usually requires joining a health club.
- A good workout requires a variety of machines.
- Some machines won't fit all body sizes.

minish in size, and the excess caloric intake will be stored as fat.

Muscle is denser than fat (a pound of muscle takes up about 20 percent less room than a pound of fat), so if you lose fat tissue but add muscle, your weight may climb. But you will probably look like you have lost weight, since muscles are firmer and more pleasing to the eye than fat, and, even though your weight may go up, your waistline may actually shrink.

Can strength-training exercises offer aerobic endurance when you perform them quickly?
The common meaning of aerobic endurance is the ability of the heart, lungs and blood vessels—your cardiorespiratory system—to deliver ever-greater amounts of oxygen to working muscles during activities like running, brisk walking, swimming or cycling. Building endurance requires performing such activities at a sufficiently vigorous pace for at least 20 minutes per session. Fast-paced muscle-toning routines—such as when you move quickly through a circuit of exercise machines—may raise your heartbeat substantially, but the training demands only short bursts of power by specific muscles, rather than continuously working large muscles.

Hence, this type of training doesn't lend itself to increased cardiorespiratory function that is sustained above a high enough threshold to produce an aerobic training effect. Studies of weight lifters indicate that their levels of aerobic endurance are about the same as those of the general population.

If you have back trouble, should you perform these exercises?
Anyone with back trouble should see a physician before doing exercises. If you do not have back problems, you should do some exercises to help you avoid these problems later in life. One of the most important things you can do is to strengthen your abdominal muscles. When these muscles are strong, they help bring your pelvis into proper alignment, which is a key to supporting the back. In general, the stronger you are, the less prone you are to injury. Of course, if any exercise causes back pain, stop doing it immediately and consult a health or fitness professional.

Do you really need to be shown how to do push-ups or other standard calisthenics?
Yes. For one thing, an exercise like the conventional straight-legged sit-up is now known to be dangerous. Keeping your legs flat on the floor arches the lower back, which overextends it and places it under undue stress. Then, too, sitting up fully during a sit-up—instead of just lifting your head and shoulders up off the floor—brings your hip-flexor muscles into play, arching the lower back again and placing it under undue stress as well. Finally, putting your hands behind your head and jerking up to get yourself started on a sit-up places a potentially damaging stress on your neck.

A number of other "traditional" exercises also carry risks (see page 283). Push-ups do not pose such hazards, but the proper techniques and several variations are crucial to getting the most from your workout.

Can anyone start a strength-training program?
Intense muscle exertion can cause a temporary rise in blood pressure, which can be dangerous to individuals at risk for heart disease. Therefore, if you are at high risk for heart disease or you have existing cardiovascular disease, you should proceed cautiously with this type of exercise, or proceed only with your physician's approval. Those with known joint or bone problems should also seek professional advice. Otherwise, there are no restrictions on strength training for adults, and you can begin a program no matter what your present level of fitness.

Of course, anyone who hasn't been in a training program should be certain to start at an easy level and build slowly in the intensity, frequency and duration of training sessions.

Sizing Yourself Up

The exercises on the opposite page evaluate the strength of muscles in the lower, middle and upper portions of your body. Based on the amount of time you can sustain each exercise, you will be able to rate your strength from High to Low. You can then use this knowledge to help you decide which exercise variations to choose in the following chapters.

Jot down the number of repetitions you are able to perform in the three self-assessment tests and retest yourself every month or so to measure your improvement. This can be a powerful tool for self-motivation—and it can be very satisfying to see your muscle strength progress.

It also helps to take a look at yourself in a mirror. Does your abdomen jut out? Does your lower back sway inward? Are your shoulders rounded? Any "yes" answers indicate bad posture that may be due to a lack of good muscle tone, which contributes to the slump responsible for many back, neck and shoulder problems. Exercises for your abdominals, back and upper body can help provide your skeleton with the support it needs.

Remember, though, that you cannot use these exercises to "spot reduce"—for example, to get rid of fat around your waist or thighs. The only way to do this effectively is to lower your intake of calories and to expend more calories with sustained aerobic exercise, which will gradually reduce body fat.

The best approach to conditioning your muscles is progressive: If your muscles are weak, they must be strengthened gradually. While the basic exercises in this section are suitable for anyone who is healthy, the advanced routines are designed for those who are quite fit. Do not attempt more rigorous exercises for any body part before you have built up adequate strength.

Before you take this test or perform any of the conditioning routines in the chapters that follow, you should do a general warm-up for at least 5 to 10 minutes. Simply run in place or do any aerobic exercise that gradually increases your heart rate and metabolism. This will allow muscles to work more smoothly, thereby helping to prevent muscle soreness and also reduce the chance of injury.

Test Your Strength

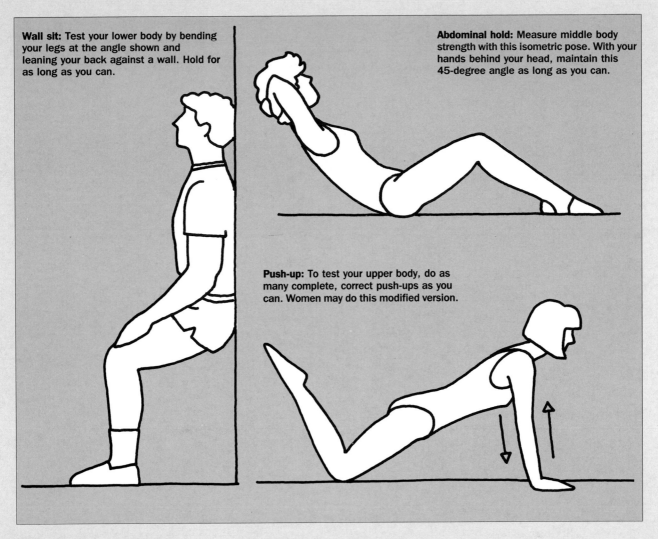

Wall sit: Test your lower body by bending your legs at the angle shown and leaning your back against a wall. Hold for as long as you can.

Abdominal hold: Measure middle body strength with this isometric pose. With your hands behind your head, maintain this 45-degree angle as long as you can.

Push-up: To test your upper body, do as many complete, correct push-ups as you can. Women may do this modified version.

Muscle strength and endurance can be measured with the simple tests above. The tests measure muscle performance in your lower, middle and up-per body. When you perform the abdominal hold, avoid undue stress on your neck.

Use the ratings below to gauge your own strength. These ratings are for men in their 20s. Values will de-crease by about 15 percent for every decade of life thereafter. Values for women will, on average, be about 20 to 25 percent less than for men.

Wall sit
High — 90 seconds
Average — 60 seconds
Below Average — 30 seconds
Low — less than 30 seconds

Abdominal hold
High — 25 seconds
Average — 15 seconds
Below Average — 5 seconds
Low — less than 5 seconds

Push-ups
High — 25
Average — 15
Below Average — 5
Low — fewer than 5

Training Terms

Overload. The only way to tone or strengthen a muscle is to place a greater-than-normal demand on it—that is, to overload it. As your muscles grow stronger you must progressively increase the overload to continue improving. You can accomplish this by increasing how often, how long or how intensely you exercise.

Reps and sets. These are the building blocks of a workout. Reps are repetitions of an exercise: To do a push-up for eight reps means performing it eight times in a row before pausing or resting. A set is one string of reps followed by a rest interval. Performing eight push-ups, resting a minute, then doing eight more equals two sets.

Range of motion. A muscle's range of motion is the angle it covers when you extend or contract it. A good exercise allows you to move the muscle through its full range of motion, since partial movement can cause uneven development of the muscle or restrict the flexibility of your joints.

Muscle balance. To work only some muscle groups and ignore others invites injury and a lack of proportion in the area of the muscle. The key is to work muscles on opposite sides of a joint. Examples of opposing muscles are biceps and triceps in the upper arm; quadriceps and hamstrings in the thigh; and pectorals and latissimus dorsi in the torso.

The Basic Regimen

HOW OFTEN

Studies show that you should exercise a muscle three to four times each week to achieve solid gains in strength and muscle tone. Exercising more than that may speed up your progress some what. However, you should be careful not to wear yourself out. Experienced body builders who work out five or six days a week exercise different muscle groups on successive days, typically alternating between lower body and upper body.

HOW LONG

The length of a training session will vary, depending upon what you want to accomplish. A starting workout of 8 or 10 basic exercises can take 20 to 30 minutes. A more advanced program will include additional exercises for one or more body parts (though you can skip working those muscles that are already firm from other forms of exercise).

If your workouts exceed 45 minutes, consider splitting them up and exercising more frequently. For example, you might train five times a week: three sessions devoted to upper body work, alternating with two sessions of exercises for the trunk and legs. This will prevent you from becoming exhausted and will add variety to your regimen. You can also vary the pace of training sessions, pushing hard and fast on some days, slower and easier on others.

HOW HARD

Do 3 sets of 10 repetitions each: That is the way to increase strength and tone in a muscle.

Take it easy at first. If you have not exercised for some time, start with a few reps of the easiest versions of each exercise. Gradually work up to 10 reps without straining.

Once you can do 10, rest a minute, then start a second set. After a few weeks, you should be able to do 10 reps on the second set and you can then start doing the third set.

This last set should thoroughly tire your muscles. As your strength improves so that doing three sets no longer brings you to the point of fatigue, you can continue to overload the muscles in several ways:

1. Make the exercise harder. Many of the basic exercises in this section include variations that increase the load of your body weight on working muscles. With exercises involving weights, you can increase the amount of weight.

2. Decrease the rest interval between sets. With less time to rest, muscles must work harder to lift the same amount of weight.

3. Increase the number of repetitions in the last set. This will continue to improve your muscle tone. And as you exceed 10 repetitions, an increase in absolute strength or muscle size gives way to gains in muscle endurance, which enables your muscles to make a sustained effort.

Ten Guidelines for Strength Training

1. WARM UP. A five- to 10-minute warm-up increases blood flow and helps prevent soreness and strains in muscles, tendons and ligaments.

2. WORK LARGER MUSCLES FIRST. The big muscles of the legs, chest and back often require heavier workloads in an exercise to achieve any result. So it is best to exercise them before fatigue starts to build. Exercising these muscles first also helps your body to continue to warm up.

3. PAIR YOUR EXERCISES. Arrange your routine so that you work one muscle group, then its opposite. For example, pair quadriceps lifts with extensions for the hamstrings, biceps curls with dips for the triceps, and push-ups for the chest and shoulders with bent-over rows or chin-ups that work the latissimus dorsi. By performing exercises in pairs, you also allow each muscle group to recover in case you want to work it in a second exercise.

4. USE VARIATIONS CAREFULLY. In many instances, you can perform slight variations on the basic movement of an exercise. These not only afford variety, but can increase the intensity or focus of an exercise. However, during any one workout, it is better to do distinctly different exercises than several variations of one exercise. Performing three versions of a push-up, for example, is not as effective as doing one type of push-up and, later, a bench press or overhead row.

5. WORK SLOWLY AND STEADILY. Slow, controlled movement subjects the muscle to relatively consistent stress during both the lifting and the lowering phase of an exercise. Quick explosive movements make you work hard at the beginning of a repetition. But that initial thrust can then carry the muscle through the rest of its motion. As well as being less productive, fast movements are also more likely to injure you.

6. BREATHE CONTINUOUSLY. You may need to hold your breath briefly during an instant of effort, but don't hold it any longer. Blood pressure rises during exercise, and can be particularly high when you are performing exercises that stress the chest and arm muscles. Holding your breath will add to the already high blood pressure, and can prevent blood from returning to the chest. Breath holding can also cause cramping during abdominal work. Generally, you should exhale during the straining part of the exercise, such as when you move weights away from your body, and inhale during the easier portion of the exercise, such as when weights move toward your body.

7. USE A FULL RANGE OF MOTION. For each rep, move the joint through its maximum extension and flexion. A muscle that makes only a partial movement performs less work and can lose flexibility. Because range of motion can differ for each joint and each exercise, you need to concentrate in each case on what your own maximum is. Do not flex or extend so far that the joint is suddenly bearing the workload: That should always be the job of the muscle.

8. REST BETWEEN SETS. After the first set, you need to restore energy to the muscle so that it can contract during the next set. If the rest interval is too short, you will exhaust yourself; if too long, the next set won't make you work harder (which it should). Generally, one to two minutes are sufficient. But if you are performing only one set of an exercise, you need to rest only a few seconds before starting an exercise that stresses a different muscle group.

9. COOL DOWN. Abruptly stopping a workout can cause blood to pool in the veins, creating a sudden drop in blood pressure that may produce light-headedness or fainting. Running in place or repeating a warm-up routine keeps blood circulating and helps the muscles recover.

10. KEEP TRACK OF YOUR PROGRESS. Record reps, sets and weights for each exercise every week. Some muscles will respond more quickly than others, so you will need to increase the overload for exercises at different rates. Every month, retest your strength and reassess your appearance. Once you have achieved the look and the strength you want, you need not increase the workload further. But you do have to keep working out to maintain the benefits.

Common Mistakes

The human body differs from other machines in that it improves with use. But exercise can break down your body rather than tone it if you are not careful. The three most common errors are to do bad exercises that may actually be harmful, to do good exercises incorrectly and to overdo good exercises.

The exercises on the opposite page are bad ones that people do routinely. Most of them do not provide the benefits they are intended to, and each is quite capable of causing injury to muscles, tendons and ligaments. Some of them have been standard exercises in schools for years, and some are still used in fitness classes. In each case, this book presents a better, safer alternative.

Choosing the right exercises but performing them incorrectly can be just as bad. If you do not maintain the correct position all through an exercise, you may fail to work the muscles you intended to. Worse, you may injure yourself by placing strain where it does not belong.

Another common mistake is to overtax your muscles, especially at the beginning of a program. Pushing muscles to their limits before they have become accustomed to exercise is almost certain to result in soreness. For an exercise to work, it should require some effort, but not strain or pain. Do not persist with any exercise that hurts, especially if the discomfort you feel is in the joints. You should feel the effort in your muscles, not your joints.

Muscles can be damaged by incautious exercise. Extreme overexertion, particularly when muscles have not been properly warmed up, may literally tear muscle fibers.

Minor muscle soreness can often be relieved by a hot bath or a massage. Muscle or joint strain may be treated with ice bags. But persistent joint pain calls for a doctor's care.

If muscles are severely or persistently sore, the cause is probably overtraining. Other signs of serious overexertion include excessive fatigue, listlessness, depression and difficulty in sleeping. If you have these symptoms and have been exercising, you may need more rest each day.

Leg lowering arches the lower back, placing it under stress that can cause backache. Instead, do the bicycle *(page 322)*.

Straight-leg sit-ups also force your back to arch, overstressing it. Try the crunch *(page 312)* or elevated crunch *(page 316)*.

The duck walk strains knees and may even rupture ligaments. Quadriceps lifts *(page 291)* are as effective without the strain.

Back arching tightens muscles that usually need lengthening. Use a safe exercise like the back diagonal *(page 340)*.

Locking your supporting knee in the donkey kick imperils your sacroiliac. Do hamstring and gluteal lifts instead *(page 295)*.

Bending your head back hard in a neck roll may hurt your spine. The seated back lift *(page 326)* strengthens your neck safely.

lifters

wrist and ankle weights

exercise mat

Equipment

Most of the basic strength-building exercises in Chapters 12-14 do not require any equipment. If you limit yourself to these, that is fine: You can strengthen all of your major muscle groups. But the items shown here, which are available in most sporting goods stores, will add variety, efficiency and comfort to your routines.

For leg or abdominal work, a mat is an excellent investment: It cushions bones and joints, and it protects your lower back. Strapping on wrist or ankle weights, ranging from one to five pounds, is one of the simplest ways of increasing the workload of many exercises.

Dumbbells focus work on specific muscles in the shoulders, arms and chest; you can start with weights of three or four pounds and move up to 10 pounds or more. A standard 15-pound weight bar adds even more resistance and makes presses and rowing exercises more efficient. If you do push-ups, lifters will intensify the exercise by allowing you to lower your body further.

dumbbells

weight bar

CHAPTER 12

The Lower Body

Powerful exercises for your body's biggest muscles

Your largest muscles—and potentially the best-developed ones—are likely to be in your lower body. The reason is simple: Your legs and hips have to support and move the rest of your body. For most adults, that means carrying more than 100 pounds.

Powerful musculature does not guarantee, however, that the lower body can be strengthened more readily than other parts of the body. In fact, your lower body can be slower to show the effects of exercise. Precisely because of their power, the body's large, high-use muscles may barely be stressed during an exercise that would easily overload smaller, less active muscles. If, on the other hand, lower body muscles have become weakened from underuse, their size makes the resulting slackness more noticeable.

Thighs and hips tend to be sites not only for oversized muscles, but also for accumulated fat.

This is often a concern for women, whose sex-specific hormones cause fat to collect in this area. Male hormones predispose men to store fat around the waist. Many people feel especially self-conscious about a condition popularly called "cellulite," the dimply ripples that appear primarily on thighs and buttocks on women, and around the abdominal area on men. Cellulite is actually nothing but ordinary fat. A number of special lotions and creams are promoted as cellulite "removers." However, lotions do not affect cellulite, nor does any other special treatment. This fat may seem to be more stubborn than fat elsewhere, but that is only because there is more of it; the upper body usually has a thinner fat layer between muscle and skin.

Muscle-toning exercises alone will not slim your thighs, but such exercises can improve your appearance by firming and shaping the underly-

Lower Body

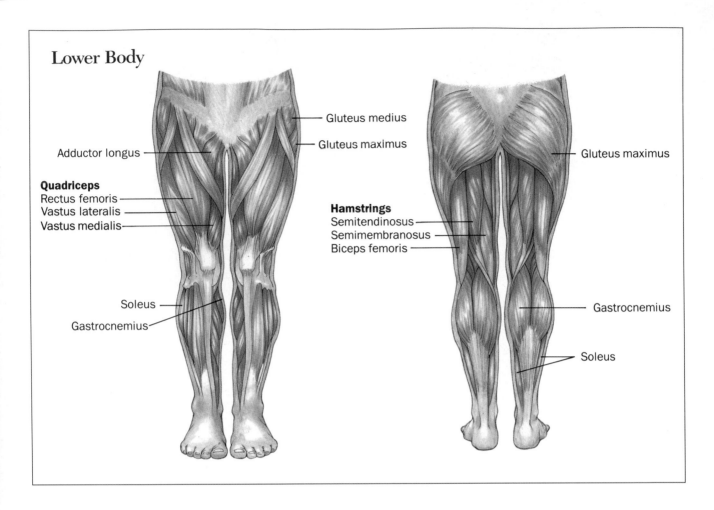

Gluteus medius

Gluteus maximus

Adductor longus

Gluteus maximus

Quadriceps
Rectus femoris
Vastus lateralis
Vastus medialis

Hamstrings
Semitendinosus
Semimembranosus
Biceps femoris

Soleus

Gastrocnemius

Gastrocnemius

Soleus

ing muscle tissue as you shed weight. The only way to lose fat and get rid of unsightly bulges is to decrease your calorie intake by consuming fewer calories and increase your calorie output through such aerobic exercises as brisk walking, running, swimming or cycling. However, while aerobic exercise tones some muscles in your lower body, it may leave other major lower body muscles virtually unused.

Research has shown that the gluteus maximus, the muscle that underlies and shapes the buttocks, works very little during walking, even brisk aerobic walking. Running and cycling do not significantly activate this muscle, either. Nor do any of these activities have much impact on the adductors—the muscles of the inner thigh. Instead, you need to perform exercises such as those on pages 294-297 and 302-303, which work just these areas.

A look at the anatomy of the lower body (see illustration above) indicates how exercises targeted at specific muscles can effectively firm the musculature of thighs and hips. The body's center of gravity is located in the pelvis, and muscles on the outside of the hips balance and support the torso and move the legs. These muscles are most efficiently toned by leg exercises. Inside the pelvis, powerful hip flexors, the strongest muscles in the body, steady hips and thighs as well as move them. Generally, these muscles do not need strengthening.

The quadriceps, a four-part muscle group, is the principal muscle in your thigh and supplies much of the power in forward movement. It is used whenever you jump, run, kick, skip, lift or push. Besides improving sports performance, training your quadriceps makes it easier to lift objects from the floor the safe way—with your legs, rather than your back, providing most of the power.

The quadriceps is also important to the knee, a hinge joint particularly vulnerable to injury because it allows movement only in a semicircular plane. This limited movement gives great stability to the lower body, but it exposes the joint to danger whenever force comes from another direction. By strengthening the quadriceps, the main connection in this hinge, you can reinforce, protect and strengthen your knees.

On the back of your thighs are the hamstrings, a three-part muscle group that opposes movement of the quadriceps with help from the gluteals. Hamstring pulls and tears are among the most common and serious sports injuries. Exercises such as sprinting and jumping build such mighty quads that they can literally tear weak hamstrings apart if these opposing muscles fail to relax when the quads contract. Normally hamstrings don't to be as strong as the quadriceps, they can be only two-thirds as strong—yet in many people, they are not.

The muscles that line the side of the hip and thigh, lift your leg away from your body and rotate it inward are the abductors. One major abductor is the gluteus medius: You can feel it when you place your hands on your hips and touch the bumps on the front of your hip bones.

The big muscles of your calf, the gastrocnemius and the soleus, join at the Achilles tendon fixed to your heel. These muscles pull on your heel and extend your ankle, allowing you to rise on your toes as you walk or run. On the front of the shin are muscles that flex the ankle, thereby lifting feet and toes. Exercises for the muscles of the lower leg help protect the shin and the ankle, frequent sites of injuries from physical activity.

In the chapter that follows, you can choose exercises to strengthen one particular area, though they should be balanced with work for the opposing muscle group. For example, toe taps for the shin muscles should accompany calf raises. Or you can choose one or two exercises for each muscle group to firm and strengthen all of your lower body.

With your foot flexed toward your shin and your leg held stiff, lift to several inches off the floor *(above)*. Slowly raise the leg to a 45-degree angle *(below)*. Pause, then slowly lower without letting your heel touch the floor. Continue raising and lowering. You may place a pillow in the small of your back for greater comfort.

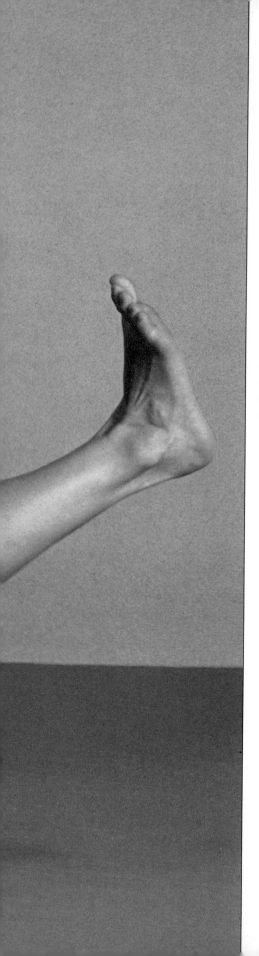

Quadriceps Lifts

Toning the quadriceps, the major muscle group underpinning the front and sides of your thigh, shapes your upper leg more effectively than working any other muscle group. A muscle that performs two jobs—straightening the knee and raising the thigh—the quadriceps can be trained either by flexing the thigh at the hip or by extending the leg at the knee.

Straight-leg quadriceps lifts, like the ones shown here, are effective strengtheners. The goal is to do both lifts of the hip and knee extensions. If you are a beginner, do these exercises lying on your back. Work up to the seated versions, which shape and strengthen faster. Beginners should alternate between sets. If you are at a

more advanced level, do all three sets for each leg before switching. As you progress, add one- or two-pound ankle weights. (People with back or knee pain, however, should not add weights.) If you want even more development, add up to five-pound weights to all quad exercises. If you cannot keep your knee straight in the lifts or extend it fully in the extensions, reduce the weights.

Straight-leg quad lifts are a good choice if your knees are vulnerable to injury or have been injured. Start strengthening with the lifts shown here (with a physician's approval). When you no longer feel undue pain or instability at the injured joint, add one of the lower-leg extensions shown on the next two pages.

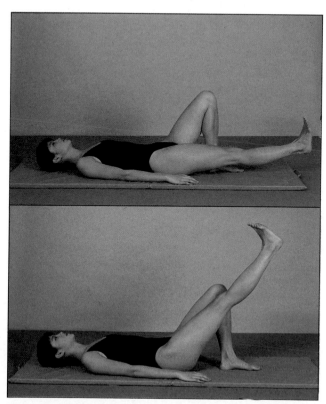

Flatten your lower back against the floor *(top)*, then slowly raise and lower your leg vertically. Do not let your leg rest on the floor. Keep your knee extended, your ankle flexed and your toes up.

Quadriceps Extensions

Lie with your lower back flat on the floor, your thighs and calves at right angles and your toes pointed *(top left)*. Straighten one leg so that your toe points toward the ceiling *(bottom left);* slowly lower to the first position. Your hips and thighs should not move.

Sit on the edge of a bench or chair with your back straight *(inset right)*. Lift one leg off the floor *(opposite)*, then fully extend it. Return to the first position, keeping your foot flexed. Avoid tilting or moving your pelvis, or tensing your upper body.

After doing the leg extension on the opposite page, finish working your gluteus maximus with this lift. Bend one leg at the knee at a 45-degree angle and point your toe *(above)*. Slowly raise your bent leg as high as possible *(below)*. Keep your hips stable. Do not rest your knee on the floor when it returns to the down position.

Hamstring and Gluteal Lifts

Working your hamstrings and gluteals will balance quad work, protect vulnerable hamstrings and continue the toning you began in the front of your thigh.

First do the leg extensions below, then finish with the bent-leg lifts at left. As with the quadriceps exercises, beginners should switch legs after each set; those who are more advanced should do two to three sets in a row for each leg. Add ankle weights as you grow stronger. The buttocks and hamstrings exercises on the following two pages work the same muscles. Choose them for variety or if you have back problems. (Their reclining position supports the back.)

Place your hands directly below your shoulders. Extend one leg straight back with your toes pointed *(below);* **bring your lower leg up to a right angle as you flex your foot** *(bottom).* **Keep your torso steady.**

Get into position with your back flat on the floor, your upper body relaxed, your feet separated and your knees bent. Tilt your pelvis, raising your hips slightly *(above)*. Do not raise your upper back off the floor. Press your legs together tightly, squeezing your buttocks hard *(below)*. Hold. Separate your knees and repeat.

Hamstring and Gluteal Squeezes

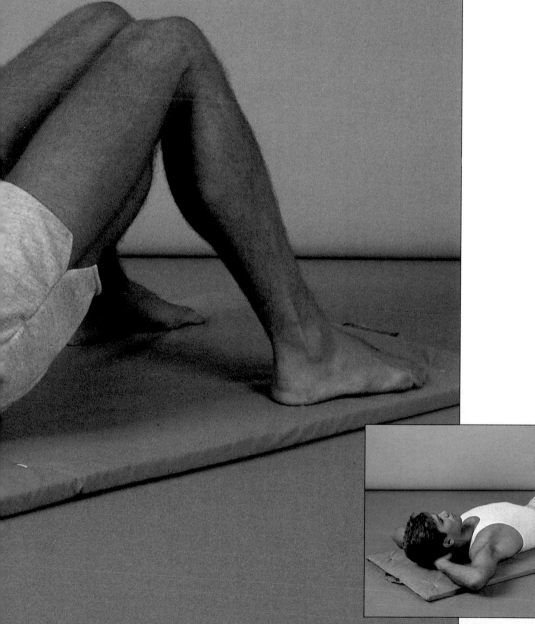

With your feet and knees together, lift your hips, leaving your upper back on the floor *(above)*. Squeeze thighs and buttocks tightly. Hold, lower slowly and relax.

With your supporting leg bent at a right angle to your body, hold your upper leg straight out parallel to your thigh *(above)*. Keep your lifted foot flexed. Make sure that your leg is rotated so that your heel is up and your toe down. Pulse your heel out slowly and rhythmically—tighten your leg muscles and press your heel out hard, then relax the muscles—at about the rate of one pulse per second. For extensions, keep the same position and bend your upper knee, drawing your upper leg in until it is directly above your bottom leg *(below)*. Then extend it fully to the starting position.

Outer-Thigh Work

Lifting your leg to the side firms not only your outer thigh, but also the side of your hip. That is the site of the gluteus medius, your second largest gluteal muscle and one of your major thigh abductors. The exercises on these two pages give you a comprehensive outer-thigh- and outer-hip-firming routine. Work them as a three-exercise set. The pulses *(inset)*, alternately tensing and relaxing, concentrate effort in the gluteals; then the extensions *(below, oppo-*

site) work all the abductors. Finally, the bent-leg lifts *(below)* isolate the outer thigh.

The straight-leg raises on the following two pages are also a classic way to work the outer thigh and gluteus medius. You may do them as an alternative. In all outer-thigh work, position is crucial. If you do these exercises wrong, you will end up working the quadriceps, rather than the abductors, or straining your lower back. As you progress, add ankle weights for extra resistance.

Finish with bent-leg lifts. Let your legs remain at right angles to your body with your ankles flexed *(top right)*. Slowly raise and lower your upper leg *(bottom right)*. Do not let it rest in the down position between lifts.

Outer-Thigh Raises

Resting on your forearm and hip, with your bottom leg bent at a 90-degree angle and your top leg raised slightly *(inset)*, slowly lift and lower your top leg in a straight line with your body. Keep your upper body erect and your foot flexed.

Starting in the position shown in inset photo, repeat the lifting and lowering, but with your toe pointed *(above)*. Do not allow your body to slump or your leg to rotate upward.

Balancing on the side of your hip with your forearm steadying you, hold your bent legs in midair *(above)*. Point your toes. Slowly bring your bottom leg up to meet your top leg *(below)*. Do not let your hips roll or shoulders slump.

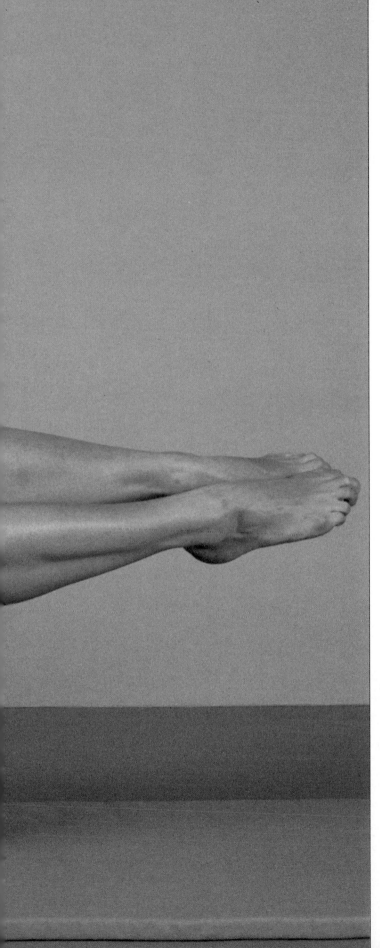

Inner-Thigh Lifts

Because they are an under-exercised area, the inner thighs show one of the quickest responses to toning exercises of any lower body area. To begin firming your inner thighs, do the leg-fanning exercise below. It is the easiest and the safest, particularly for anyone troubled by back pain or weak knees. The hip lift at left should be added as soon as you are able: It stresses the muscles in a slightly different way. After you have built up some strength, you can do the inner-thigh leg raises on the following two pages. If you have adequate flexibility, do the raises with your leg behind the bent leg.

With your lower back flat on the floor, your arms by your sides and your upper body relaxed, lift your legs to form a V over your hips *(top)*. Separate them as widely as you can without pain *(above)*, then draw them back into the starting V.

Inner-Thigh Raises

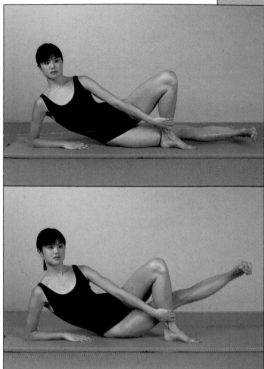

The most difficult inner-thigh raise
and the fastest strengthener, this exercise
requires flexibility. Start in the same
position as that described on the opposite
page, but place your bent leg in front
of your extended leg. Then lift. Be sure your
hips do not sag, your knee stays up and
your foot is flexed.

Rest on your hip with your forearm and bent upper leg helping you to balance. Rotate your bottom leg out so that your heel is turned up and your toe down. Keeping your foot flexed, lift your leg as high as you can without rolling your hip back. Do not allow your leg to rest on the floor.

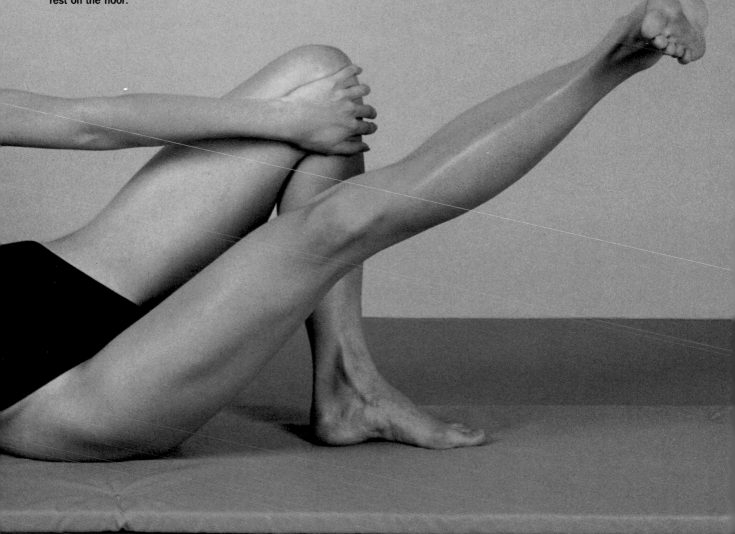

Calf Lifts

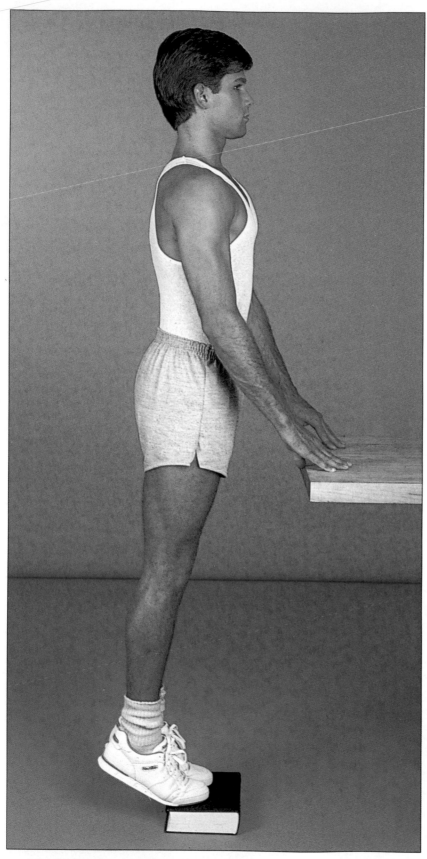

Stronger, better defined calves are best built with calf lifts, which you should do with the balls of your feet on a raised object like a book. This position allows the ankle to move through a full range of motion, thereby promoting flexibility and minimizing the risk of injury. Balance calf lifts with the toe-tapping exercises below. This tones the muscles in the front of your lower leg and helps prevent the condition called shin splints, which often afflicts runners and those who do high-impact aerobic movement routines. In addition to strengthening the major calf muscles like the gastrocnemius and soleus, lower-leg work builds the muscles that control toe and foot movement and subtly steer our bodies direction.

With your toes pointed straight ahead, slowly rise on the balls of your feet, then lower your heels completely to the floor *(left)*. Use your hands only for balance, not support. Be sure that your ankles do not roll outward.

Sitting in a chair, lift the front of your foot as high as you can and tap your toe rhythmically to the floor at a rate of about one tap a second *(below)*. Continue for 30 to 60 seconds.

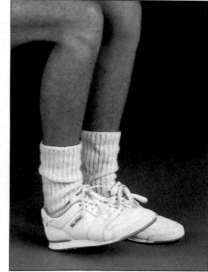

Intensify the effort by strengthening one calf at a time. Balance on the ball and toes of one foot with the other foot wrapped around the back of your ankle as you lift and lower. Don't let your foot roll inward (that is, in the direction of your big toe).

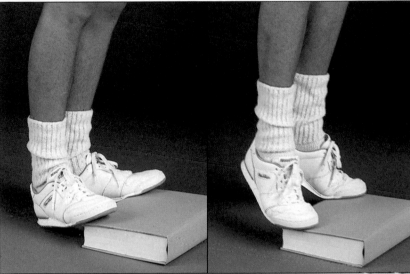

Lift with your heels together and toes pointed out to work major calf muscles and the outer peroneals, which help steady the leg and turn the foot out.

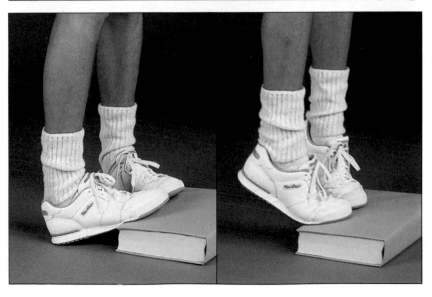

Do calf lifts with your toes together and your heels apart to add the inner tiboals to your workout. Strength in these muscles helps roll your feet in, enhancing agility as well as ankle stability.

CHAPTER 13

The Middle Body

A flatter stomach and a stronger back

———

Everyone wants a trim waistline. Both men and women, according to one survey, express more concern about the shape of their midsections than about any other part of their body. For most of us, the concern may be purely aesthetic, since taut, well-muscled middles look attractive. But this appeal also has a sound basis in physiology. A firm waist is generally considered an accurate signal of overall fitness.

The abdominal muscles are important to many everyday movements involving the torso. Walking, sitting, jumping, squatting, reaching—even breathing and good posture—depend on abdominals. These muscles stabilize or power your body in virtually every type of exercise, whether you are hitting a tennis ball or kicking a football. Like powerful rubber bands, the abdominals help properly transfer force between your upper and lower body. Strong abdominal muscles make you a faster sprinter because your pumping arms help pull your legs into a burst of forward movement. And they mobilize force from your lower body that gives strength to upper body movements. Moreover, when working properly, they are like a natural girdle that supports both your organs and your back. You cannot have a healthy back or good posture without strong abdominals.

Unique among muscles, the abdominals influence certain joint movements, even though they aren't attached to the relevant bones. The rectus abdominis, for example, is a principal mover of your spine. Stretched between rib cage and pubic bone, this long muscle bends your spine forward and stabilizes the chest and abdomen in almost every movement. The rectus abdominis is also the muscle responsible for the "washboard"

Middle Body

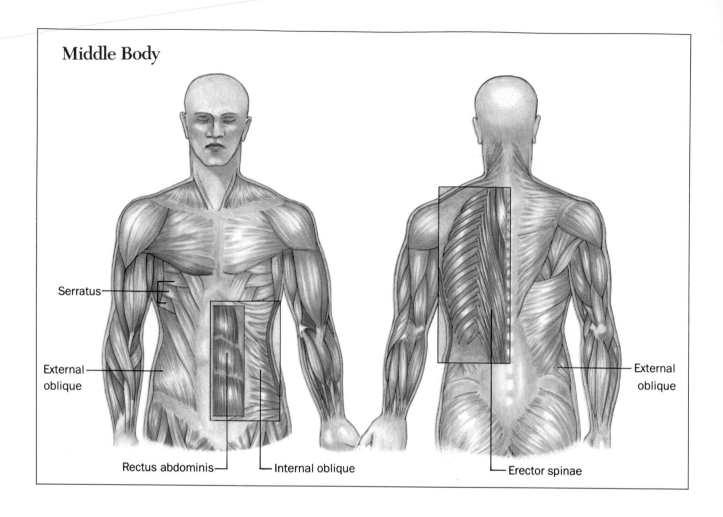

Serratus

External oblique

Rectus abdominis

Internal oblique

External oblique

Erector spinae

look seen in well-toned abdomens, an appearance caused by the tendinous bands that cross the muscle. It is the rectus that basically flattens the abdomen, though no one has a truly flat abdominal wall: Its curves accommodate internal organs. Because some exercises work the top of the rectus harder than the bottom—or the bottom harder than the top—strengthening the muscle requires exercises that involve both legs and upper body.

Assisting the rectus in flexing the spine are the external obliques, which also twist, turn and bend the middle body, and keep it erect. These sheetlike muscles overlap. On top, the external obliques wrap around your sides, coming to a V in front. Along the sides of your rib cage, they intersect in a sawtooth fashion with the serratus muscles. The serratus muscles help stabilize your rib cage when you breathe, but they get the

most work from exercises or activities that involve raising your arms. Underneath the externals, the internal obliques run diagonally opposite and form an upside-down V. All of the obliques are best developed by exercises that work your body at an angle, such as diagonal crunches (pages 314-315).

Even the most well-exercised abdominal muscles cannot tame a bulging belly area that is the site of excessive fat storage. If you are very overweight, these muscles, no matter how well toned, will remain hidden by fat stored below your skin but above the muscles. And pressure from fat stored internally will ensure that the muscles are stretched, making your abdomen protrude. To reduce fat here, as anywhere on the body, you have to diet and increase your overall caloric expenditure, primarily by performing an aerobic exercise such as walking, jogging, swimming or cycling. But a protruding abdomen can also be the result of poor posture that exaggerates any fat surplus and often contributes to an aching lower back. Strengthening your abdominal wall can help correct this condition by pulling your pelvis into better alignment and away from the common arched, swayback tilt or an overly forward thrust that is often associated with lower back pain. Your abdomen will appear flatter as well.

Of course, you also need to develop your back muscles for good posture and a pain-free back. The relevant muscles are primarily the erector spinae group, which runs along both sides of the spine from the base to the chest. This group consists of many intertwining, superficial muscles; none of them is very long or strong, but together they are crucial for good posture and for a back that does not ache.

Misconceptions abound about how to condition the hard-to-reach muscles of the middle body. For example, many people still regard the conventional bent-knee sit-up as the best all-around abdominal exercise. But as explained on page 312, the crunch, an alternative to the sit-up, is a safer, more effective exercise. Moreover, there is no "best" exercise, since no single movement can maximally engage all of the muscles involved in firming the midsection. In fact, more than one exercise is required simply to work the rectus abdominis thoroughly. In addition to the crunch, this chapter presents several crunch variations along with other abdominal exercises and a special program of exercises for the back.

When doing these exercises, inhale during the relaxed phase and exhale during the exertion (which should allow you to pull your abdomen in). You can also try breathing in your upper chest, using rapid puffs, when abdominal work grows intense. Work the muscles through their full range of motion in each exercise, though this movement may be small in certain positions. Not returning completely to a rest position will help keep tension in the muscles throughout the exercise. And rather than let gravity pull you quickly back to earth, roll down as slowly as possible, using your muscles to resist the pull of gravity. This will also help protect your back from strain. Be sure to balance your abdominal work with back-strengthening exercises.

The Crunch

The crunch is the safest and most efficient way to condition abdominal muscles. This exercise focuses effort on the crucial layer of muscle covering your midsection from rib cage to pubic bone. It bypasses muscles that may well be strong enough already, like hip flexors. It avoids stressing the small of the back, which can happen when your back arches as you rise. And if done correctly, without jerking the neck, the crunch protects you from upper cervical strain as well.

All of these reasons make the crunch superior to a traditional sit-up when the sit-up involves a lift of more than 45 degrees from the floor—the level at which scientists have determined that hip-flexor involvement occurs. Holding your feet down does not help. This only emphasizes the hip flexors and detracts from the work of the abdominals. And if you do a traditional sit-up with your legs straight, you risk lower back strain.

Technique is everything with crunches. The results you get will depend not on how many you do, but how well you do them. Start with one of the crunches for the rectus and one diagonal crunch, done to the left and to the right, for your obliques. Beginners or people with back problems should perform the elevated crunches on pages 316-317 for both muscles.

To perform the basic crunch, shown below, lie with your back flat on the floor and your legs comfortably drawn up to about a 90-degree angle. Support the back of your neck just below your skull with your hands. Point elbows forward. Slowly lift your upper body with your abdominal muscles, raising yourself no higher than the bottom of your shoulder blades. Let the weight of your head hang, supported by your hands. Use alternative arm positions to vary the amount of effort. For the least effort, reach your arms forward *(top right)*. Add exertion by folding your arms across your chest *(middle right)*. Or spread your elbows, placing your hands behind your head for more difficulty *(bottom right)*. When using alternative arm positions, be sure not to jerk your neck up as you lift.

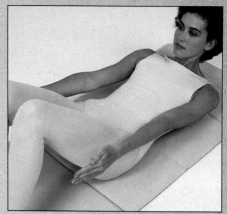

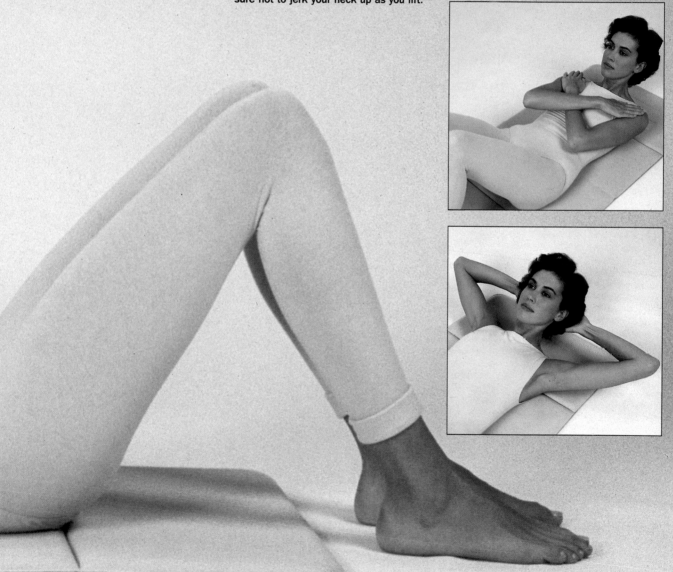

The Diagonal Crunch

To tone the muscles that shape the sides of your waist and provide the power for torso twists and turns, you must pull across your abdomen as if tightening an X-shaped band, one crosspiece at a time. This enlists your obliques to their maximum.

Start with your head and shoulder slightly raised *(above)* and twist your elbow toward your knee *(below)*. Complete sets for one side of your torso before switching to the other side.

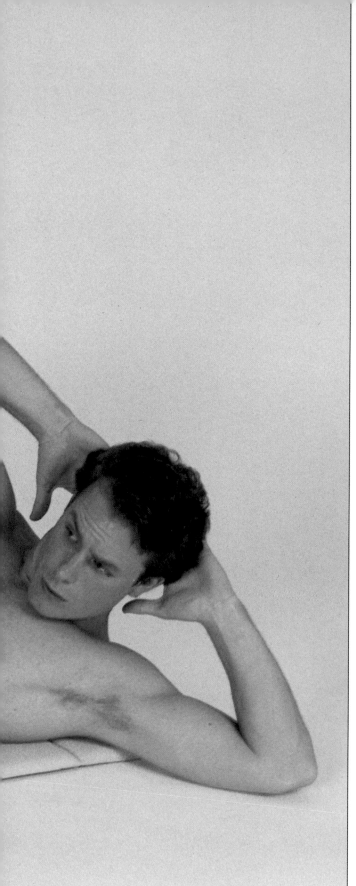

Support your neck by placing your hands at the base of your skull. Bend your legs, letting them flop to the left, the bottom one resting on the floor *(top)*. Lift, letting your head hang *(bottom)*.

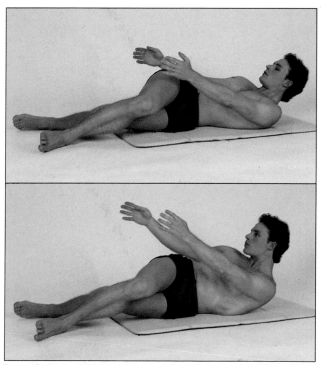

Intensify diagonals by lying on one hip with your bent legs crossed to the side. Begin with your head and shoulders slightly lifted, arms reaching out *(top)*. Continue reaching as you roll up slowly *(bottom)*. Never roll all the way down.

The Elevated Crunch

I f you have back trouble or especially weak abdominal muscles, safeguard your back by performing crunches with your legs raised and supported. Beginners should start with elevated crunches, too. This position keeps your lower back securely on the floor and defeats any attempt to use hip flexors rather than abdominals. You may use any bench, chair or sofa of the right height. Do the basic version, shown on the opposite page, to work the rectus abdominis or the variation shown below to work the obliques.

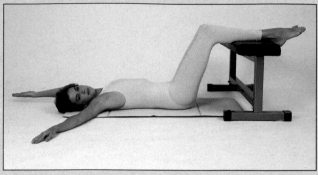

To work your obliques, lie on your back with your bent legs resting on a stable support and your arms raised to form a wide V over your head *(above)*. Lift your left arm slowly and reach across your torso to the right of your knees *(below)*. Do all the sets on that side before switching to your right arm.

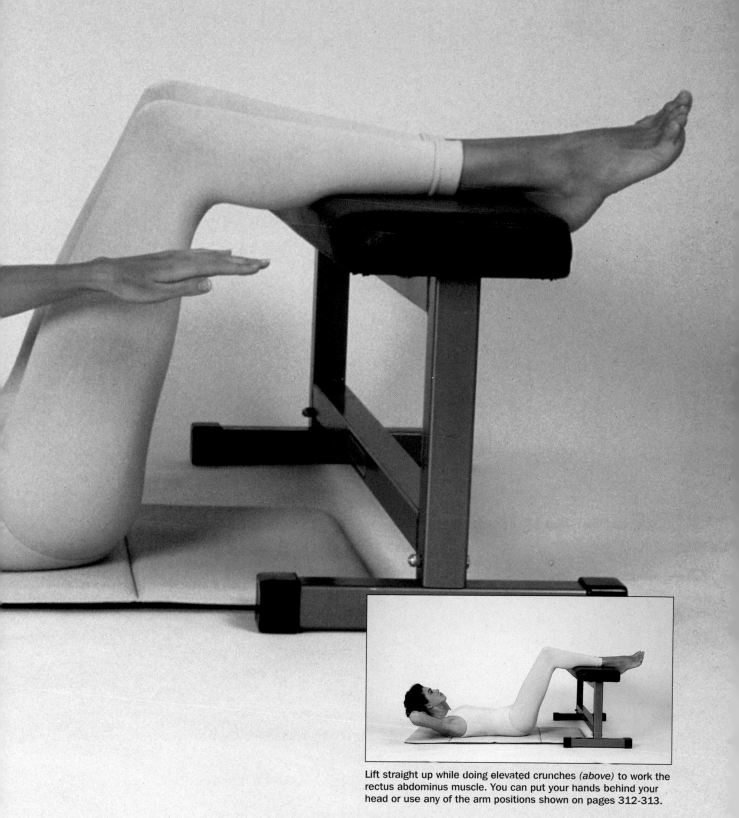

Lift straight up while doing elevated crunches *(above)* to work the rectus abdominus muscle. You can put your hands behind your head or use any of the arm positions shown on pages 312-313.

The Diamond Crunch

If your torso is long or your back inflexible, this will help you focus on abdominals and avoid exercising hip flexors. Put the soles of your feet together and spread your bent legs. Support your head with your hands *(below)*. Contract your abdominals and lift *(bottom)*. Do not jerk your head forward.

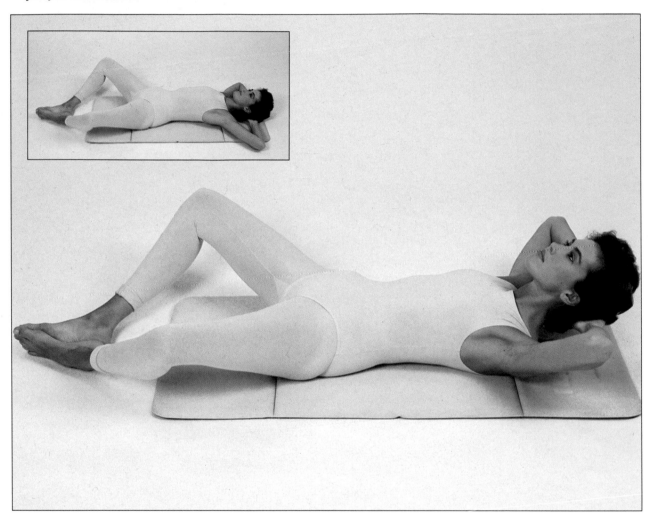

The Hip Lift

Do this exercise for the lower rectus on your back with your legs raised and ankles crossed, your head lifted and supported by your hands *(opposite)*. Contract your lower abdominals to raise your hips slightly off the floor.

The Negative Sit-Up

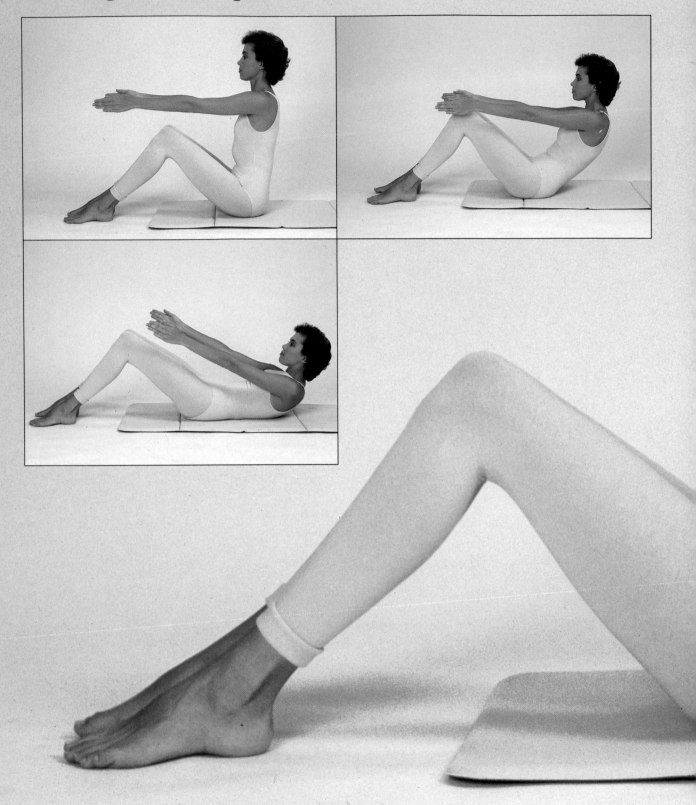

If the preceding abdominal work is too difficult or if you simply want to add variety to your program, do this sit-up. It rolls down, not up, and does not endanger your back or overemphasize hip-flexor work. Start by sitting with your legs bent at approximately a 90-degree angle and your arms reaching forward *(inset, top row at far left)*. Slowly lower yourself vertebra by vertebra to the floor *(insets, top row at near left and below left)*. After you are completely down, use your arms to push yourself back up *(left)*.

The Bicycle

These versions of the bicycle effectively stress both upper and lower abdominals simultaneously. In addition, they work both the rectus and the obliques. Any of the three degrees of difficulty shown can provide a thorough abdominal workout. Attempt the intermediate and advanced versions only if you can do them without lifting your lower back from the floor. Try the intermediate once you can do three sets of 20 in the beginning position. Move on to the advanced version when you can do three sets of the intermediate.

With hands behind your head, legs bent and toes pointed, touch one elbow, then the other, to the opposite knee *(above and below).*

To do the intermediate version, fully extend each leg in turn after you pull your knee in toward its opposing elbow *(above)*.

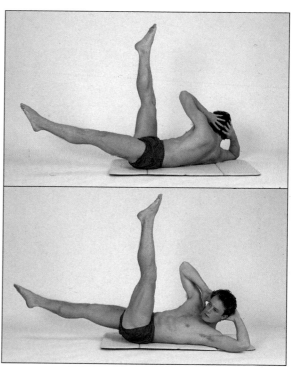

Do the advanced version with legs straight and toes pointed. Alternately bend one leg at the hip and then the other, drawing each leg toward the opposing elbow *(above)*.

The V-Up

A classic exercise, the V-up targets the lower abdominals when you perform it properly. Many other types of V-ups require leg lifts, but these start with legs raised to avoid engaging the hip flexors. Because they don't require you to jerk your legs into the air as do standard V-ups, these are also safer for your back. However, if you have a weak back or feel back strain, choose an easier exercise like the beginning bicycle on page 322.

To do the beginning V-up, lie flat on your back, hands behind your head, your legs bent at a right angle *(top)*. Lift your head and shoulders *(middle)*. Straighten your legs and point your toes *(bottom)*.

Start the intermediate V-up on your back with hands stretched behind your head, your bent legs held at an angle of about 90 degrees *(above)*. Bring your arms over your head, raise your upper body and reach your hands beyond your knees, parallel with lower legs *(below)*.

Back Strength

Because strong abdominals should be balanced by a strong back, your midsection program should include work to develop the erector spinae muscle group. (However, if you suffer back pain, consult your doctor before doing these strength exercises.) Start by sitting on the edge of a weight bench or chair. Put your hands behind your head and bend forward (*inset*). Lift up slowly to about a 45-degree angle but do not go any higher (*right*).

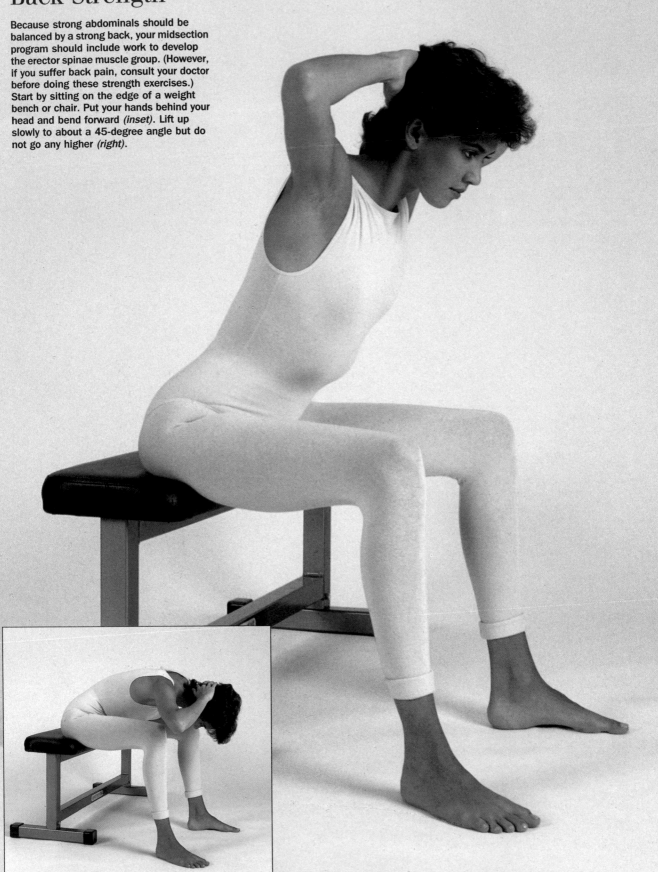

Lie face down on a weight bench or sturdy table, your hands behind your head, with the top of your chest over the edge *(right)*. If you are on a table, use a folded towel for padding. Lift your upper body until you are about parallel to the floor *(below)*.

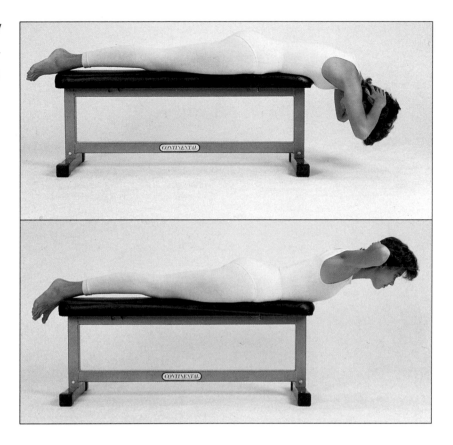

Lie stomach down on a weight bench or heavy table with your head lifted. Hang your bent legs over the end of the bench from the hip joint. Hold onto the bench for support *(right)*. Then extend your legs and point your toes until you are parallel to the floor or a little higher *(below)*.

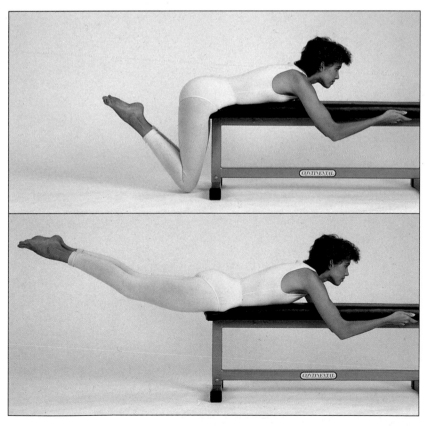

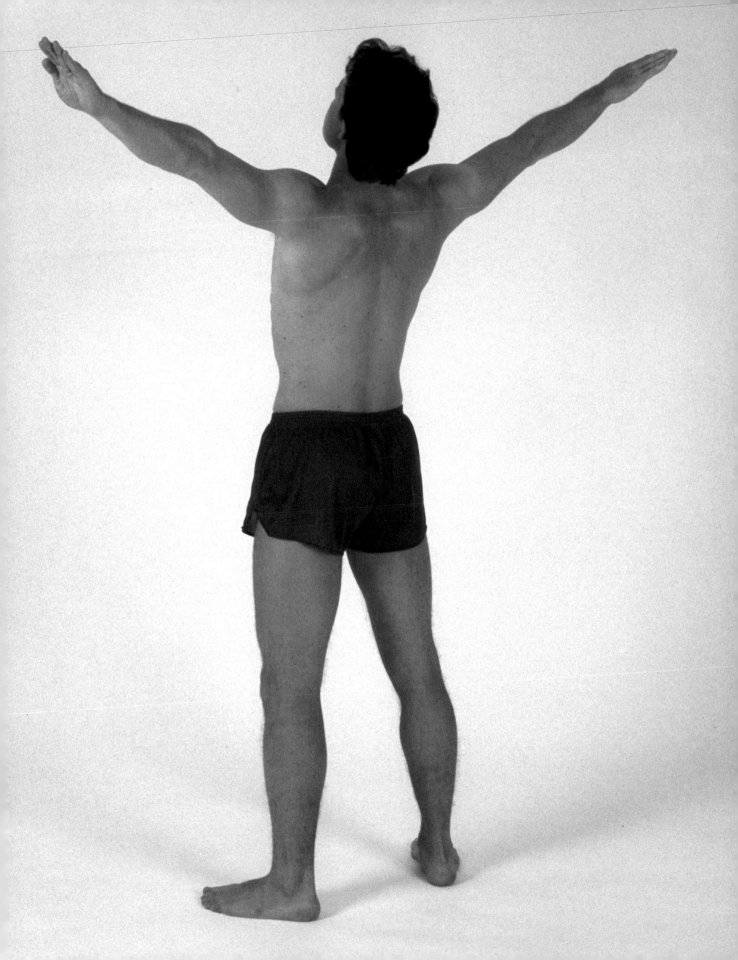

The Good-Back Program

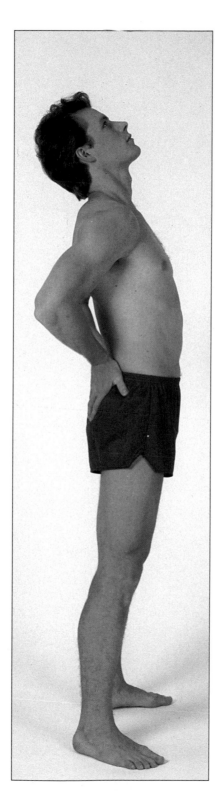

Though they are vital, strong abdominal and back muscles together cannot give you all the protection you need against common causes of back strain, including poor posture. Adding a few simple exercises to your program can help you avoid the back pain that afflicts an estimated 80 percent of adults.

The exercises in this section help counteract problems created by too strong or too tight hip flexors and extensors, which join your pelvis and your spine to your thighbones. Leg exercises such as walking, running and bicycling build strong hip flexors and extensors that pull on the pelvis. If not resisted, the pelvis tilts, over-stressing muscles in the lumbar spine region. The result: muscle strain, spasm and ache. In addition, your abdomen protrudes, putting more strain on the small of your back.

Counteracting this problem calls for loosening hip flexors and extensors along with strengthening abdominal and back muscles. The final important step is to train the muscles that support your pelvis to assume the correct tilt. This helps ensure good posture and avoid a lumbar-stressing swayback.

These exercises are designed not only to prevent back trouble, but to help relieve stiffness or soreness in your back without overtaxing weak muscles. However, if you suffer back discomfort, consult a physician before beginning this program.

Most of the exercises in this section may be done as often as you wish, no matter what your level of fitness. The final three strengtheners (pages 338-343) are more taxing, and you should gradually work up to performing full sets.

Begin to warm your back with this soaring reach *(opposite)*. Stand with your feet shoulder width apart, so that your weight is distributed evenly. Reach up and back, spreading your arms like wings. Lift your face. Keep your hips right below your rib cage. Breathe in and out deeply 10 times.

Align your pelvis properly *(right)*. Stand at ease. Rest your hands on the small of your back. Lift the top of your chest, raise your chin and keep your hips directly below your rib cage. Hold this pose one minute, breathing normally. This position eases the strain on your back.

Knee Press

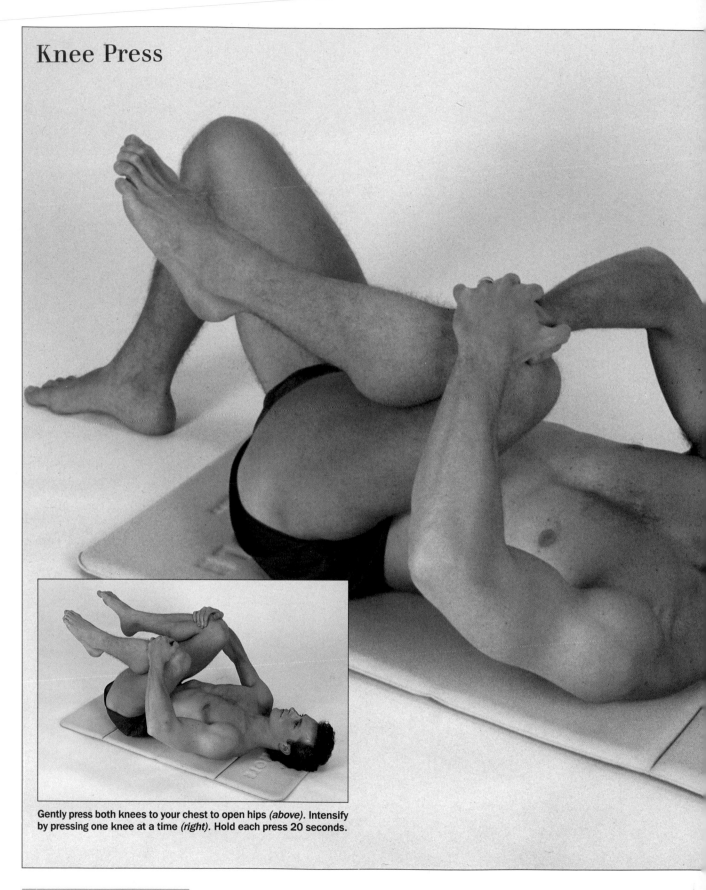

Gently press both knees to your chest to open hips *(above)*. Intensify by pressing one knee at a time *(right)*. Hold each press 20 seconds.

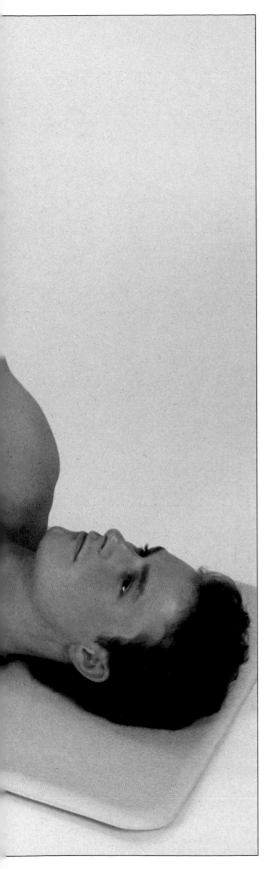

Pelvic Tilt

Place your hands comfortably under your head. Bend your legs up, rest your feet on the floor and flatten your lower back *(top)*. Then slowly roll your hips up until you reach your waistline *(above)*. Feel your lower spine lengthen as your pelvis tilts. Hold for 10 seconds, then slowly roll back down. Repeat three times.

Cobra and Sphinx

To perform the cobra, place your hands under your shoulders and slowly raise your upper body *(above).* Use the muscles along your spine as well as the strength of your arms. Rise as high as you can without experiencing discomfort. Keep your head up, your elbows bent and your shoulders down *(right).* Hold for 10 seconds or longer.

If the cobra is too difficult, do the sphinx *(above)*. Lie face down with your arms bent by your sides. Lift your head and chest as you slide your forearms up until your elbows are directly below your shoulders. (It should feel as if there were a string lifting the top of your head toward the ceiling.) Do not hunch your shoulders. Hold for at least 10 seconds.

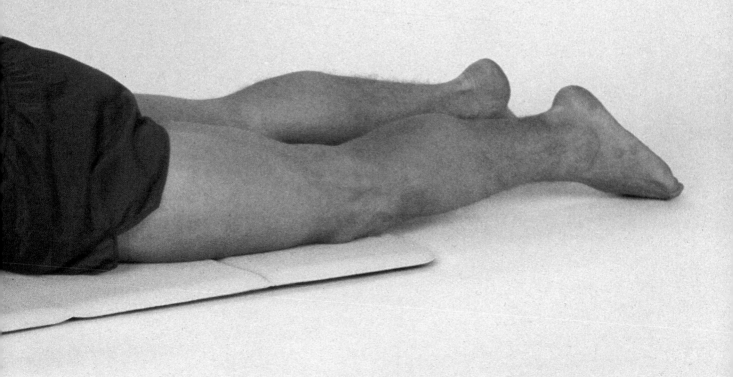

Spinal Curl

Start on hands and knees, placing each hand directly below your shoulder and your knees just below your hips. Lift your right hand toward the ceiling with your palm facing out, turning your head to follow the movement and keeping your eyes on your hand *(below)*. Slowly sweep your hand out to the side and down, aiming for the space between your left arm and leg *(opposite top)*. Follow the motion with your eyes. Continue the curl by sliding the back of your hand along the floor as you lower your shoulder. Curl through as far as you can, resting your shoulder, arm and head on the floor *(opposite bottom)*. Hold 10 seconds or longer. Repeat with your left arm.

The Child

Rest your forehead on a mat or rug, stretch your arms out in front of you and lift your hips so that your bent knees support most of your weight *(left)*. Relax your back completely. Remain in this posture for half a minute. Then let your upper body slide toward your knees as your hips sink onto your lower legs *(below)*. Stay in this pose as long as you wish, letting all the tension in your body evaporate.

The Cat

Assume a catlike position with your hands beneath your shoulders and your knees under your hips (right). Bend your spine down so that your rib cage sinks, your pelvis tilts toward your legs and the top of your head rises. Hold for a count of five. Then arch your spine, bending your head down and drawing your abdomen in as far as you can (below). Hold for another five count. Repeat this sequence twice.

Advanced Back Work

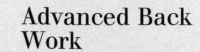

After you have increased the strength and flexibility in your back with the preceding exercises, you may try the exercise shown here, along with those on the next four pages. They can build power into your back and give you extra protection against aches and injury. However, do not attempt these exercises unless you have no back pain.

Start in a comfortable position on hands and knees. Curl your head down as you draw your knee in toward your face *(left)*. Then lift your head and extend your leg up and out behind you *(opposite)*. Do not let your hips shift. Repeat with the right leg. Work up to three sets of 10 to 12 reps.

Back Diagonal

Begin on all fours with knees below hips and hands below shoulders *(right)*. Without shifting your torso, reach forward with your right hand and point your left foot to the rear. Do not let your hip or shoulder sag, move forward or move back *(below)*. Return to the starting position. Reach forward with your left hand and point back with your right toe, maintaining the same posture *(inset opposite)*. Work up to three sets of 10 repetitions of this sequence.

Diagonal Back Lift

Lie flat on your stomach with your hands stretched in front of your slightly lifted head *(left)*. Slowly raise your extended right arm and left leg, toes pointed, as high as possible without twisting your torso *(below)*. Lower and repeat with the other arm and leg *(inset opposite)*. Work up to three sets of 10 repetitions.

CHAPTER 14

The Upper Body

Developing broad shoulders,
a taut chest and well-shaped arms
—the right way

To most of us not well versed in anatomy, the biceps, triceps and pectorals are probably the best known muscles in the body. They, along with the deltoids and trapezius of the shoulder and the latissimus dorsi of the back, are the muscles associated with a classic physique. Yet studies show that the upper body suffers the most neglect. People who make the effort to do something about their waistlines may be unable to do a single push-up. Typically, women are especially weak in upper body strength, with weakness along the back of the upper arm a common problem. And men whose biceps are firm from regular use may have weak and essentially shapeless muscles in their shoulders, chest and back.

Precisely because they are often the most neglected, the muscles in the upper body often respond most noticeably to conditioning, and the results can be impressive. That this area generally stores less fat than other areas also makes the results of strength training appear more readily.

The illustration on the next page shows how these muscles shape your upper body. At the back of your shoulders and neck, and descending between your shoulder blades, is the trapezius. It draws your head back, rotates your head and shrugs your shoulders. The deltoids shape the tops and sides of the shoulders. They lift your arms to the side, help raise them above your head, and swing them forward and back. The biceps, the familiar two-headed muscle in your upper arm, flexes the elbow and lifts your forearm. The three-part triceps, covering most of the back of your upper arm, opposes the biceps to extend the elbow, thereby straightening the arm.

Your chest and back are shaped by much larger muscles. The pectoralis major, the big muscle

Upper Body

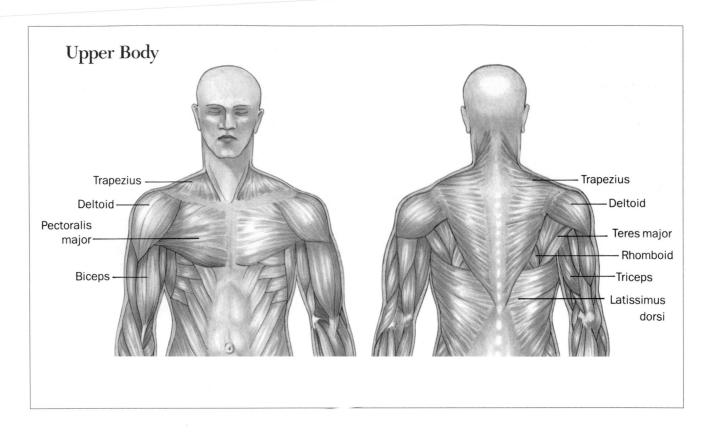

Trapezius
Deltoid
Pectoralis major
Biceps

Trapezius
Deltoid
Teres major
Rhomboid
Triceps
Latissimus dorsi

of your chest, moves your arms front and center and gives you force to push. The latissimus dorsi covers a broad portion of your back. Although activities like chopping wood or swinging a pick-ax work this muscle, it is generally underexercised, and its weakness often contributes to shoulder problems. The teres major and the rhomboids, which act on the shoulder blade, also frequently suffer from disuse and from being forced into the hunched-over position associated with sitting at a desk all day.

Exercising these muscles produces notable improvements in appearance as well as strength. Developing the latissimus dorsi, for example, gives definition to your middle back and strengthens your pulling power. It is the latissimus dorsi that produces a V-shaped torso, which you can accentuate with broader-looking shoulders by working the deltoids. For firming the upper arm, many people concentrate on the biceps, the muscle in front. But the triceps in the back of the upper arm also enhances definition, and since that muscle generally gets little work

from day-to-day routines, it often responds quickly to exercise training.

A toned chest, a result of working the pectorals, improves the appearance of both sexes. Women may notice that pectoral exercises make their breasts look firmer and higher as they receive better support from underlying tissue. Strengthening your upper body muscles will also enhance your posture. Toned muscles hold your head more erect, lift your upper chest and draw your shoulders down and back. And both men and women will find that any number of daily tasks, from carrying groceries to opening heavy doors, become easier.

Women worry needlessly that they will overdevelop muscles from working their upper bodies. For muscle to bulk up heavily, high levels of testosterone, a male sex hormone, are required. Although women's bodies do produce testosterone, it is in minute quantities. Men who do not wish to look like power lifters can also relax: The exercises in this chapter do not lead to excessive muscle growth.

Because people differ in their strength and their goals, this chapter contains a wide range of exercises. In addition to helping you avoid the tedium of performing the same routine, variety is necessary for dealing with the complexity of the upper body. Many people will choose to start their routines with the push-up (pages 348-349). This versatile exercise, which requires little or no equipment, combines work for shoulders, chest and arms, and has variations that may be used to emphasize the triceps, deltoids or pectorals. In addition, abdominal muscles, gluteals and leg extensors must work hard to hold your body rigid for the push-up.

You should pair any pushing exercise with a pulling exercise to prevent imbalances that put weaker muscles in jeopardy. Good exercises to oppose the push-up are the dip (pages 356-357) or the chin-up, which may also be done as a bent-arm hang (pages 370-371). Both help strengthen a weak latissimus dorsi. The chin-up also works the major flexors of the elbow, including the biceps, while the dip works the triceps harder. You can also do pulling exercises with weights in a bent-over position (pages 360-361).

In upper body work, you may train either the latissimus dorsi or the pectorals of the chest first, since both are large muscles. Bench presses and bench flys (pages 358-359) target the pectorals if you want to intensify or concentrate on chest work. The lift to the front with the weight bar (which may also be performed with dumbbells) is a good choice for combining chest and shoulder work (pages 366-367).

It is particularly important in working this part of the body to maintain your position as you perform the exercises. Leaning forward and backward when doing curls, for instance, not only makes the exercise easier and hence less effective by dividing the work among a number of bigger muscles, but it may also cause undue back strain. And if you "cheat" by not performing exercises through the full range of motion, you may deprive yourself of flexibility.

The Push-Up

Push-ups can quickly strengthen shoulders, arms and chest. Using the weight of your body for resistance, this classic exercise overloads the front deltoids, pectorals and triceps. Moreover, push-ups work abdominal and back muscles, which stabilize your body and keep it rigid during the exercise. Even your legs and buttocks get a workout.

In addition to quick, effective strengthening, adaptability is one of the push-up's advantages. No matter how strong or weak you are, one of the variations here and on the following six pages will help develop strength. And by shifting to different positions, you can use push-ups to concentrate the work on your deltoids, pectorals or triceps.

The push-up is not an easy exercise. Many women cannot initially do one full push-up, and men who do not exercise their upper bodies regularly may also have trouble. But after having practiced the modified push-up shown here until you can do 20 without pause, you should be able to master the classic push-up shown on the following two pages. If even the modified version is too taxing, do the exercise while standing up and leaning against a wall. Increase the angle and the number of repetitions until you can switch to the floor. Later you can vary the push-up to increase its intensity or to focus on muscles you want to target.

Do the modified push-up on your knees with your hands underneath your shoulders and your ankles crossed. Keep your torso straight as you lower your chest to the floor (*inset*) and push back up. Do not lock your elbows in the up position (*right*).

The Classic Push-Up

To concentrate work on the front of your shoulders, balance your weight between your hands (placed under shoulders) and your toes, which are flexed. Align your body so that it is straight *(below)*. Keep it rigid as you lower your chest to the floor *(left)*. Do not rest between push-ups or lock your elbows.

To work on your chest, space your hands widely, point your fingers straight ahead and hold your elbows close to your body *(top right)*. A close-grip push-up shapes and tones triceps faster *(bottom right)*.

The Deltoid Push-Up

By bringing the weight of your torso to bear on your shoulders, this push-up tones the deltoids and also firms the trapezius. Make your body into a bridge, bending at the hip and dividing your weight between your hands and toes. Keep your elbows slightly bent even when you are fully raised *(left)*. Keep your body bent at the same angle as you slowly lower yourself toward the floor *(above)*.

The Raised Push-Up

Place arm lifters at a right angle to each other and spaced slightly wider than your shoulders *(below)*. Lower yourself as far as you can without bending your body *(above)*.

When doing push-ups with your feet lifted, maintain rigidity in your back as you lift and lower *(below and bottom)*, but do not hyperextend your elbows. The higher you raise your feet, the more weight shifts onto your upper body, intensifying the effort. Similarly, by allowing you to descend lower, lifters — or any sturdy, untippable hand supports — intensify work for your arms, back and chest. The ultimate upper body builder is a handstand push-up done against a wall. But most people will find the versions shown here sufficiently challenging.

The Dip

An extremely effective exercise that requires limited equipment, the dip focuses effort on the rear deltoids, lower pectorals, triceps, lower trapezius and latissimus—important shapers of the shoulders, arms, chest and back. Like the push-up, the dip uses body weight to overload muscles that do not usually have to provide much body support. When performing the dip, use a weight bench, a stool or a sturdy well-balanced chair.

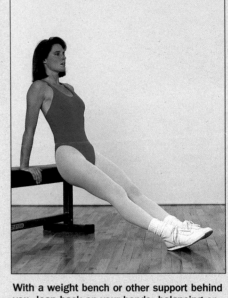

With a weight bench or other support behind you, lean back on your hands, balancing on your heels. Keep your shoulders down, the top of your chest up and your back straight. Bend your arms and lower yourself without letting your shoulders rise toward your ears *(left)*. Extend your arms to push yourself back up *(above)*.

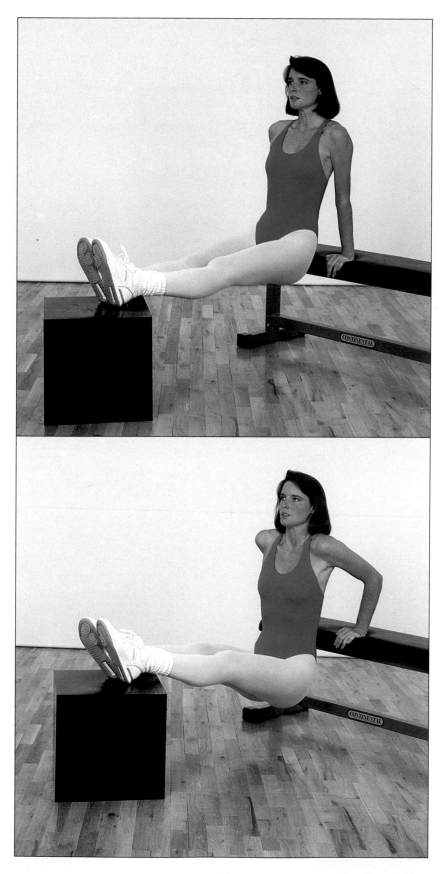

Elevating your feet for dips adds lower body weight to the exercise, making it harder. Lean on your hands and place your heels on the support *(top left)*. Dip without allowing your shoulders to rise *(bottom left)*, then push back up.

Small Weights

Using small weights lets you work isolated muscles better than exercises that rely on body weight alone. You can, for instance, isolate the triceps to firm the back of your arms. Concentration curls target your biceps. Three- to five-pound weights work well for most women, though many will want heavier loads for bench and military presses and for upright and bent-over rows. Most men will prefer seven- to 10-pound dumbbells for flys, curls and single weight lifts, but may want to use heavier weights in the same exercises as women.

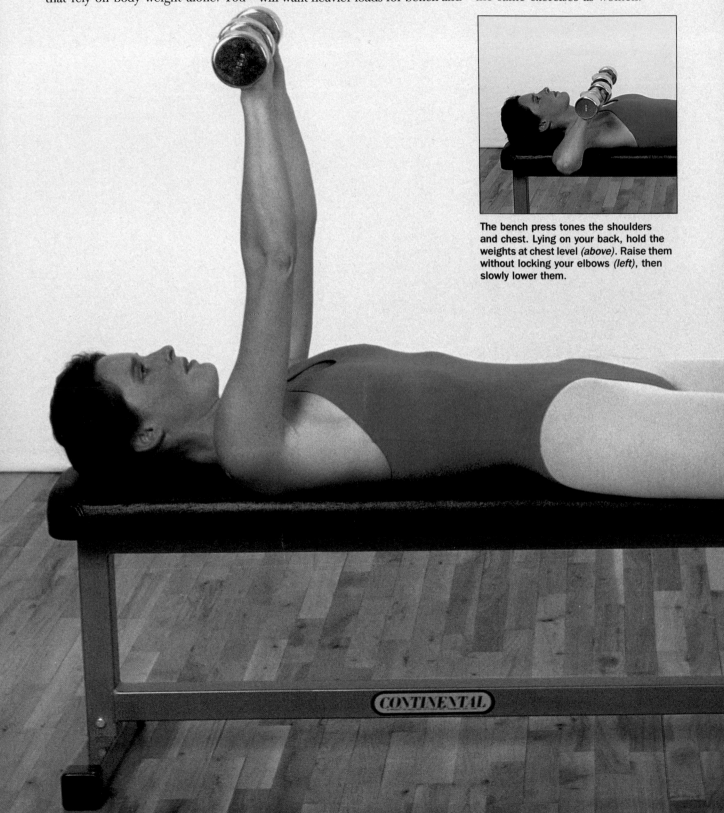

The bench press tones the shoulders and chest. Lying on your back, hold the weights at chest level *(above)*. Raise them without locking your elbows *(left)*, then slowly lower them.

Bench flys, shown at right, isolate the pectorals, the major muscles that shape the chest. Hold your arms out to your sides, forming a cross *(top left)*. Keep your elbows slightly bent and your back flat on the bench. Lift the weights through a semicircular arch until they are side by side above your chest *(top right)*. Breathe evenly throughout the work. To isolate your triceps, grasp both ends of a single dumbbell and hold it several inches behind your head so that your forearms form a right angle *(middle left)*. Raise the weight until it is high over your chest *(middle right)*. To exercise your latissimus dorsi, thereby shaping your back and sides, hold one end of a dumbbell in both hands and extend it as as far as you can beyond the top of your head *(bottom left)*. Slowly raise the dumbbell until it is over your chest *(bottom right)*. Keep your elbows unlocked.

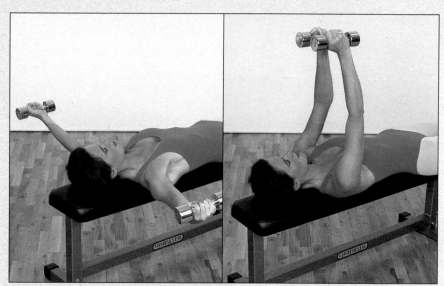

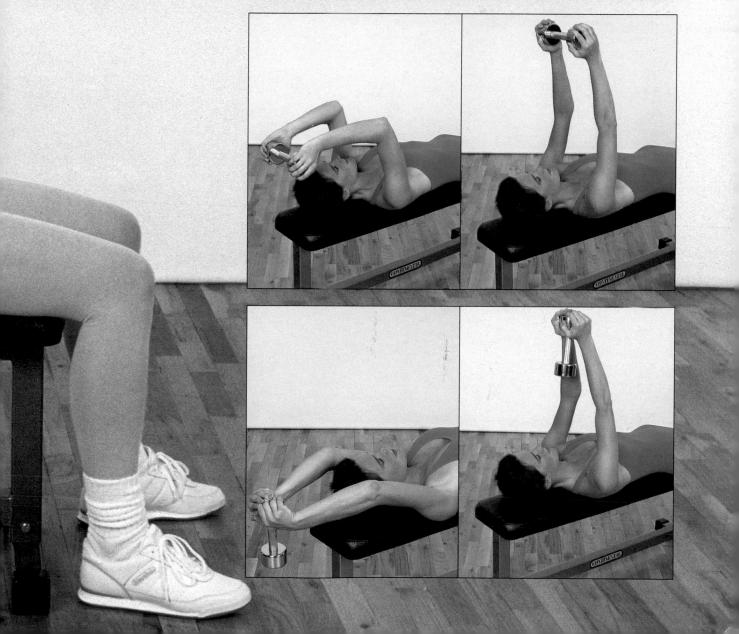

Bent-Over Lifts

To do a bent-over row, which will firm your latissimus, trapezius, rhomboid and biceps, bend your knees and lean forward at the hip. Keep your back straight and buttocks high. Let the weights hang down, but keep your elbows slightly bent *(left)*. Lift weights straight up *(below)*.

Single rows *(below and bottom)* stabilize your body, focus the effort on one side and protect the lower back. Bend over with your knee and hand on a weight bench.

Do single-arm flys for latissimus, triceps and trapezius by supporting your knee and hand on a bench. Start with the weight in the bent arm at the side of your chest *(above)*. Extend arm to the rear *(left)*.

With your back straight, knees bent and buttocks high, do bent-over double flys, which concentrate work on the latissimus. Let weights hang easily below your shoulders *(far left)*, then slowly lift up and to the rear *(near left)*.

Standing Lifts

Upright rowing works the shoulders, biceps and forearms. Stand with your feet slightly farther apart than your shoulders *(below)*. Lean forward slightly to avoid arching your back. Hold weights at thigh level. Then slowly lift them straight up the front of your torso as far as your collarbone *(left)*.

To do a lateral raise, stand with the same relaxed good posture as described opposite, but with dumbbells parallel to each other *(below left)*. Slowly lift out to the sides to focus work on the deltoids *(below right)*. Keep your elbows slightly bent.

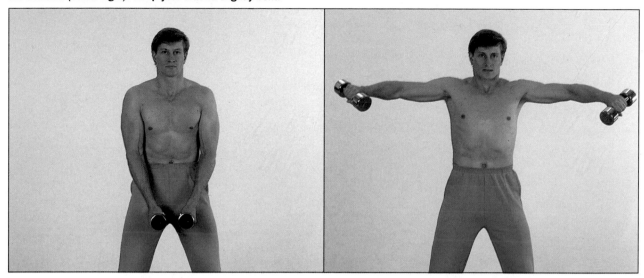

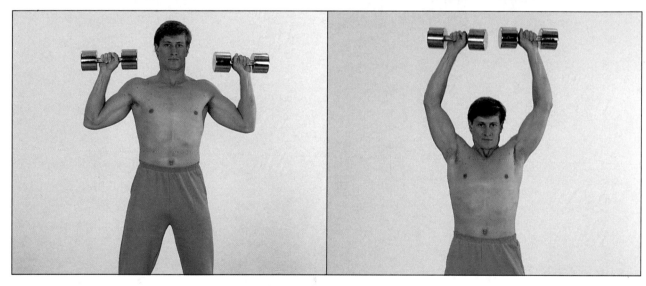

For the military press, hold the dumbbells horizontally a few inches above your shoulder *(above left)*. Slowly raise them straight up without locking your elbows or arching your lower back *(above right)*.

Biceps and Triceps Lifts

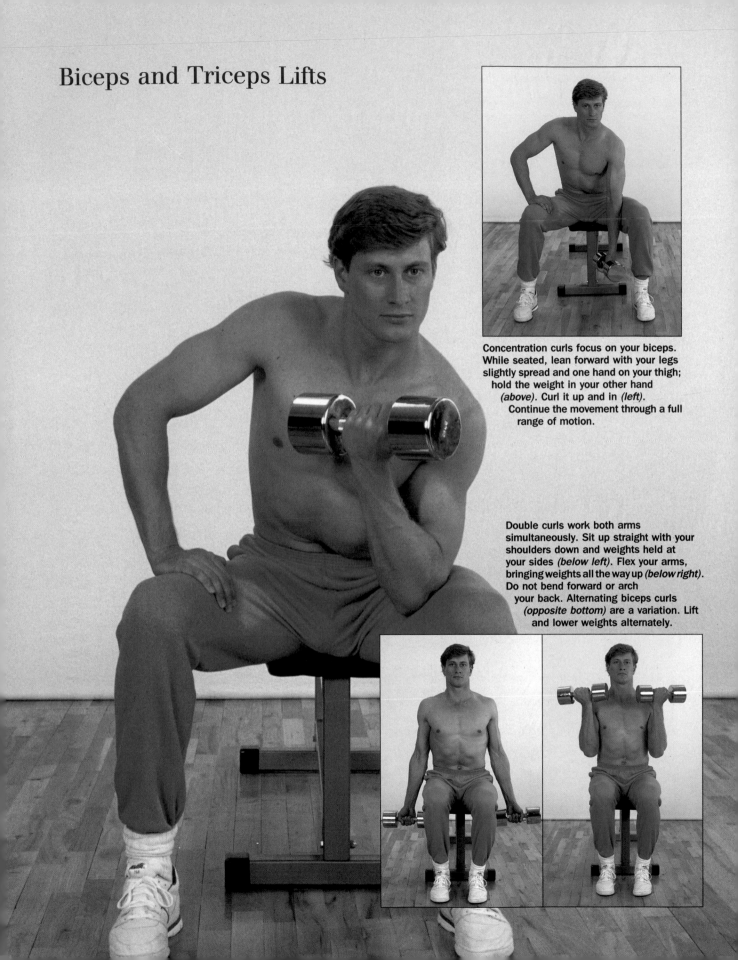

Concentration curls focus on your biceps. While seated, lean forward with your legs slightly spread and one hand on your thigh; hold the weight in your other hand *(above)*. Curl it up and in *(left)*. Continue the movement through a full range of motion.

Double curls work both arms simultaneously. Sit up straight with your shoulders down and weights held at your sides *(below left)*. Flex your arms, bringing weights all the way up *(below right)*. Do not bend forward or arch your back. Alternating biceps curls *(opposite bottom)* are a variation. Lift and lower weights alternately.

Isolate your triceps. While straddling a bench with your back straight, fold your arms over your head. Hold the end of the dumbbell in one hand and use the other hand to steady the weight-bearing arm *(above)*. Raise your arm without locking your elbow *(right)*.

Bar Lifts/1

A weighted bar — the standard one is 15 pounds — helps overload upper body muscles, efficiently working many muscles together, and it can be used in place of dumbbells for several exercises. You may also find it easier to balance.

Work the entire shoulder muscle with this lift. Start with the weight bar held parallel to shoulders with palms facing out *(above)*. Lift slowly over your head *(near right)* and to the rear of your head *(far right)*. Return to the first position.

Do upright rowing for shoulders and upper chest with your feet placed slightly wider than your shoulders and the bar held in front of your thighs *(below)*. Your palms should be in, your elbows slightly bent. Lift the bar straight up your torso to your collarbone *(right)*. Do not arch your back.

Bar Lifts/2

Work front deltoids and upper pectorals with a forward lift while seated. Hold the bar at neck level with palms facing forward *(below left)*. Extend your arms out and up so the bar is slightly above your head *(below right)*.

Do a behind-the-head press to focus on rear deltoids and trapezius. Start with the bar at neck level and your hands spaced far apart *(bottom left)*; lift straight up *(bottom right)*. Be sure that you do not lock your elbows.

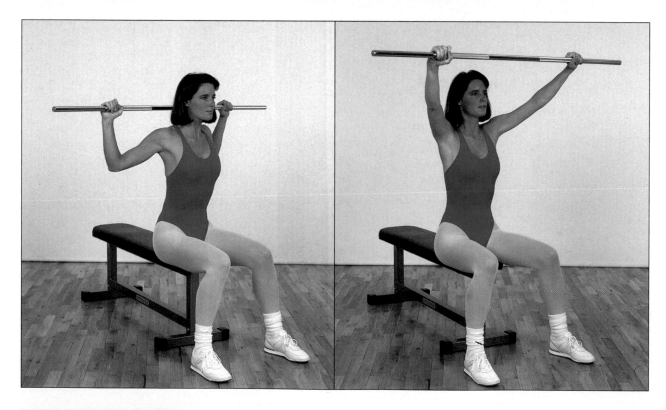

Bent-over rows with a weight bar work the latissimus, triceps, biceps and rhomboids. Bend your knees and lean forward at the hip *(below)*. Keep your back straight and buttocks lifted. Raise the bar straight up, close to your chest *(left)*.

Do standard chin-ups with your palms facing toward you *(left)*. Be sure to lift all the way up to collarbone level. Turn your palms out *(above)* to work your forearms harder, your biceps less hard.

Chinning

With a chinning bar, you can use your entire weight for upper body resistance. The chin-up quickly gives muscles an intense workout. A chin-up requires so much strength, however, that most women and some men will have to work up to it. But even the easiest version, the supported bent-arm hang, can give you a good workout, and you can stay with it if you find it sufficiently intense. (To increase strength and tone, you can extend the time you hang.)

A bent-arm hang with your legs supported is the easiest way to work the chinning bar. Place your feet or calves on a stable object to support part of your weight *(below)*. Hold the bar with palms in, elbows bent. Hang in this position for 30 seconds or as long as you comfortably can. Rest 30 seconds and repeat. When you can do this easily, chin yourself with your legs supported.

A bent-arm hang with legs free is the next level of difficulty. Grasp the bar with your palms facing in and your elbows bent slightly. Lift your legs and hang for as long as you can *(above)*. Work up to 45 seconds; when you can hang for that long, try a full chin-up.

CHAPTER 15

Exercising with Machines

Strengthening and shaping muscles with variable resistance

In recent years, many fitness enthusiasts have come to prefer working out in health clubs, commercial gyms and fitness centers. Such establishments have grown in number—there are an estimated 14,000 in the United States—as well as in the kinds of facilities they provide. Of course, going to a club or gym cannot match the convenience of exercising at home, but a club is likely to have machines that are too bulky or expensive for most homes. Machines to build strength come in a variety of sizes and designs, and new models appear constantly. At many health clubs, though, the most popular machines are likely to be referred to as variable resistance machines. These include machines made by Nautilus, a widely recognized maker, and similar machines from other manufacturers. Because muscles and bones function as levers, a given weight on a barbell or dumbbell may be easier to move when your joint is in one position and harder to move in another position. The position in which a weight feels heaviest is called the sticking point. In order to exercise a muscle through its full range of motion with free weights, you need to select a weight that is light enough for you to move it through its sticking point. By doing so, however, the muscle is stressed with less than maximum resistance through much of its range of motion, and your strength gains may take longer. Variable resistance machines have been designed to compensate automatically for a muscle's changes in strength by utilizing cams or levers to vary the resistance, keeping it at maximum throughout the full range of motion (see box, page 374). Furthermore, by maintaining your body in a particular position and by making you move a weight along a predetermined path, the machines apply

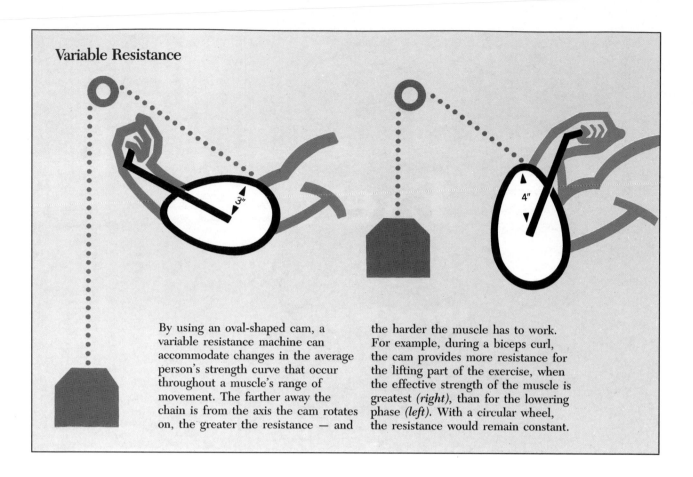

Variable Resistance

By using an oval-shaped cam, a variable resistance machine can accommodate changes in the average person's strength curve that occur throughout a muscle's range of movement. The farther away the chain is from the axis the cam rotates on, the greater the resistance — and the harder the muscle has to work. For example, during a biceps curl, the cam provides more resistance for the lifting part of the exercise, when the effective strength of the muscle is greatest *(right)*, than for the lowering phase *(left)*. With a circular wheel, the resistance would remain constant.

resistance directly to the muscle being worked, isolating that muscle more efficiently than is usually possible with free weights.

Whether training on variable resistance machines develops strength faster or to a greater degree than working with free weights has yet to be established. Both methods of training have produced positive results, and it may be that certain machines are more efficient than others, which may also be true of certain barbell exercises; however, machines do offer some advantages. For people beginning a weight-training program, machines are usually easier to work with and safer to use than free weights. This is because the machines are designed to utilize weighted plates held in place by pins that slide back and forth along a fixed path. You adjust the amount of weight for an exercise simply by inserting a pin at a particular point in the weight stack, rather than by having to load and unload weights onto a barbell. This frees you from wor-

rying about dropping a weight or maintaining your balance during an exercise. The use of pins also allows you to move quickly from machine to machine, so that you can complete your workout in 20 to 30 minutes.

Some advocates of machine training have claimed that, because machines are highly efficient, you can get the best workout by performing only one set of each exercise—and this single set should be intense enough to achieve momentary muscular failure on the last repetition. In other words, at the end of the set, your muscles should be so fatigued that they cannot move the weight through another repetition. To work this intensely, you will need to experiment to find the right amount of weight you need on each machine. But you will find that working to muscular failure can be difficult and even painful. Therefore, it is recommended that you take more time and perform two or three sets at 80 or 90 percent of your maximum ability.

If you are interested in using machines at a gym or health club, make sure that there is a sufficient variety to give you a full workout. You should be able to perform four to six exercises for the lower body and six to eight for the upper body. Machines should be arranged so that you can work larger muscles before smaller ones, since this is the desirable sequence for the most efficient workout. Your gains in strength will be greatest if you rest a few minutes between machines. By moving quickly, you may elevate your heart rate, but this kind of circuit training, typically, will not provide you with any true aerobic or endurance benefits.

The routine shown on the following pages is primarily on Nautilus machines, but many exercises on other brands of machines are similar. It is a good idea to have a trainer at your club show you how to adjust any machine you use to suit your height, physique and strength. Keep in mind that, while a machine steers you through the movement of an exercise, you must still observe good form to get the maximum benefit from this type of equipment.

As with free weights, you will need to experiment to find the proper amount of weight for each exercise. For the first five or six sessions, keep the weight at levels that you can lift comfortably for 12 to 15 repetitions. You can then select a heavier weight load that allows you to reach momentary muscular failure in one set. Or, if you do not wish to work to failure, adjust the weight so that you can perform 8 to 12 repetitions, stopping just short of failure, and perform each exercise for two to three sets.

For beginners and intermediates, three exercise sessions a week on machines are optimal, though many people will derive some benefit from working out twice a week. Be sure to rest at least 48 hours between workouts.

Training Techniques

Start your workout with a five-minute warm-up such as running in place. Then begin your machine circuit by conditioning the large muscles of the thighs, using a machine such as the one on these two pages, which works the quadriceps and hamstrings. You should then move on to the lower legs and the upper body.

On each machine, focus on the muscles you are exercising; do not grip the handles tightly, tense your face or overly contract other unengaged muscles. Be sure to move through the exercise in a deliberate, controlled manner; keep your body aligned and avoid twisting or shifting during the movement. In general, take two seconds to raise a weight

and four seconds to lower it, pausing slightly between the two movements.

Although on some machines it may take longer to move through the full range of motion, you should always move more slowly through the lowering phase than through the lifting phase. Exhale as you raise the weight; inhale as you lower it.

Sit in the leg extension machine with your back firmly against the base and with a folded towel behind your neck. Fasten the belt and place your feet behind the rollers *(below)*. Extend your right leg *(below right)*, pause briefly and return. Finish with one leg before you work the other.

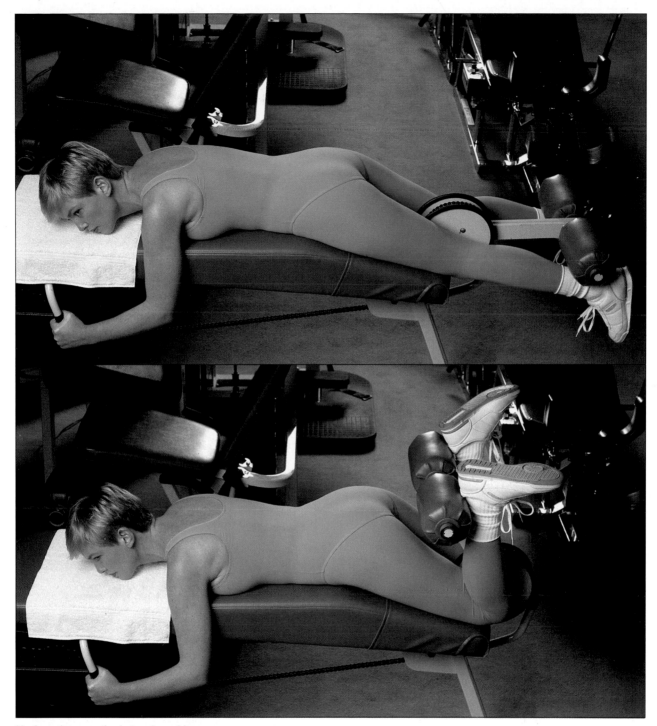

Lie face down on the leg curl machine, slip your feet under the rollers and grasp the handles lightly *(top)*. Draw the rollers toward your buttocks without raising your hips more than one or two inches *(above)*. Pause briefly and return.

Abductor and Adductor

To work your outer thighs, sit down in the abductor machine, place a folded towel behind your neck and lightly grasp the handles *(below)*. Using your thighs, not your ankles, press outward against the machine *(below right)*. Pause briefly and return to the starting position.

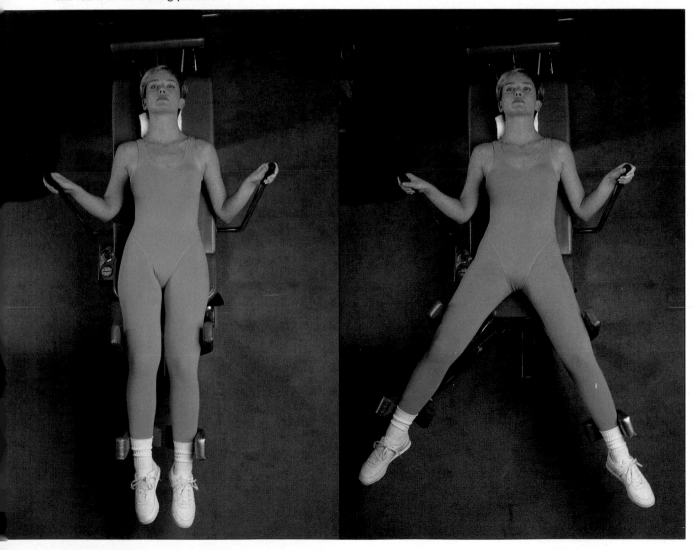

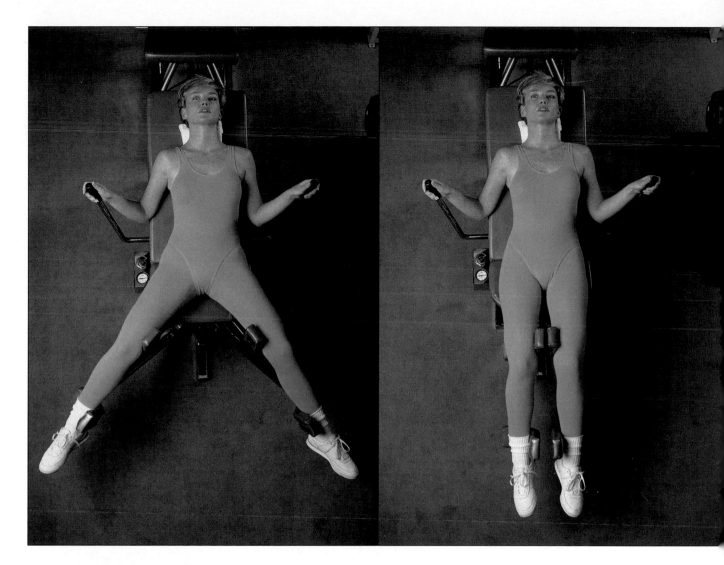

Sit in the adductor machine — which
works the inner thighs — with a towel
behind your neck *(above)*. Squeeze your
legs together, using only the force of your
thigh muscles to resist the force of the
machine *(above right)*. Pause briefly and
return to the starting position.

Multi-Exercise

To condition your calf muscles, attach the hip belt to the multi-exercise machine and adjust it around your waist. Grasp the handles and step onto the platform with the balls of your feet so that your heels drop *(right)*. Rise up on your toes as high as you can without leaning forward or backward *(inset)*. Hold for a second and return. Perform 15 to 20 repetitions of this exercise.

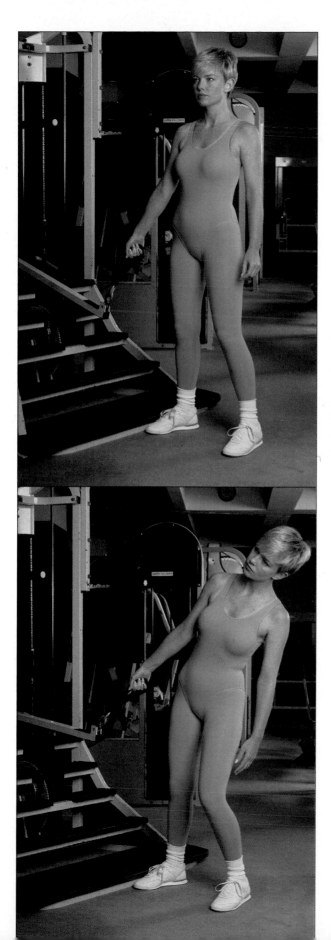

To work the oblique muscles in your sides, attach a hand grip to the multi-exercise machine. Hold the grip in your right hand and stand with your right side facing the machine, your feet about 12 inches apart *(left)*. Keep your right knee straight, bend your left knee and pull away with your body *(below left)*. Return to the starting position. Perform about 15 to 20 repetitions.

Lat Pull-Over

Sit in the lat pull-over machine, which conditions the latissimus dorsi muscles in your back. Tighten the belt and bring the crossbar into position by depressing the footplate *(left)*. Raise your arms over your head, place your elbows in the pads and rest your fingers lightly on the cross-bar *(below left)*. Release the footplate and slowly draw the crossbar down *(inset opposite)*. Be sure to push with your elbows, not your hands, as you draw the crossbar to your waist *(opposite)*. Pause briefly and return to the starting position.

Lat Pull-Down

Sit in the lat pull-down machine and fasten the belt. Reach up and pull the bar down, grip the handles and lean forward, keeping your elbows slightly bent *(inset opposite)*. Pull the bar behind your neck *(opposite)*. Pause briefly and return to the starting position.

An alternative lat pull-down machine has a padded leg brace to keep you in place. Sit down and slip your legs under the pads so that they hold your lower body firmly on the bench. Reach up and pull down the bar, gripping both handles and keeping your elbows slightly bent *(top right)*. Lean forward and pull the bar down behind your neck *(right)*. Pause briefly and return to the starting position.

Sit in a rowing torso machine to condition the muscles in your shoulders and upper back. Place your arms through the rollers and cross your forearms *(above left)*. Push back as far as you comfortably can and try to squeeze your shoulder blades together *(above right)*. Pause briefly and return to the starting position.

Rows and Raises

To strengthen the deltoid muscles in your shoulders, sit in a lateral raise machine and fasten the belt. Lightly grip the handle and push out and up with your elbows *(opposite top)*. Raise your elbows until your forearms are parallel to the floor *(opposite)*. Pause briefly and return to the starting position.

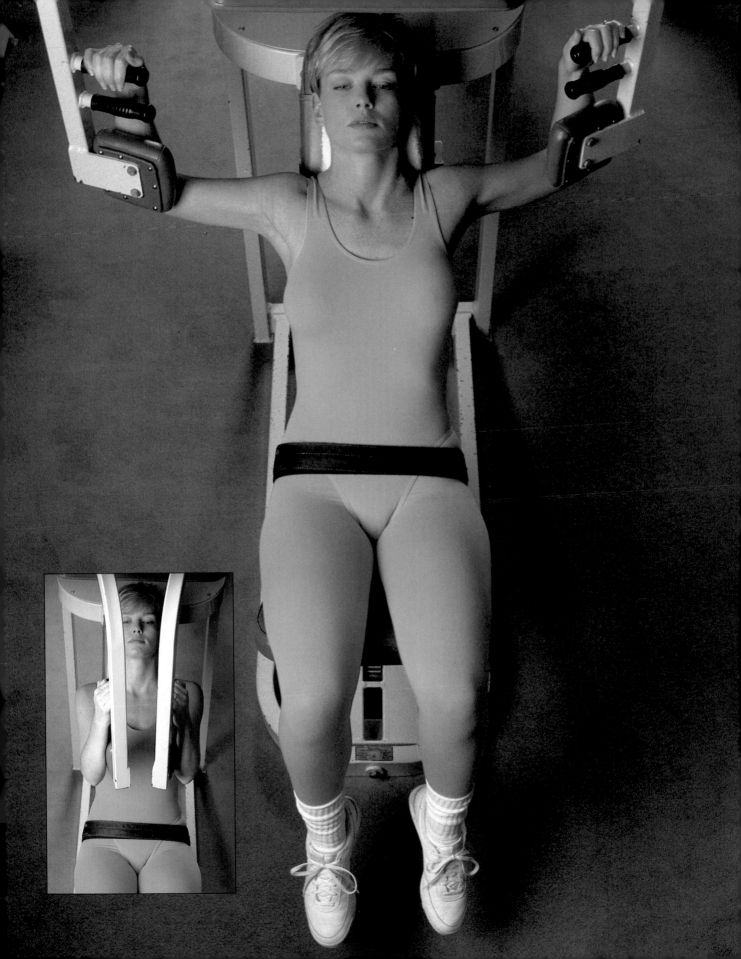

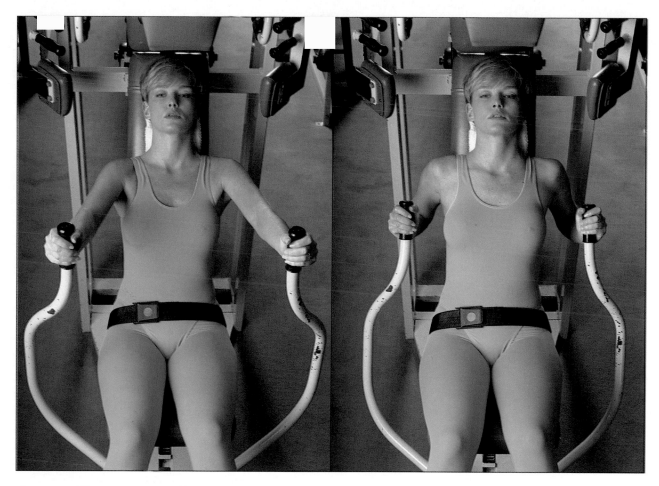

Arm Cross and Decline Press

To strengthen your chest and shoulder muscles, use the arm-cross machine. Place a towel behind your neck and fasten the belt. Place your forearms against the pads and hold the handles lightly *(opposite)*. Press with your forearms toward the center of your chest *(inset)*. Pause briefly and return to the starting position. A similar machine offers both the arm-cross exercise and a decline press. Complete a set of arm-cross repetitions first, then perform the decline press. Place your feet on the footplate and push the handles into position. Grasp the handles, release the footplate and push the handles forward *(above)*. Pause briefly, then allow the levers to move back slowly until you feel a stretch in your chest muscles *(above right)*.

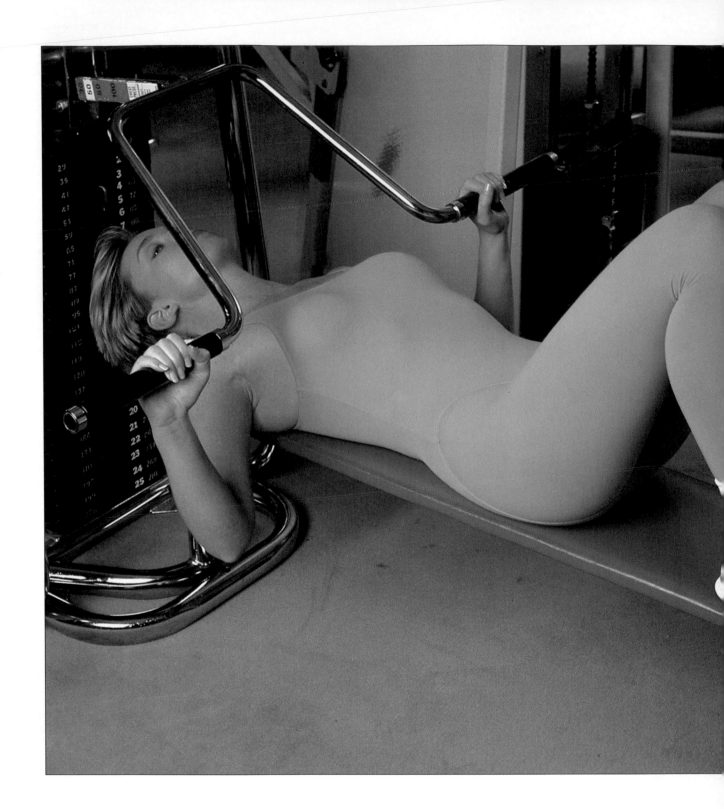

Bench Press

Use a bench-press machine to condition your pectorals, deltoids and triceps; the wider your grip is, the more you will emphasize your pectorals. Lie down with your knees bent and your feet flat on the bench. Place a towel behind your neck and grasp the handles *(left)*. Apply pressure to the handles so that the weights begin to lift off the weight stack *(below left)*. Press the handles up and extend your arms without locking your elbows *(below right)*. Pause briefly and return to the starting position.

Triceps and Biceps

Sit on the triceps machine, place your elbows on the pad and your hands in the grip, palms facing in *(top)*. The seat should be adjusted so that your shoulders are slightly lower than your elbows. Extend your arms together, but do not lock your elbows *(above)*. Pause briefly and return to the starting position.

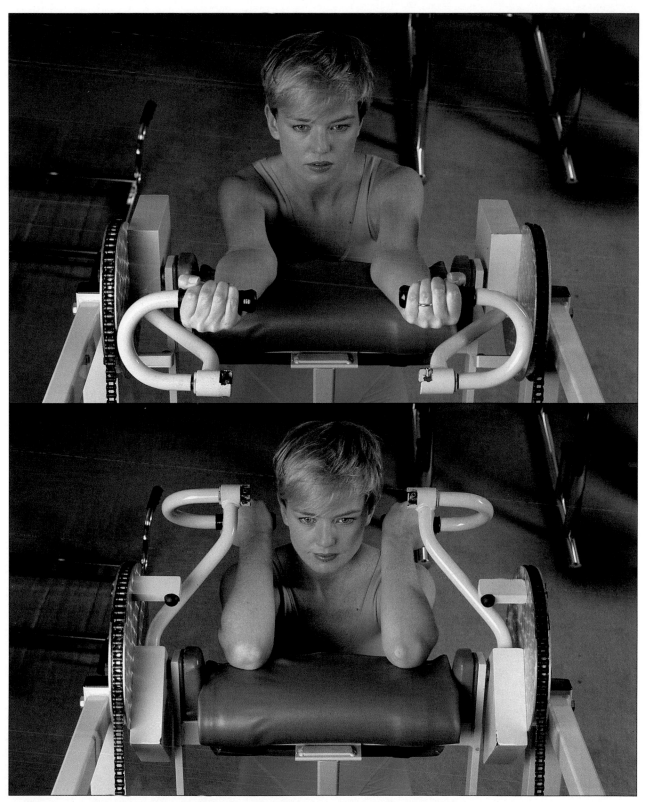

Straddle the biceps machine, place your elbows on the pad, grip the handles and pull them halfway up. Then sit and lower the handles until your elbows are slightly bent *(top)*. Curl the handles back together until your hands just about touch your ears *(above)*. Pause briefly and return to the starting position.

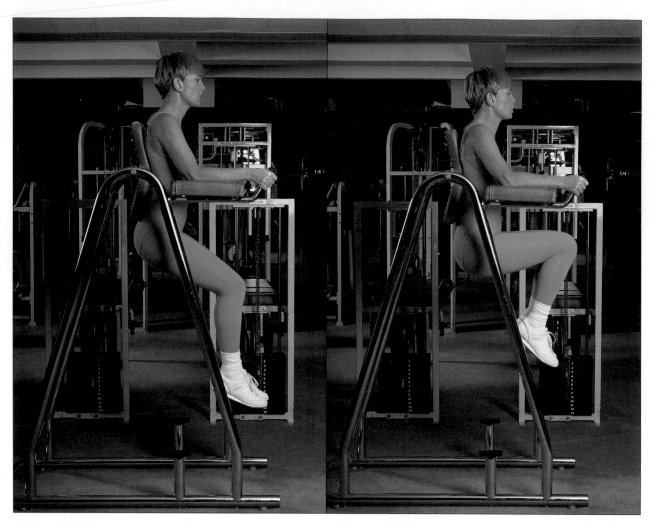

Hip Flexors and
Lower Back

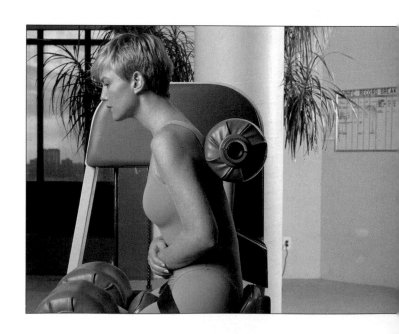

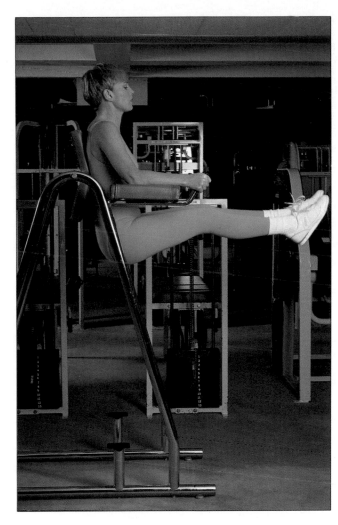

If you have had back pain, do not perform this or the exercise below. Stop doing either exercise if it causes any back pain. Step up in a hip-flexor apparatus, grip the handles, place your forearms on the pads and let your legs dangle. Draw up your knees slightly (far left). Raise your knees so that your thighs are parallel to the floor (center left). Pause briefly and return to the starting position. As an advanced exercise, keep your legs extended with your knees slightly bent. Raise your legs slowly until they are parallel to the floor (near left). Pause briefly and return to the starting position.

Sit straddling the lower back machine. Place your thighs under the rollers, attach the belt and cross your hands over your abdomen *(far left)*. Push against the pad until your back is straight, at about a 45-degree angle to your lower legs *(left)*. Do not arch your back. Pause briefly and return to the starting position.

PART 4

FITNESS ANYTIME, ANYWHERE

Making Time for Fitness

The 20-Minute Routine

Fitness Anywhere

CHAPTER 16

Making Time for Fitness

Preserving the benefits of exercise with routines that are efficient, comprehensive—and brief

Lack of time is the most common explanation that people offer for giving up an exercise program. They think that exercising requires setting aside inconveniently large blocks of time. But few people realize that, even if they do not have time for thorough workouts, they can stay fit with an abbreviated exercise routine.

Once you have achieved a moderate level of fitness, you can essentially maintain it despite a busy schedule. Even if you spend long hours working or caring for children, or if your work week is interrupted by business travel, there are exercises that you can do almost anywhere to keep in shape. And several studies indicate that exercisers whose regimens require little equipment and can be done at home, at work or nearby are more likely to stick with exercising than people whose routines are less convenient.

How is it possible to stay fit with relatively short exercise sessions?
The key is the intensity of each exercise—that is, how hard you exert yourself. By increasing the intensity, you can decrease the amount of time and the frequency you devote to an exercise—whether it be a set of push-ups or an aerobic activity such as running or swimming—and thus reap the benefits more rapidly.

Although quick routines are most useful for those times when your usual exercise schedule is disrupted—when traveling, for example, or working extra hours—you can perform an abbreviated workout if you have only limited time to devote to exercise. Keep in mind, though, that people who let their exercise training lapse completely may have to reestablish the benefits they have lost, which demands much more time and energy than maintaining fitness.

Do quick routines provide a total fitness regimen?

A 20-minute session does not constitute a complete fitness program. So, for maximum results, each session should be devoted either to aerobic or strength exercises, but not both. And each type of exercise should be accompanied by stretches for flexibility and an easy cardiorespiratory warm-up.

Most exercise experts believe that while strength, flexibility and aerobic training are all crucial for total fitness, aerobic exercise is the most important. If your time is severely restricted, you should devote all or most of your workouts to vigorous aerobic activities such as running, walking, cycling and swimming. But whenever possible, you should arrange a schedule that allows you to switch between aerobics and strength exercises on alternate days, or to squeeze two quick workouts—one aerobic, the other for strength—into one 40-minute exercise session three times a week.

Can you really get an effective aerobic workout in only 20 minutes?

The effectiveness of a short workout depends in part on how fit you already are. If you are out of shape, you should exercise aerobically for 30 minutes at least three times a week to increase your cardiorespiratory fitness level. Such a workout begins with a five-minute warm-up and concludes with five minutes of cool-down and stretching. According to recent findings by exercise physiologists, working out less than this produces little or no training effect in unconditioned individuals. However, even without fitness benefits, there can be health benefits conferred by a minimal amount of exercise—a little is better than none.

Once you have achieved an acceptable level of cardiorespiratory fitness, which generally takes two to six months for someone who is healthy but has not exercised consistently, you can maintain it with less exercise. In one study, aerobically fit subjects were able to stay in shape by exercising every third day. In another study, exercising just twice a week was sufficient to maintain aerobic capacity in a group of fit subjects. In that same study, exercising even once a week was found to help slow the decline of cardiorespiratory fitness, although a weekly workout was insufficient to maintain fitness at optimal levels. Other research shows that endurance training at low intensity less frequently than twice a week and for less than 10 minutes per session is inadequate for fitness maintenance.

It takes less time to maintain fitness than to build it. One study examined subjects who had been training three times a week to build cardiorespiratory fitness—as measured by VO2max. When the subjects cut back their training, those who worked out twice a week were able to maintain their fitness gains. The once-a-week group showed a 40 percent loss in aerobic capacity in 10 weeks but were still in better shape than the nonexercisers, who dropped back to the fitness levels they had before training.

If you are out of shape, will quick workouts offer any benefit?

For people who exercise rarely or not at all, short but frequent bouts of aerobic exertion can improve fitness somewhat. In one study, for example, sedentary subjects were able to increase their aerobic capacity by about 15 percent in three months by running in place for just 10 minutes a day.

Nevertheless, it requires more effort to get into shape than it does to maintain fitness once you have achieved it. Most exercise experts advise people who are unfit to undertake an exercise program slowly but steadily. The program should gradually become more demanding, so that you reach your optimal level of cardiorespiratory conditioning over a period of months.

Brief aerobic workouts must be performed at a relatively high level of intensity (measured in terms of heart rate) to be beneficial. Unfit individuals should not start exercising at such levels.

Studies show that engaging abruptly or sporadically in any vigorous activity—shoveling snow, for example—may increase the risk of heart attack in sedentary people, particularly those with unidentified coronary problems. Being out of shape also increases the likelihood of muscle or joint injury during an intense workout. Therefore, quick workouts are best suited for maintaining fitness in those who have already established a reasonable level of fitness.

If you stop exercising, how quickly will you lose aerobic fitness?

The benefits acquired over months or years do not vanish overnight when an exercise program is interrupted, but the effects of aerobic conditioning are definitely reversible. A number of studies have found that VO_2max, a measure of aerobic fitness that reflects the maximum volume of oxygen the body can use per minute of intense exercise, drops by up to 10 to 15 percent after two weeks without aerobic exercise. After 4 to 12 weeks of not exercising—which physiologists refer to as detraining—participants in one study experienced a marked drop in VO_2max.

Scientists believe that this loss of cardiorespiratory conditioning varies from person to person. And the speed at which your fitness drops off during a slack period also depends on how well trained you were when you gave up exercising: If two people stop exercising for the same amount of time, the person who was fit for only a few days or weeks will drop to a lower level of fitness, as measured in VO_2max, than someone who had been fit for a year or more. Still, researchers note that even a highly trained athlete who stops working out will, over the course of several months, lose the fitness gains that he or she had achieved through training.

How long does it take to regain aerobic fitness?

It takes about as long to retrain your cardiorespiratory system as it takes to become aerobically fit in the first place. There is apparently no transfer of fitness benefits from one training period to the next if a significant period of detraining has intervened. A study of students who had increased their aerobic capacity during seven weeks of training, for example, showed that seven additional weeks without exercise decreased their aerobic capacity to within 3 percent of their pretraining levels. Afterward, it took them another seven weeks to regain the fitness level they had lost. Clearly, it is much more efficient to use brief exercise sessions to maintain fitness than to stop exercising until detraining has become almost complete.

The best way to stay motivated is to set aside time for exercise within an existing framework of activity. A Gallup poll showed that people who find the time to exercise regularly tend to squeeze it into their schedules, rather than altering their routines by getting up earlier or otherwise changing their lives.

Are strength and flexibility lost as easily as aerobic fitness?

Only a few studies have been done on strength retention. These suggest that it takes longer to lose strength and flexibility than it does to lose aerobic capacity; one study found that, without strength-building exercise, muscular power underwent a slow, steady decline resulting in a 35 percent loss in five weeks.

Similarly, maintaining muscle strength is less time-consuming than maintaining aerobic fitness. In fact, in an experiment using isometric exercises (described on the next page), participants needed to exercise just once every other week to maintain the gains they had attained during a previous daily training regimen.

The data on flexibility are scant, but many exercise scientists believe that muscles and joints deprived of exercise grow less flexible.

What is the quickest way to build strength?

Isometric, or static, exercises, in which you contract muscles against a fixed resistance, such as a wall, take only a few seconds to perform. More-over, they require no equipment and are inconspicuous enough to be done anytime, anywhere. An isometric workout can substantially boost your muscle strength. In one study, subjects using isometrics increased the power of a hand muscle by an average of 51 percent, compared to a 19 percent gain among subjects doing another type of strengthening exercise. The gains from isometrics are also easy to maintain: Most experts say that working out isometrically once a week is enough for maintenance, and one study found that doing isometric contractions for two seconds every two weeks was sufficient.

Isometric exercises are quick: You can strengthen and tone a muscle by contracting it against a stationary object—like a shelf or a wall—for just six seconds. But there are limitations. In one study, subjects performed an isometric contraction with their arms at a 170-degree angle. After six weeks, their muscle strength had increased by 18 percent, but only when measured with the arm at the same 170-degree angle. When arm strength was measured with the elbow flexed at 90 degrees, the gain was only 5 percent.

Isometric exercise is not without its drawbacks, however. Most important, muscular development achieved by isometrics occurs only at the specific angle within a joint's range of motion at which force is applied. Therefore, to gain strength uniformly, even within the same muscle group, you must perform isometric contractions at four or five angles throughout the joint's range of motion. Even though each contraction takes only a few seconds, having to repeat it in a number of positions obviously prolongs your workout. In addition, researchers have found that blood pressure tends to shoot up during and just after an isometric contraction. Physicians therefore warn heart patients and anyone with high blood pressure to avoid isometrics, as well as other strenuous strengthening exercises like weight lifting, without prior consultation.

Do quick exercise sessions yield long-term health benefits?

One of the most comprehensive longevity studies ever undertaken—a long-term survey of nearly 17,000 Harvard alumni by Dr. Ralph S. Paffenbarger, Jr. and his associates—revealed that even a moderate amount of physical activity, particularly when it has an aerobic component, made a difference. In his study, men who expended 500 to 1,000 calories a week—roughly the equivalent of walking 5 to 10 miles a week, or about 20 minutes a day—had a 22 percent lower risk of death than those who got no exercise (a group the researchers used as a benchmark for assigning a 100 percent risk of death).

Is there a best time of day to exercise?

Almost any time is fine, as long as it fits into your schedule. However, you should not exercise vigorously right after a meal, when your blood is at work absorbing nutrients from your food and therefore is not as readily available to flow to your exercising muscles or skin for thermo-regulation. Nor should you perform aerobic exercise right before going to bed, since such exercise stimulates the release of adrenaline, a hormone that may keep you awake.

Some evidence does suggest that people who exercise in the morning tend to stay with their exercise routines more consistently than those who work out at other times of day. And many corporate fitness program directors have found that the morning is virtually the only time when a busy person can fit exercise into his or her schedule, especially if the workday extends into the evening.

If you do not have time for even a quick exercise session, can other day-to-day activities help maintain fitness?

First of all, be honest with yourself. When you consider the fitness and health benefits conferred by exercise training—even modest amounts—you will likely reassess your priorities and make time for exercise.

Realize, too, that any vigorous physical activity will help you stay fit, whether it is part of a formal exercise program or connected with your job or leisure-time pursuits. Within the scope of your daily routine, there are many ways to create opportunities for developing your aerobic fitness as well as your strength and flexibility.

A primary requirement for deriving aerobic benefits is that you perform an activity at a pace that would burn 200 to 400 calories in an hour. You can accomplish this with activities usually considered to be exercise, like running or cycling, but raking leaves, shoveling snow, gardening or scrubbing a floor can be done vigorously enough to serve as exercise.

You can also develop or maintain strength with ordinary everyday tasks. Books and other objects can be used for dynamic strength exercises, or, if you have no items available that you can lift or move around, you can perform isometric exercises anywhere or at any time by simply opposing one part of your body with another or by pressing against an immovable object.

What can you do to keep in shape when you travel?

During the past few years, many businesses that cater to travelers have added facilities that make it easier to exercise while you are on the road. Many hotels now either offer exercise rooms and equipment or are affiliated with local health clubs that hotel guests can use. Even some airports have health clubs. In addition to providing guidebooks that include information on where to exercise, some hotels and motels will advise runners about safe routes; some even provide jogging maps with distances marked. You can inquire at your hotel about renting a bicycle or cross-country skis, or you can consult a local telephone directory. You can also use your hotel or motel room as a personal gym for quick workouts. The exercises in the following chapter are designed for this purpose.

Most of these quick routines also require little or no equipment. As a rule, you will need a pair of running or aerobic shoes, a T-shirt, shorts, a towel and, for some exercises, a table and chair.

CHAPTER 17

The 20-Minute Routine

A convenient total-body regimen

The effectiveness of a fitness program is often perceived as directly proportional to the amount of time spent exercising. But, in fact, you can maintain your level of fitness with exercise sessions that take only 20 minutes each. A thorough program should include exercises that strengthen and tone muscles as well as aerobic routines that benefit the heart and lungs. You can perform these two types of exercises on alternate days. Or you can combine them into one longer workout that you should perform two or, better yet, three days a week. And, whenever you perform strengthening or aerobic exercises, you should incorporate warm-ups, cool-downs and flexibility-enhancing movements.

The exercises shown in this chapter provide a workout that lasts 20 minutes. This workout focuses on strengthening and stretching all of the body's major muscle groups. It maximizes the benefits you can derive in 20 minutes and minimizes the equipment you need. A few of the exercises require light weights, for which you can substitute commonplace items like books. (Travelers may wish to use hollow weights that they can fill with water in their hotel rooms.) The only other equipment the exercises in this chapter call for are such readily available items as towels, tables and chairs.

The 20-minute workout includes warm-up and cool-down exercises. Many people, in an effort to save time, overlook or dispense with these two essential components. Warm-ups are meant to loosen inactive muscles gradually and increase their temperature without causing undue stress. When your muscles and joints are more pliable, the benefits you derive from strengthening exercises increase. Once your muscles and joints are warmed, their range of motion expands, and you can perform the exercises more effectively and with less chance for soreness or injury.

Cool-downs, on the other hand, keep your muscles from tightening up too quickly after you complete your workout. By keeping muscles loose, both warm-ups and cool-downs help prevent injuries. If you move stiff muscles too vigorously, they will not give easily. Eventually tears may form in the muscles or in the surrounding tendons that connect them to bone.

After completing the brief warm-up, you may begin the stretching and strengthening routine. The exercises first work the larger muscles of the lower body, further increasing blood circulation and preparing your body for the exercises that follow. The workout emphasizes the thighs, stomach and arms, which, in most people, are areas that require added flexibility and strength. Other benefits of this routine include improved coordination and reduced muscular tension.

Some of the exercises may improve your carriage and overall appearance by building up the muscles that contribute to correct posture. The push-ups and sit-ups included in the workout are among the best ways to strengthen your chest, upper arms, shoulders and abdomen. The workout demonstrates variations of these two exercises that range from moderately demanding to quite difficult. Choose the variation that is the most appropriate for your level of strength.

Interspersed with the strengthening exercises are stretches that will maintain the flexibility of the body areas being developed. During each stretch, you should push just to the point of resistance, relax slightly, then hold the stretch until the feeling of tightness diminishes, from 30 to 60 seconds. Do not attempt to stretch farther than you comfortably can. Stretching your leg muscles to the point where they begin to shake, for instance, could cause injury.

If you suddenly feel tired at any time during the 20-minute workout, stop and rest before you continue. Extreme fatigue may be a sign that you are exercising too strenuously and should slow your pace.

Breathe slowly and steadily as you perform the exercises. Avoid holding your breath during strengthening exercises, since this may produce large increases in blood pressure. Erratic changes in blood pressure may also occur after you've held your breath; when this happens, the blood flow to your brain suddenly slows, which will cause you to feel dizzy.

Aerobic activities are just as vital to your fitness as the strengthening exercises. Performing a 20-minute aerobic activity three times a week will not only maintain your cardiovascular fitness, but will also use calories more efficiently than any other form of exercise. The box on the following page suggests some ways to fit aerobic activities into your week.

Even though the exercise routine in this chapter is meant to save you time, you shouldn't rush through it. The program has been designed to give you full-body conditioning when you perform the exercises at an even pace—not at breakneck speed—for 20 minutes.

A 20-minute routine like the one shown here is not intended to replace longer, more intense workouts, but it can form the basis of an effective exercise program. If you have trouble finding a convenient time and place to exercise consistently, combining these essential activities into a quick, efficient routine will keep you feeling fit and in shape.

THE EASY ROAD TO FITNESS

Some recent studies suggest that you need to exercise for 30 minutes every day; others recommend exercising enough to expend a certain number of calories each week.

For instance, Dr. Ralph S. Paffenbarger's long-term study of Harvard alumni showed that those who expended about 2,000 extra calories per week in physical activity were healthier, had fewer heart attacks and lived longer than their more sedentary counterparts. A University of Minnesota study came up with 224 calories per day (1,568 per week) as the minimum number to expend in order to stay fit. And a recent study at the Institute for Aerobic Research in Dallas found that brisk walking for 30 to 60 minutes a day kept people healthy: that's the equivalent of using about 1,100 calories weekly at the low end, 2,250 at the high.

Of course, the benefits of simply not being sedentary are so great that all you have to do is be moderately active: In the Paffenbarger study, using even 500 to 1,000 extra calories per week was associated with a lower risk of death. But if you want to expend 1,500 to 2,000 calories a week, what would you have to do? The following plan is a sample: It shows activities that, when performed briskly, help expend a fair number of calories and also increase cardiorespiratory fitness. Caloric expenditure is calculated for a body weight of 150 pounds; for every 10 pounds lighter or heavier, subtract or add about 7 percent to the calories used.

This shouldn't be a particularly tough schedule. Spreading the activities over fewer days would be acceptable; so would doing different activities, whether jumping rope, playing tennis or hiking.

ACTIVITY	CALORIES
MONDAY	
Walking, brisk, to and from work, 30 minutes total	160
Stair climbing, 5 minutes	35
TUESDAY	
Cycling, stationary, 15 minutes (10 mph)	105
WEDNESDAY	
Walking, brisk, to and from work, 30 minutes total	160
THURSDAY	
30 minutes at gym:	
Stair climbing, fast, 10 minutes	85
Rowing, on machine, 10 minutes	65
Running, treadmill, 10 minutes	95

ACTIVITY	CALORIES
FRIDAY	
Swimming or basketball, 20 minutes	180
Cycling, 20 minutes	135
SATURDAY	
Walking, brisk, 30 minutes	160
Gardening, 20 minutes	110
Housecleaning, 20 minutes	80
SUNDAY	
Brisk walk, 15 minutes	80
Mowing lawn, 20 minutes	150
Raking grass and yard work, 20 minutes	135
Washing car, 20 minutes	65
GRAND TOTAL	**1,800** (IN ABOUT 5 HOURS)

Getting Started

Begin your workout with the warm-up exercises on these two pages, which should take two to three minutes. If you do the workout as soon as you get up in the morning, you can prepare for it by walking around the room for a few minutes to wake up your body.

Even with an abbreviated routine such as this, warming up is important because it increases your heart rate, promotes blood flow to your muscles and prepares your tendons and ligaments for the demands of exercise.

Injury prevention is another benefit of warming up. While cold muscles tend to be stiff and relatively hard to contract, you can work warm muscles vigorously without undue risks of tears or strain.

Warming up also helps safeguard your heart. Studies show that three out of four people who engage in sudden, vigorous exercise without warming up show abnormal cardiovascular activity, including irregular heartbeat. But researchers have found that warming up will minimize these problems, regardless of the exerciser's level of fitness.

After warming up, you will be ready for the strengthening and stretching exercises that begin on page 410. The routine first works the thighs and lower legs, then the abdominal muscles (pages 416-421) and concludes with the upper body (pages 422-429).

The exercises combine stretching and strengthening activities. By alternating these two types of exercise, you will find the workout less fatiguing. The stretches will not only help speed your recovery from the more strenuous exercises, but they will also help you stay loose and flexible as the workout proceeds. Hold each stretch for 30 to 45 seconds, except when otherwise indicated.

Stand with your arms hanging loosely at your sides. Shrug your shoulders, lifting them toward your ears five times.

Lean your head to each side five times, bringing your ear toward your shoulder without straining your neck.

Put your hands behind your head. Let the weight of your hands pull your chin toward your chest. Hold it, but don't strain.

Standing with your feet spread about shoulder width apart and your arms hanging loosely at your sides, lean forward as far as you comfortably can, keeping your head above your waist *(far left)*. Rotate each arm in a circle five times, alternating arms. Next, lean first to one side and then the other, and repeat the arm circles on each side *(center)*. Then, leaning forward once again, do 20 double-arm circles, moving both arms at the same time *(near left)*.

Knee Press and
Outer-Thigh Raise

Lie on your back. Lift your upper body,
bracing yourself with your forearms resting
comfortably on the floor. Keep your legs
straight and your feet flexed. Bring one
knee toward your chest and lift the other leg
slightly. Straighten the bent leg and bend
your other leg. Perform the entire sequence
five times.

Lying on your right side, with both hands and your right forearm on the floor, bend your right leg to form a 90-degree angle. Keeping your left leg straight, flex your foot and raise the leg to about a 45-degree angle *(above)*, then lower it to just above the floor *(right)*. Do five repetitions, then turn over and repeat with your right leg.

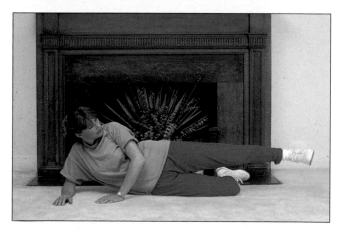

Inner-Thigh Raise
and Stretches

Lie on your back with your legs straight out. Prop up your upper body with your forearms, taking care not to overarch your back. Alternate bending each knee slightly, without lifting your heel off the floor. Perform five repetitions with each knee.

Lie on your right side, with your right forearm on the floor. Bend your left leg, keeping your left foot on the floor. Your right leg should be straight and your right foot flexed. Grip your left knee with your left hand. Raise your right leg to about a 45-degree angle *(right)* and slowly lower it, but not all the way to the floor *(below)*. Perform five times, making sure that your leg moves steadily up and down. Roll over and repeat five times with your left leg.

Sit on the floor with your legs extended straight out *(left)*. Place your hands behind you so that your weight rests on them; keep your arms straight. Rotating your ankles, slowly move your toes in a circle outward as far as you can and then back to the center. Do five repetitions.

Thigh and Hamstring Stretch

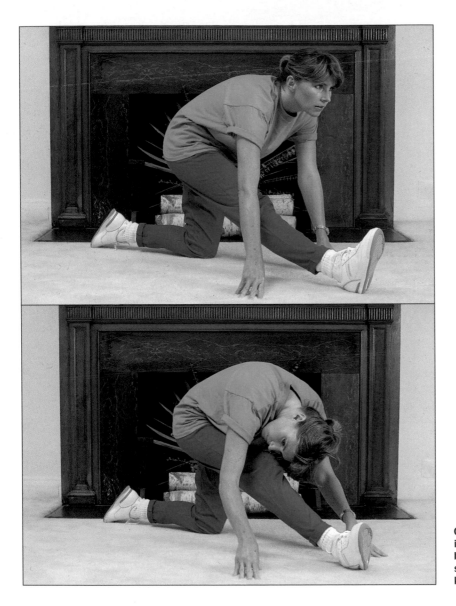

Crouch down so that your right leg extends in front of you and your left leg is bent behind you *(top left)*. With your arms at your sides, bend your head toward your right knee *(left)* and hold. Switch legs and repeat.

Sit on the floor, cross your legs and lean
back slightly, supporting your weight with
your hands. Gently arching your back, lift
your lower body until you feel a slight
stretch in your thighs. Keep your arms
straight and lower legs on the floor. Hold.

Stomach Crunch

Lie on your back with your hands clasped behind your head. Bend your legs so that your feet are flat on the floor *(top)*. Move your chin and knees toward each other *(above)*. Slowly lower your feet and head back to the floor. Perform 10 repetitions.

Lie on your back, hands clasped behind your neck, knees bent and feet on the floor *(opposite)*. Pointing your elbows up, lift your upper body until your shoulder blades clear the floor. Slowly lower yourself back down. Perform 10 repetitions.

Hip and Back
Stretches

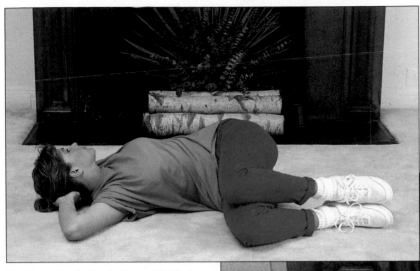

Lie on your back, hands clasped behind
your head, legs together, feet off the floor
(right). Roll your knees to the right as far as
you comfortably can and hold *(above)*. Roll
to the left and hold.

Get down on your hands and knees, placing your hands on the floor shoulder width apart and your back straight *(above left)*. Hang your head down while you round your back and hold *(above right)*.

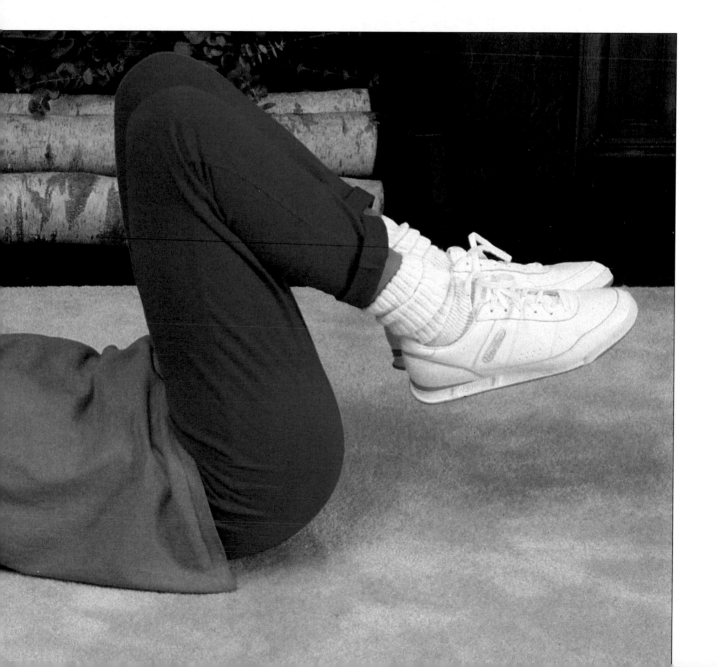

Diagonal Crunch

Lie on your right side with your legs extended but relaxed. Bend your knees slightly. Cross your left leg over the right so that your left foot just rests on the floor. Point your hands toward your feet, your lower hand slightly off the floor *(opposite)*. Reach for your feet as you lift your upper trunk off the floor. Focus your effort on the muscles on the side of your trunk *(below)*. Slowly lower yourself back down. Perform five times on each side.

Push-Up
Variations

These versions of the push-up are of varying difficulty. In the easiest version *(top),* begin on your hands and knees, placing your knees slightly farther back than your hips and your fingers pointing forward. Bend your arms and slowly lower your chest to within three inches of the floor, then return to the starting position. Point your fingers toward each other *(center),* or cross your legs and lift them off the floor *(above)* to increase the effort. Do one of these push-ups or the more difficult classic push-up *(right)* five times.

Keeping your back and arms as straight as possible, rest your weight on your hands and toes. Bend your elbows and lower your chest to within three inches of the floor. Then raise yourself back to the starting position. Do five repetitions.

Sit on the floor with your legs outstretched. Place your left hand on your hip and extend your right arm to the side; your palm should face the floor and your fingers should point to the side *(top)*. Moving from the waist, slowly rotate to the right as far as possible while keeping your arm straight and parallel to the floor *(right)*. As you turn, look over your right shoulder but do not force your head back. Hold and repeat on the other side.

Standing with your feet slightly more than shoulder width apart, hold the ends of a towel behind you and bend slightly from the waist *(inset opposite)*. Lean forward, bringing your head no lower than waist level, and raise the towel *(opposite)*. Hold this position and pull on the towel.

Arm and Upper Body Stretches/2

Holding a towel stretched out behind your head, lean as far to the right as possible and hold. Repeat on the left side.

Hold a towel behind your head. Stand with your feet shoulder-width apart and your elbows bent *(top)*. While pulling on the ends of the towel, raise it as high as possible and hold for a count of five *(above)*; lower slowly. Do five repetitions.

Stand with a towel stretched out overhead, your feet slightly farther apart than shoulder width. Without locking your elbows, pull on the towel *(top)*. Slowly turn to the left, shifting your weight to your left foot, which should be turned out to the right at a 90-degree angle *(left)*; most of the turning should be done from the waist. Hold and repeat on the other side.

Dip and Arm Stretch

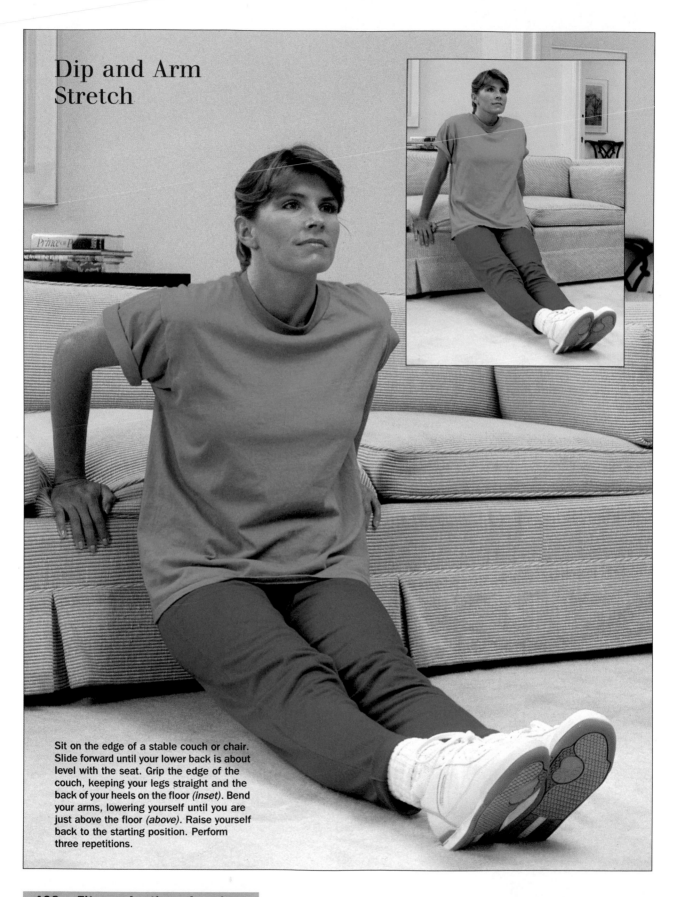

Sit on the edge of a stable couch or chair. Slide forward until your lower back is about level with the seat. Grip the edge of the couch, keeping your legs straight and the back of your heels on the floor *(inset)*. Bend your arms, lowering yourself until you are just above the floor *(above)*. Raise yourself back to the starting position. Perform three repetitions.

Stand with your hands behind your head, fingers touching and elbows bent *(left)*. Slowly raise your hands as high as possible, keeping your fingers together *(above)*. Hold this position, then slowly lower your hands to the starting point.

Cool-Down

Stand with your knees slightly bent and your feet slightly farther apart than shoulder width, and make 10 large arm circles in front of you, keeping your shoulders relaxed. Your hands should cross at the top and bottom of the circles.

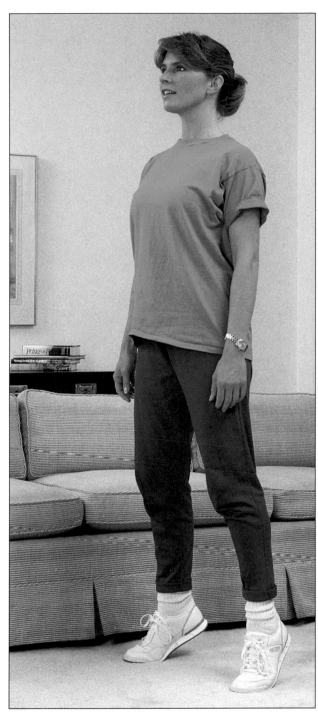

Standing with your arms hanging loosely at your sides, raise yourself slowly on your toes and hold for about two seconds. Keep your head straight and your shoulders loose and relaxed. Perform 10 repetitions.

Stand with your hands on your hips, your right foot forward, your right knee slightly bent, your left foot back and your left knee straight. Lean forward until you feel a stretch in your lower left leg. Hold, then switch legs.

Indoor Aerobics

If you do not have access to a swimming pool, exercise bicycle or rowing machine, the most convenient indoor aerobic exercises you can do are running in place, jumping jacks and jumping rope. Although such activities are useful for increasing your cardiovascular capacity, they do place some degree of stress on your lower body and back. Proper footwear is therefore essential when you do these exercises. Never perform them barefoot or in worn-out shoes. Wear running or aerobic shoes that have adequate resiliency. And, if possible, do your aerobics on a rug or other padded surface. Women should wear a sports bra when doing these exercises.

To avoid boredom, do not limit your aerobic routine to one indoor exercise. For instance, you can start with seven minutes of running in place, switch to jumping jacks for three minutes, jump rope for three minutes and then switch back to running in place for the last seven minutes of your 20-minute aerobic workout. The warm-up and cooldown should consist of two to three minutes of any of these exercises performed slowly.

Run in place at a slow pace for two to three minutes, then pick up speed. Raise your knees higher to make the exercise more challenging. For variety, alternate running in place with moving around.

To do jumping jacks, start with your feet together and your hands relaxed at your sides. Jump up, moving your feet apart wider than shoulder width as your arms rise. Land with your hands over your head. Then jump again and resume the starting position.

CHAPTER 18

Fitness Anywhere

Exercise routines for work and travel

The vast majority of Americans spend most of their days seated, or at least sedentary. The conveniences offered by modern offices as well as the transportation that most people take to work tend to reinforce an inactive lifestyle. Elevators, escalators and word processors may contribute to your productivity, but they reduce the amount of physical work in your life.

Sitting for prolonged periods can adversely affect physical fitness in several ways. First, it contributes to weight-control problems by expending fewer calories than moving around. Second, long stretches of sitting, whether in an office or in a car or some other mode of transportation, can weaken your stomach and back muscles. Lower back problems are compounded by badly designed chairs or poor posture. Finally, sitting reduces the range of motion through which you move your joints. Desk work in particular restricts movement and deprives you of exercise.

Even if you do not sit all day, chances are that your office environment and work schedule present little opportunity for getting sufficient activity, so that you must make a conscious effort to fit extra movement into your everyday routine. One way to compensate for this lack of activity is to exercise before or after you are at work or on the road. If possible, you can also take advantage of fitness facilities near your office or at hotels you will be visiting when you're traveling. Many hotels have exercise clubs and spas, and some even offer aerobic classes. If you can perform an aerobic activity such as walking or jogging, along with an efficient routine like the one shown in the previous chapter, you can stay relatively fit.

In addition, you will feel better and have more energy if you make a point of moving around and

Unless you prepare in advance, it is difficult to stay in shape while traveling. Disruptions in your every-day routine, the stress of unexpected delays and the lack of adequate exercise facilities on the road can all interfere with exercising consistently when you go away on vacation or business. While planning ahead cannot entirely counteract the negative effects of travel on your exercise regimen, it can mitigate them and save you from abandoning your commitment to fitness.

• When you arrive at your destination, try to exercise first thing in the morning, before you become involved in meetings or other activities. An early work-out will help you establish a fitness schedule you can follow while you are on the road and also help acclimate you to any changes in time zones.

• As a general rule, you should not exercise as intensively while you are traveling as you do at home: Aim for maintaining rather than improving fitness. While you are traveling, cut back to about two-thirds of what you are used to; build back up to your normal level once you get home. For instance, if you are used to running for 30 minutes a day, run for the same length of time but at a slower pace while you are away. If you need advice on where to run, a local running club may be able to provide maps with recommended routes of varying lengths. Be mindful of personal safety in urban areas.

• Take the area's climate and altitude into account. At altitudes above 5,000 feet, for example, the air is so thin that you may experience nausea, a loss of appetite, dehydration and headache. Do not exercise as soon as you arrive when visiting high altitudes; give your body at least a day or two to get used to the decreased air pressure. If you usually exercise at or near sea level, you should also initially cut back on the duration and intensity of your exercise at high elevations.

• If you experience unusually rapid heartbeat or difficult breathing while working out in high altitudes, stop exercising immediately. These are both signs that your body is having trouble coping with the thin air. Don't forget that being at a high altitude will affect you indoors as well as out.

• Take similar precautions while visiting climates hotter and more humid than your own. In order to prevent dehydration, drink more fluids than usual, moderate your consumption of alcohol and caffeine, which have a dehydrating effect, and try not to exercise outdoors during the hottest part of the day. To avoid sunburn, apply a sunscreen and wear a hat. In big cities, you should forgo exercising outdoors during morning and evening rush hours, when air pollution reaches its daily peak; listen to local weather reports for smog alerts.

• If swimming is your preferred exercise, remember that swimming in the ocean can be dangerous for those who usually swim in a calm lake or pool—strong swimmers included. Do not swim alone or at beaches where there are no lifeguards.

exercising during the rest of the day. The stretches illustrated on pages 438-441, for example, are excellent for retaining or restoring range of motion to your joints. Stretching is particularly important for those who work with electronic devices like computer keyboards. You may not move for long periods of time, and even your hands may stay in place while only your fingers move. As a result, when you work at a computer terminal for several hours, tension builds up in your hands, shoulders and forearms, making you vulnerable to cramps or stiffness.

In addition, neck and back problems can arise from staring at a computer monitor, talking on the telephone or sitting in one position in a car, train or plane for an extended period. The stretches included in this chapter can stimulate blood flow to your muscles, thereby relieving muscular tension. And they emphasize bending and reaching in ways that most people neglect during the typical workday. You can also perform strengthening exercises while sitting. Strengthening the upper body can be accomplished with isometrics that pit the arms against the hands, or with more dynamic exercises that involve lifting books or similar objects.

Standing in long lines at terminals or sitting in the same position for hours in planes, buses, trains or cars can cause muscle cramps, fatigue and feelings of malaise. The best antidote to the confinement of long trips is to get up periodically and walk around. Walking works the large muscles in your legs and restores circulation to your extremities. In tight spaces like the cabin of a crowded plane, where walking around frequently may not be possible, the exercises presented in this chapter will be especially beneficial. These movements include stretches, isometrics and other exercises you can perform almost anywhere—even while you are waiting in line. Regardless of your mode of transportation, these exercises will offset the boredom and help to counteract the debilitating effects of long trips. As a result, they will make you feel better when you reach your destination than if you had simply sat still.

Approach these stretches and strengtheners as carefully as you would any new set of exercises. Move into them gently and do not push yourself farther than you can comfortably go. Over several weeks, you will find that your strength and flexibility will gradually improve as you become more experienced with the routines, and you will be able to reach and stretch farther.

In the Office

You can perform most of the exercises in this routine without even getting up from your chair. The stretches here and on pages 440-441 will release some of the tension that builds up during the workday. As you stretch, remind yourself to loosen tight facial muscles, straighten hunched-over shoulders and relax your neck and hands. Do these stretches gently; otherwise, you may injure muscles unused to being stretched. Hold each stretch for 15 seconds to a minute.

The exercises that use books (pages 442-445) are designed to strengthen your arms and shoulders. The first time that you perform these exercises, be careful not to select objects that are too heavy for you. Always err on the side of caution, at least until the exercises are comfortable and familiar. Begin with five repetitions of each exercise, making sure to perform any exercise you do with your right arm or leg with your left as well.

When you are ready to make these exercises more difficult, you can either lift heavier objects or increase the number of repetitions.

Sit on the edge of your chair, firmly grip the back and straighten your arms. Keeping your back straight, let your upper body gently pull you forward to stretch your shoulders, upper back and chest.

Reach up with your hands side by side *(right)*. Then reach forward and down *(top inset),* and move your hands apart. Keep your arms parallel to each other and let your chest fall forward, your hands hanging at your sides *(bottom inset)*. Reach down as far as you can comfortably go but do not force yourself to touch the floor. Beginning this stretch with an upward reach benefits the shoulders and upper back more than would merely reaching downward.

Shoulders

Reach up with one hand as you allow the other hand to fall toward the floor. Focus attention on the upper hand and imagine that it is floating gently upward.

Sit upright with your hands clasped behind your head *(top)*. To stretch the upper back, gently pull your elbows back as far as you can and hold them in position *(above)*.

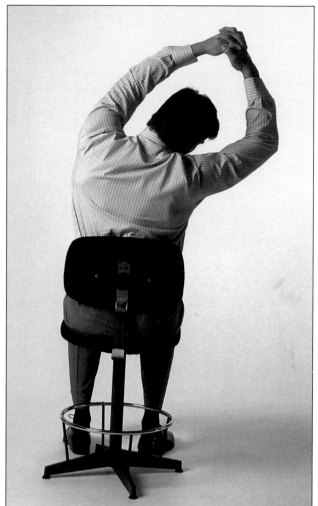

Clasp one elbow behind your head and pull down toward the back of your neck. Repeat with the other elbow. This increases flexibility in the shoulders and triceps muscle in the back of the upper arm.

With your hands clasped overhead, lean from your waist to the left and then to the right, holding the lowest position each time. This stretches the middle back and sides.

Arms/1

To increase strength in your triceps, sit down and hold a book with one hand to reach behind your shoulder; keep your palm facing up and the opposite hand supporting your elbow *(above)*. Raise the book until your arm is straightened *(right)* and then slowly lower your arm to the starting position.

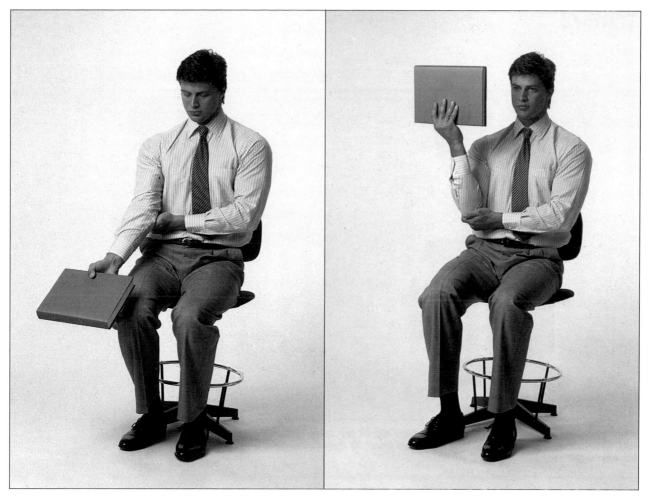

With your palm up, hold a book level with your knee. Use the opposite hand to support your elbow *(above)*. Raise the book to your shoulder *(right)* and then lower it, working your biceps.

Arms/2

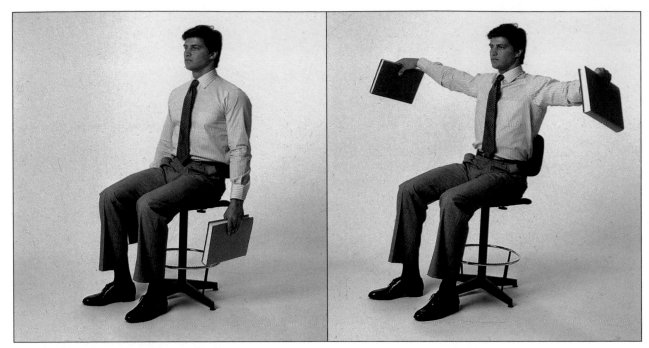

To work the shoulders, start with a book in each hand and let your arms hang down *(above)*. Keeping your arms straight at all times, lift them to shoulder height *(right)*.

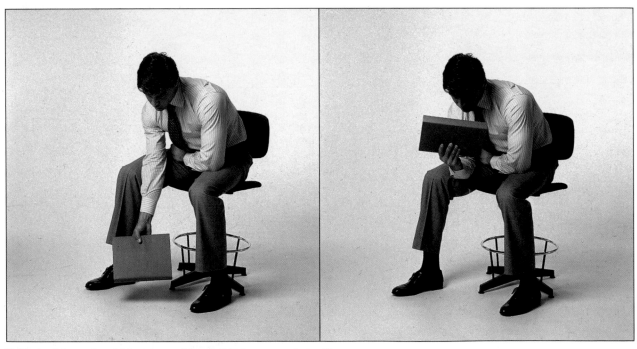

Hold a book in one hand. Lean over and dangle it between your legs with your arm straight *(above)*. Then lift the book to your chest *(right)*, keeping your elbow on your upper leg.

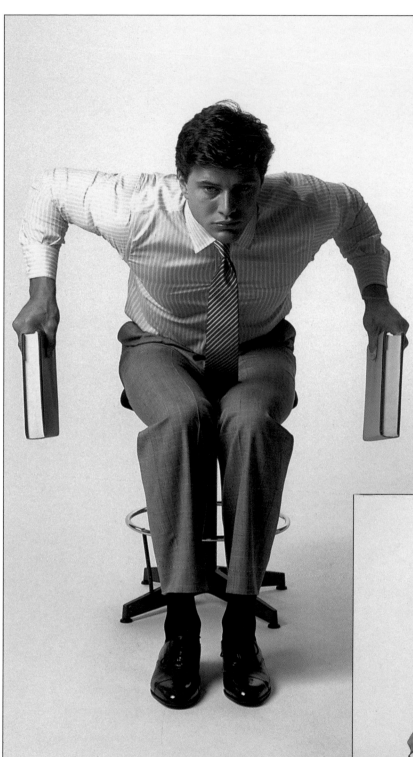

Lean forward with books in both hands at your sides, keeping your arms extended *(below)*. Bend your elbows to lift your arms, bringing the books to chest level *(left)*. Lower the books and repeat nine times. This motion works the triceps and shoulder and upper back muscles.

Legs

Sit down, grip the seat of your chair and raise one leg while you flex your foot *(bottom)*. Slowly move your leg outward *(inset)*, then back toward the center and down. This will tone your thighs.

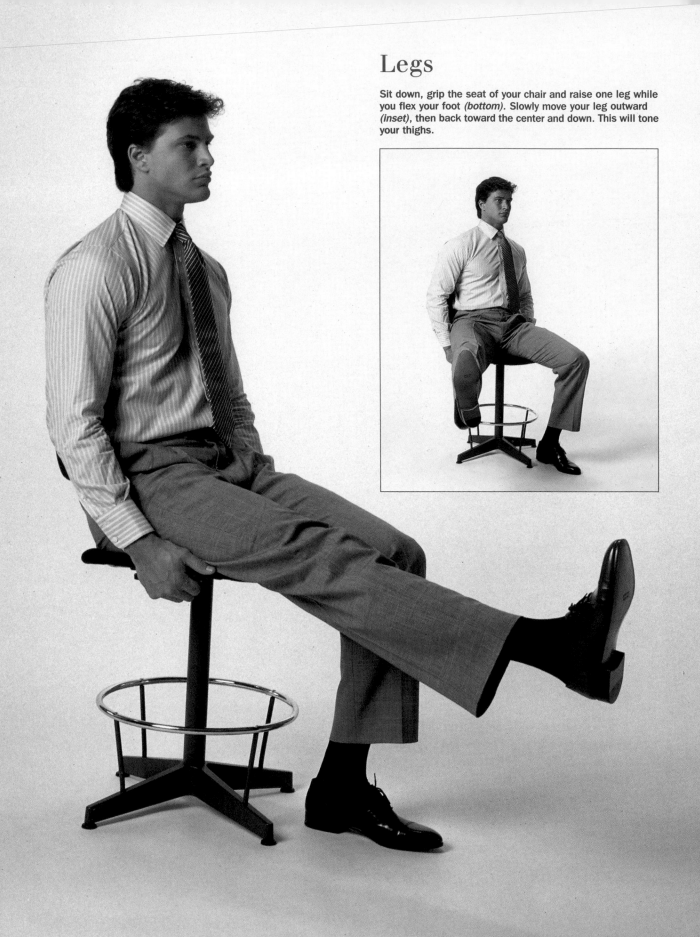

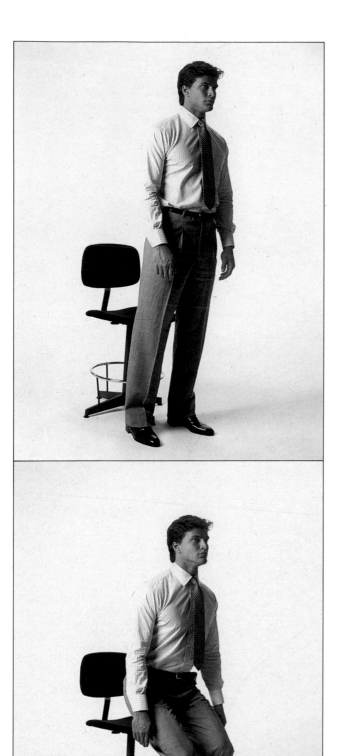

Do a shallow knee bend for your upper legs. Stand up with your back straight *(top)*. Bend your knees but not so far that your buttocks drop below knee level *(bottom)*.

On the Road

Cramps, stiffness and numbness can be problems for travelers who are confined to their seats during long rides in cars, buses, trains or airplanes. Car and bus travelers, whose muscles may be subjected to jarring motions in stop-and-go traffic, are especially vulnerable to muscle spasms, particularly in the back. But exercises that involve gentle stretching will alleviate such discomforts. Sitting in an aisle seat will give you more room in which to perform these movements.

A technique that increases the effectiveness of stretching is to momentarily contract the muscles you are about to stretch and then, as you stretch, consciously relax them. The brief contraction stimulates a reflex that helps lengthen the muscles. Consciously relaxing them increases your awareness of the tension that had built up.

If you have time for nothing else, at least try to do the loosening and flexibility-enhancing routines shown on these and the following four pages. The stretches focus on the areas that tend to tighten the most when you are traveling—the muscles of the neck, shoulders and lower back. Whenever you perform these stretches, the movement should be relaxed: Do not force your joints beyond a comfortable range of motion. Above all, do not stretch so far as to cause pain. Hold each stretch for 30 to 45 seconds.

The strengthening exercises on pages 454-458 require a minimum of space because they are isometrics, which involve static muscle contractions and entail no movement once you have assumed the proper position. Most of them oppose one body part with another, and you can perform them on virtually any kind of chair and in any vehicle, although one or two of these exercises may require a chair with a wide back or seat, depending on your size.

As you perform the isometrics, remember to do each one at several different angles, since isometrics develop strength only at the particular angle at which they are performed. For each isometric exercise, push as hard as you can for about 10 seconds. Continue to breathe evenly; holding your breath throughout the contraction can cause dizziness.

Sit up straight and interlace your fingers behind your head, pointing your elbows out to the sides *(opposite)*. **Bring your elbows toward each other and press gently with your hands until your chin reaches your chest** *(inset)*. **Hold.**

Place your hands over one knee. Pull your leg up until you feel a slight stretch in your thigh. Hold. Repeat with the other leg.

Turn to one side, rotating from the waist, until you feel a stretch in your lower back. Hold and repeat to other side.

Sit with your arms hanging loosely at your sides. Gently let your chin fall to your chest. Hold this position.

Shoulder Stretches

Look straight ahead and cross your arms in your lap, keeping your shoulders relaxed *(near right)*. Slowly bring your arms up in front of you *(far right and below left)*. Lift your hands above your head *(below middle)* and bring them up and out to the sides. Making as large a circle as possible with your hands and arms *(below right)*, slowly bring them back to the starting position. Do five repetitions.

Extend your arms and grasp the bottom of your seat. Keeping your back as straight as possible, pull up firmly on the seat without straining *(opposite)*. As you pull, lean back until you feel a slight stretch in your shoulders. Hold.

Chest Stretches

Curl your hands into fists and hold them in front of your chest, your elbows out to the sides. Reach back with your elbows *(left)* until you feel a stretch across the middle of your chest and upper chest. Hold. As you move your elbows back, you may have to lean forward slightly to have enough room to complete the stretch.

Place your hands on your shoulders. Bring your elbows together in front of you as your shoulder blades move apart *(left)*. Hold.

Press your hands together in front of you, the fingers pointing up *(opposite)*. Look straight ahead. As you continue gently pressing your hands together, lift them over your head as high as you can *(inset)*. Then slowly lower them to the starting position. Do five repetitions.

Arm Isometrics/1

Lean forward and place your hands on your shins. Keep your back straight and push against your legs.

Place your hands on top of your thighs and press down. To work your thigh muscles, resist by trying to lift your legs.

Fold your arms. Grasp your right upper arm with your left hand and pull as your right arm resists. Repeat on the other side.

Put your hands on your seat, fingers pointing behind you. Keep your arms straight and push down on the seat.

Arm Isometrics/2

Hold your arms straight out in front of you. Make two fists and hold them together with knuckles touching. Push your arms together. To vary the angle, move your fists slowly toward your chest and then away from you as you press them together.

Cross your arms and grasp each forearm with the opposite hand. Pull outward and then push the other way.

Put one hand on top of the other in front of you. Push your hands against each other, then switch hands.

Place your palms together in front of you, fingers pointing up. Press your hands together.

Interlock your fingers in front of your chest and pull outward. Reverse directions and push your hands toward each other.

Leg and Stomach Strengtheners

Rest your palms against your seat. Lift your knees toward your chest and then slowly lower them. Do five repetitions.

Hold the edge of your seat with both hands. Alternately raise and lower each knee six inches. Do 20 repetitions.

With both feet on the floor, first lift the heel *(opposite)* and then the toe *(inset)* of each foot in a rocking motion. Do 10 repetitions with each foot.

Standing Stretches

When standing in line or waiting for an elevator, keep moving. Do not hold the same position for an extended period. Move your hands, step back and forth, stretch, take off your jacket or coat, put down your bag and pick it up, and devise other strategems to keep yourself from standing still. The motion of your arm and leg muscles will aid your circulation and keep blood from pooling in the veins in your legs.

Curiously, standing still can be more stressful than moving around. For example, standing in one place with your knees locked and your legs straight places too much of the burden of support for your body on your back. It is better to stand with one leg slightly extended in front of the other and your knees bent. By doing so, you place demands on the muscles in your thighs, abdomen and hips.

Waiting for an elevator in any uncrowded place gives you the chance to perform the stretches shown on these two pages. The stretch shown opposite is good for relieving the tension and stiffness that carrying a heavy briefcase or handbag for a long time can produce in your shoulders. The lunge shown on this page stretches the muscles in the lower legs. Hold each stretch for 30 to 45 seconds.

Stand with your right foot about 12 inches in front of the left. Let your arms hang loosely at your sides *(above)*. Lunge forward gently, bending your knees so that you lower your upper body about six inches *(right)*. Keep your back straight. Hold. Reverse feet and repeat.

Stand with your right shoulder near the wall, your right foot slightly in front of the left. Reach out with your right hand and place the palm on the wall, fingers pointing to the rear *(opposite)*. Keeping your hand at the same spot on the wall, slide your right foot and shoulder forward until you feel a stretch in your shoulder *(inset)*. Hold. Then turn around and repeat.

One-Minute Routines

Waiting in a lobby gives you an opportunity to do isometrics and dynamic strengthening that you cannot do in the confines of a crowded bus, train or plane. Pushing against a wall while standing, for example, uses most of the major muscles of the upper body. After doing these exercises, you should relax by doing one or more of the stretches on pages 466-467. Hold each stretch for 30 to 60 seconds.

The exercises that involve pushing against a wall can be done as isometrics when you push and hold a steady position, or as dynamic exercises when you move slowly as you push. The isometrics should be held for about 10 seconds. Dynamic exercises can be done for 10 to 20 repetitions.

Stand with your hands together over your head. Press them against each other and hold.

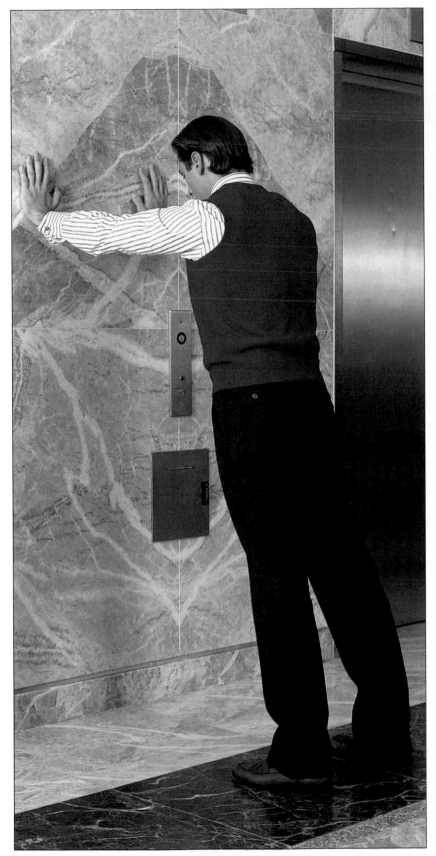

With your feet about three feet from a wall, place your hands on the wall at shoulder level, keeping your arms and back straight and fingers pointed up. Push *(left)*. From the same starting position, rotate your hands so that your fingers point inward. Bend your elbows slightly and push *(top)*. Place your forearms on the wall, fingers again pointing up, and push *(above)*.

Strengtheners

Face a wall, standing flush against it, your head turned to one side. With your arms at your sides, rest your palms against the wall, fingers pointing down. Push your hands against the wall.

Stand with your back to the wall with your arms hanging down. Keeping your arms and legs straight, place your palms against the wall and push with your hands.

Stand a foot away from a wall. Lean forward, placing your forearms on the wall, hands pointing up. Bend your right knee and bring your left foot back about two feet, keeping your left leg straight. Push as hard as you can, concentrating all the effort in your legs.

Stretches

Stand with your arms relaxed at your sides and let your chin fall to your chest *(far left)*. Rotate your head to the right until your chin is level with your shoulder *(near left)*. Return to the center position. Do five repetitions on each side.

With your knees slightly bent, gently lean forward. Let your hands reach for the floor *(left)*, but do not force yourself down or bounce in an effort to touch the floor. Keep your knees slightly bent.

Stand up straight with your feet shoulder width apart. Reach up as high as you can and hold *(opposite)*.

growth of, 274
in bodybuilders
of lower body, 287-289
of middle body, 309-311
soreness of, 72, 198, 282, 406
stretch reflex and, 197, 208
of upper body, 345-347
music, for aerobic movement, 159

N

Nautilus machines, 373, 375
neck stretches, 232-233, 448, 449, 466
neuroma, 73

O

obliques, 310
exercises for strengthening, 314-316, 322-323
machines, 381
office exercise routines, 435-447
chest stretches, 438
leg strengtheners, 446-447
leg stretches, 447
quadriceps strengtheners, 447
shoulder strengtheners, 444, 445
thigh strengtheners, 446
upper arm strengtheners, 442-445
upper back strengtheners, 445
upper back stretches, 438, 439
off-road cycling, 150-155
Olympic athletes, 36
orienteering, 35-36, 60-65
overexertion, 282
overflexibility, 198
overstretching 202

P

pace, 84, 93
jogging, 71
pacelines, in cycling 148-149
pain, 198, 199, 282, 329
and running injuries, 72-73
pairing of exercises, 281
partners, training with, 56, 89-95
see also fartlek training, games, partner
partner stretching, 235-251
advantages of, 235
for calf muscles, 238-239
for chest muscles, 238-239
contract-relax method and, 235-237
for hamstrings, 238-241

for hip flexors, 244-247
for inner thighs, 242-243
for lower back muscles, 240-241
for quadriceps, 244-247
for upper back muscles, 250-251
passing, 95
passive stretching, *see* static stretching
Peachtree Road Race, 70
pectoralis major, *see* chest muscles
pedaling, 134-135
pelvic tilt exercises, 331
pelvis, 311
pivot joints, 195
plow stretch, 202, 203
pins, 374
posture, 196, 214, 228, 273-274, 311, 329, 346,
aerobic movement and, 159
in cycling, 130-131
in running, 71
in swimming, 102-103
in walking, 44, 50
power, flexibility and, 253-254
power phase of swimming, 104, 108-113
prancing, as running conditioner, 86
President's Council on Physical Fitness, 67
progress tracking, 281
proprioceptive neuromuscular facilitation (PNF), *see* contract-relax stretching
psychotherapy, and running, 69
pull-down machine, 384-385
pull-over machine, 382-383
push-ups, 347, 348-355
push-up test, 279
push-up variations, 422, 423

Q

quadriceps, 198, 199, 288-289
exercises for, 290-293
flexibility test for, 201
machines, 376
partner stretching for, 244-248
static stretching for, 220-225
see also leg strengtheners
quick exercise routines
and aerobic fitness, 400, 401
defined, 399, 400
duration of, 400
equipment for, 403
flexibility retention, 401

for the office, *see* office exercise routines
for travel, *see* travel exercise routines
frequency of, 400
intensity and, 399-400
isometrics, *see* isometric exercises
long-term health benefits of, 402
strength building, 401-402
strength exercises, *see* strength exercises
time management, 402-403
time of day for, 402
20-minute routine, 405-433

R

race walking, 36-37, 52-57
errors, 56-57
lifting, 51, 52
rules for competition, 52
range of motion, 281
recovery rate, 70
recovery phase of swimming, 104, 114-115
rectus abdominis, 309
exercises for, 312-313, 316-317
relaxation, 438
reps, in strength training, 280
resting between sets, 281
resting heart rate, aerobic fitness and, 23
rhomboids, 346
exercises for, 348-355, 360, 369
road touring bikes, 129
rowing machine, 31
rowing torso machine, 386
runner's knee, 73
running
biomechanical action of, 68, 69
cardiorespiratory benefits of, 67
choosing the right shoe, 15, 68
common errors, 84-85
conditioning routines for, 86-87
injuries, 69-70, 72-73
on hills, 82-83
pace and posture, 71
psychological benefits of, 67, 68, 69, 89
tips for getting started, 69
stride, 78-81
technical mistakes, 84-85
warm-ups and streches for, 74-77
with a partner, 71, 89-95
running surfaces, 70

Photography Credits
Cover: top, center; middle, left; bottom, center: Steven Mays
top, right; middle, right; bottom, right: Andrew Eccles
top, left; middle, center; bottom, left: © 1993 David Madison

page 17: Andrew Eccles; pages 40-155 © David Madison except
pages 38-39, 128-129 by Steven Mays and 148-149 © David
Epperson/WILDPIC; pages 160-191: Andrew Eccles; pages
192-371: Steven Mays; pages 376-395: Andrew Eccles; pages
369-467: Steven Mays

Illustration Credits
Page 27, walking test charts: Brian Sisco, Tammi Colichio; page
29: David Flaherty; page 31: Susan Blubaugh; page 37: Phil
Scheuer; pages 50-51, 56-57: David Flaherty; page 68: Tammi
Colichio; pages 84-85, 200-203, 208, 236, 254: David Flaherty;
pages 279, 283: Durrell Godfrey; pages 288, 310, 346: Dana
Burns-Pizer; page 374: David Flaherty

Acknowledgements
The One-Mile Walk Test on page 27 is reprinted courtesy of
The Rockport Company, © 1987 The Rockport Company

Cosmetics and grooming products supplied by Clinique Labs,
Inc., New York City

Location for pages 376-395 courtesy of Ralph Anastasio, The
Printing House Fitness Center, New York City

Many thanks to Paul Klein, Department of Human
Biodynamics, University of California at Berkeley

Production by Giga Communications, Inc.